'An essential book about repression and resistance, bold, lucid and deeply inspiring'
Olivia Laing, author of *The Garden Against Time*

'The British police thought it could use and discard Kate Wilson, but it messed with the wrong woman. Her courage, determination, clarity and insistence on justice are absolutely awe-inspiring'
Oliver Bullough, author of *Butler to the World*

'It is rare that an exceptionally gifted writer should find herself at the epicentre of such a huge story . . . The result is a highly intelligent memoir that reads like a psychological thriller'
Rob Newman, author of *Neuropolis*

'When I say "everybody should read this book", I don't mean everybody who is interested in human rights, in police ethics, in feminism, in the future of the planet, in freedom of speech . . . I mean everybody'
Louisa Young, author of *You Left Early*

'A searing page-turner . . . *Disclosure* firmly places the British police on the wrong side of history'
Peter Hain, former Secretary of State for Northern Ireland

'Exposes one of the most shocking abuses of state power in modern British history . . . a must-read for anyone who cares about our fundamental rights'
Jeremy Corbyn

'Important history and a brilliant read'
Vera Baird, former Victims' Commissioner for England and Wales

Kate Wilson is a lifelong campaigner. Her landmark victory in the trial 'Wilson v the Commissioner' established that the British undercover police operations targeting her movements were unlawful and unnecessary in a democratic society, and systematically violated basic human and political rights. She now works as a nurse.

DISCLOSURE

Unravelling the Spycops Files

KATE WILSON

WEIDENFELD & NICOLSON

First published in Great Britain in 2025 by Weidenfeld & Nicolson,
an imprint of The Orion Publishing Group Ltd
Carmelite House, 50 Victoria Embankment
London EC4Y 0DZ

An Hachette UK Company

The authorised representative in the EEA is Hachette Ireland,
8 Castlecourt Centre, Dublin 15, D15 XTP3, Ireland (email: info@hbgi.ie)

3 5 7 9 10 8 6 4 2

A CIP catalogue record for this book is
available from the British Library.

ISBN (Hardback) 978 1 3996 1429 0
ISBN (Ebook) 978 1 3996 1432 0
ISBN (Audio) 978 1 3996 1433 7

Printed in Great Britain by Clays Ltd, Elcograf S.p.A

www.weidenfeldandnicolson.co.uk
www.orionbooks.co.uk

For Lily, Esme and John

Contents

Author's Note

The events covered in this book span twenty years, and more than ten years of litigation. Inevitably the timeline has been collapsed and some phases of the court processes have been simplified to make a more coherent story and a less confusing and more interesting read. My cases and those of other victims of these police units deal with deep intrusion by the state into people's intimate, private lives. I do not want to compound that intrusion here. Where identities are protected by court orders in other proceedings, I have used those pseudonyms or ciphers. In other places I have simply changed or removed people's names. For the same reason, countless stories will be left untold. Many other people took part in the events (past and present) recounted here, and I don't claim to speak for them. Where possible, when telling someone else's story, I have drawn from their own words.

The same goes for the police. I have quoted from the police files as accurately as possible (including leaving spelling and grammar errors intact). Their redactions are shown, as they were in the disclosure, using black rectangles. Edits I have made (for brevity or privacy) are indicated by an ellipsis or square brackets.

Most of the officers involved in these events remain anonymous. Over the years, the police and different judicial authorities have used a purposefully baffling array of codes and ciphers to refer to them. In places I have had to choose which name or cipher to apply. That could be the officer's real name, the Cover Name they were known by in their undercover roles, the 'Elter

Number' – (EN) ciphers created by Operation Elter (the official police investigation into wrongdoing by the National Public Order Intelligence Unit (NPOIU)) – or an 'Officer' (O-number) cipher that was unique to the Investigatory Powers Tribunal (IPT). Where possible, I have opted to use the cipher most commonly used to refer to that officer in public discussions.

None of the officers referred to in this book were willing to give evidence to the IPT. Some may eventually speak to the Public Inquiry, but many will do so behind closed doors. The files that were disclosed in the IPT may therefore be the only source we have to understand their role. We found enough provable errors in their reporting to know that those files were not the truth we were looking for. Nevertheless, the only way to really tell this story is to give you both their version and our own.

PART ONE

PART ONE

CHAPTER 1

'Did you feel that?' he said. 'The engine's skipping.'

She glanced at him, the muscles of his jaw visible in the glow from the dashboard. They had passed the Welsh border about two hours ago. In the blackness behind their reflections, she tried to make out the terrain. There was nothing out there but trees. Mark sat forward, hands high on the wheel, pumping the pedal, and she held her breath, looking up the hill and willing the road to keep passing beneath them.

Just as they crested the brow of the hill, there was a shudder, a mechanical cough, and then quiet. Neither of them spoke. Gravity took over, tyres shushing as the van rolled slowly down into a deep valley.

Near the bottom, the road curved and a golden glow spilled across the tarmac. The van drifted to a stop in front of maybe the only petrol station in a hundred-mile radius. Katja stared. Newspaper stands, flower bouquets, bundles of firewood in a metal rack. Two neat rows of pumps. Who was all this for? She hadn't seen any houses or signs of life for miles, couldn't remember when they'd last seen another car. Mark grabbed a can and jogged across the road. It took a bit of fumbling to get enough into the diesel tank to start it. Then he turned the ignition and pulled a U-turn, spinning the wheel with the heel of one hand. The headlights swept the tarmac, and he pulled up smartly next to a pump.

'Do you think this would still be here if we came back tomorrow?'

3

He didn't answer, but the tension in his face had gone. She could see that his swagger was back. If pushed, he would probably say he had planned it.

He went off to pay, then carefully stashed the receipt in the glove box.

'For my tax return,' he said, winking his good eye.

No longer troubled by the need to find fuel, her thoughts strayed back to their cargo. She peered through the wire mesh into the dark space beyond. Passing lights hinted at shiny round surfaces, poorly concealed beneath camping gear.

'How the hell will you explain those if we get stopped?' she asked. 'It looks bad, even to me. I mean, Jesus, do they not have motorbikes in Ireland?'

Mark leant back on the headrest and closed his eyes for a moment.

'Relax, will you? I've taken worse things across borders. Trust me.'

Several decks below, figures in yellow jackets were stowing dock lines thick as their arms. She leant on the iron rail, slightly sticky from the salt air, and played over in her mind what had happened.

Just as she feared, the border guard had stepped out from the shelter of his little hut and waved at them to stop. Mark wound down the window. She stared at her feet.

'Cycling,' Mark had told him. 'And camping, in the Wicklow Mountains.'

Then she watched as the van was opened. There was no way to explain why they were taking a dozen motorbike helmets on a camping trip. They weren't even going to Wicklow.

From Seattle in 1999 to Prague in 2000 to Genoa in 2001, meetings of global leaders had become the scenes of massive protests. On May Day 2004, it would be Dublin's turn. Ireland held the Presidency of the European Union, and twenty-five European prime ministers would be gathering in the country's capital for a summit meeting. People were mobilising, but the Irish police had made it clear they wouldn't let the protests happen. The collection of helmets was to protect the front line of demonstrators from police attacks. Fuck knows where Mark had got them.

The border guard shone his torch over the contents of the van. It seemed impossible that he wouldn't see through Mark's lie. She felt sick. And yet, a moment later, he waved them up the ramp and onto the ferry, wishing them a pleasant trip.

'Piece of cake,' Mark gloated. 'You worry too much, you know?'

Mid-morning, they parked up in front of a large town house in Leeson Street. Boarded windows made it look abandoned, but they knew better.

Mark knocked. A man dressed in black answered, long dark hair visible beneath a hooded sweater. He glanced up and down the street before ushering them inside. There was some urgent conversation as Mark explained that he wanted help unloading.

The house was gloomy. It had been squatted just a few days previously, and it would take hours of work with brooms and dusters before they could set up all the dormitories, cooking facilities and meeting rooms they were going to need. It turned out there were only two people holding the fort, waiting for others from the UK. They clearly weren't happy about storing Mark's cargo, which could easily be used as evidence that activists were planning a fight. Mark was adamant though, they weren't staying in his van, so the helmets were unloaded and stuffed into a cupboard under the stairs. As soon as they finished, Mark turned to leave. He looked at her with his hand on the door latch.

'Come on then.'

'Where? This is the convergence space, right?'

'I've arranged to stay with a friend.'

Katja could see dust motes drifting in the air.

5

'I think we should stay and help out,' she said. 'At least until more people arrive.'

Mark's mood shifted. He had spent a lot of time organising this trip, and he wanted her to go with him, to meet his friends. He was raising his voice. It wasn't usual for him to get so angry. When he had finished, Katja picked at a dirty piece of wallpaper, looking from Mark to the drawn faces of the couple guarding the space. They had a big responsibility and there was a lot of work to do. She hadn't even wanted to come, but the squat was obviously short-handed, and it was basic solidarity to stay and help get it up and running. But in the murky light filtering through the glass in the door, Mark looked grim. She followed him out into the street, promising to come back in the morning with cleaning supplies.

In the van, he apologised.

'I'm just a bit tense. I think we might be being followed.'

She felt her chest tighten, but he reached out and took her hand.

'Don't worry, I'm probably just tired.'

It had been at least three days since they'd properly slept.

Mark's friend answered the door wearing a pink glittery cowboy hat. She invited them in, chatting in a soft Irish accent about the Dublin Grassroots Network, filling them in on preparations for the demo. The gloom they had been carrying since the squat dissipated in the face of her enthusiasm. Eventually she noticed how exhausted they were and showed them to her spare room.

Mark fell asleep almost immediately, his arm thrown across Katja's waist. She lay beside him for some time, brain humming at the strange new surroundings and the tensions of the day.

They probably would have slept until noon, but they were woken early by their host sticking her head round the door. She looked agitated and a little dishevelled. The cowboy hat was gone. She apologised for waking them, but she thought they would want to know. The police had raided Leeson Street, and everyone at the squat had been arrested.

Mark and Katja sat up, exchanging a glance.

'I've made coffee, and there's a crisis meeting in a bit,' she said. 'You'd better get up.'

The only large space left where they could gather was the court-yard of a warehouse on Dublin's Northside. Top of the emergency agenda: housing all the people who could no longer stay in the squat, and supporting the prisoners. It was clear they weren't going to be released.

'Just as well we stayed at my friend's place,' Mark muttered.

'Jesus Christ, Mark. Those people are on remand because of your bloody helmets.'

The meeting moved on to logistics. One of the Dublin crew pointed out a field kitchen in the courtyard. 'Since the eviction, we've been welcoming new arrivals and preparing food here, but that can't carry on.'

The warehouse was owned by a local media company and had only been intended for communications work. Now it was suddenly the centre of the mobilisation, and was drawing a lot of police attention. There was talk of finding a new building to squat. Mark offered to help, slightly mollifying Katja. Then the meeting moved on to plans for the weekend: street-theatre protests, a picnic and mass trespass into a privatised city-centre park, a Reclaim the Streets party, and the big demonstration: 'Bring the Noise'.

A young man stood up, cropped hair and a T-shirt bearing a screen print of a clenched fist. 'We want it to be a colourful march, and loud,' he said. 'We're asking people to bring saucepan lids and spoons, whistles and kazoos, foghorns, musical instruments, drums, anything to make noise. The idea is to get as close to Farmleigh House as we can. There's a black-tie dinner there for Europe's leaders. We want them to hear us as they eat their expensive meal.'

The police had other ideas. In the days that followed, while the protestors painted banners and held meetings, cooked food for the masses, handed out leaflets in the city centre and practised their street-theatre routines, taking advantage of the rare spring sunshine to do as much of it as they could outdoors, the police began raiding people's homes. Determined not to be embarrassed, all Gardaí leave was cancelled, and they were gearing up for a fight. A wing of a Dublin prison was emptied in readiness for new prisoners; hospitals were told to get ready; body bags were ordered, and space was cleared in the city morgue. Then, at the last minute, they declared the meeting point for the demonstration a no-go zone: the police would attack anyone who showed up.

Dublin Grassroots Network press release, Friday, 30 April
Dublin Grassroots Network, the group organising the 'Bring the Noise' march to Farmleigh House at 6 p.m. on Saturday evening, has condemned Garda measures announced yesterday evening which amount to the banning of the march. They have called on everyone with an interest in civil liberties to gather at the General Post Office instead, at the same time, for a meeting to protest the ban.

In the gathering dark, Katja could barely make out the faces on the far side of the circle. It was the night before the rally at the General Post Office and decent places to meet had become hard to find, so the padded bloc had assembled on a car park entry ramp. Discussions had been long and difficult, but they had eventually reached a decision, and it was a brave one. Everyone knew that they would be facing militarised riot police, and they had lost all their protective clothing in the raids, but the police threats and the media hype around the demonstration were intended to scare people and stop them mobilising. The group was determined not to let state violence silence protest.

From the Black Bloc statement 'Dublin Mayday: Why we pushed through police lines'
We are some of the people who participated in the bloc that pushed through the police lines on the demonstration to Farmleigh. This bloc was not formed spontaneously. It came as a result of a meeting the night before, called by both international and Irish people planning to join the march . . .

We have no leaders and we reject authority . . . We also reject the media division of demonstrators into 'violent' and 'non-violent' . . . Violence comes from the state. Violence comes from a system where profit takes priority over humanity . . . We feel that it is appropriate, on a weekend of demonstrations against borders, to confront the lines of police creating a border between ourselves and those who create the policies which result in the deaths of thousands of desperate people on the borders of Europe . . . to confront the decision to prevent our protest from going ahead. We decided that we would not cause property damage and we would not be an aggressive bloc or attack the police. However, we decided not to turn and walk away as soon as police blocked our path and not to allow ourselves or others to be attacked . . .

The morning dawned bright, and Katja and Mark set off to leaflet a Trade Union demonstration, drumming up support for the evening's rally and spreading the word about the new meeting point at the General Post Office. The Gardaí were targeting anyone publicising the event, but they proved easy to dodge. It felt like a small victory when the last flyer had been given out.

At 6 p.m. people began to assemble outside the General Post Office on O'Connell Street. The sun was shining on the thousands under the statue of Jim Larkin. Someone with a megaphone suggested that they defy the police ban and march to Farmleigh. It was met with a cheer and a rising chant of 'Whose streets? Our streets!'. Katja could hear drumming and the keening of over a thousand whistles, all merging together into a single mass of sound that rolled back and forth over their heads. She raised the flag she was carrying and took Mark's arm. A thrill of excitement ran through the crowd, and as one, the tide of people began to move.

From the Black Bloc statement 'Dublin Mayday: Why we pushed through police lines'
Demonstrations where people are herded from one place to another, miles from where decisions are being taken, can be ignored. We took our protest to Farmleigh House to directly disrupt the gathering of the EU . . . Our intention was to reach Farmleigh and make our protest with dignity . . .
When the police formed a line to stop the demonstration at the Ashton Gate roundabout, the Dublin Grassroots Network stopped their march 200 yards from the lines . . .

The crowd bunched together, as the police moved in to close the road up ahead. This was it. The official demonstration was over, but a group of protestors had resolved to defy the roadblock and keep marching, come what may. Katja tied a T-shirt over her head to hide her face. She hoped it made her look a little more intimidating, not as vulnerable as she felt. Mark covered the lower half of his face with a bandana, donning his sunglasses and pulling his cap low over his eyes. They formed up behind a red-and-black banner proclaiming 'Resist the Europe of Capital', and linked arms on the front line.

Laying the wooden poles of the flags they had been carrying horizontally across the top of the banner to form a solid rail, they began to move forward.

The police line was made up of ordinary, uniformed Gardaí in hi-vis jackets and flat caps. The bloc pushed and the Gardaí pushed back. But beyond the line, hundreds of riot police with shiny black visors filled the road. Katja's thoughts flashed to the vanload of similar helmets now sitting in an evidence locker.

There had been rumours that British police hardware would be used on the streets of Dublin for the first time since Irish independence. She had secretly thought that the symbolism was too dreadful for the Irish government to allow it, yet here they were: Northern Irish water cannons, rumbling down the street. They were a lot bigger than she had expected, white and boxy, and sporting an imposing array of spotlights, metal grills and dark windows. The jets themselves were mounted like guns on the roof. The mass of shields parted, as though to make way for royalty.

As she watched, she noticed a riot squad close to her tooling up and getting into formation. A sudden image came into her mind of a poster she had seen as a child. It was a painting of a demonstration that, viewed from afar, looked like a bearded man lying face down on the ground. Red flags became blood flowing from an open head wound under a banner reading 'Who Killed Blair Peach?' The poster was a tribute to a young teacher who died in 1979 after he was hit over the head by police during an anti-racism march in Southall. She recoiled at the thought, throwing her weight back.

And that was the only reason she managed to stay on her feet. The line of yellow-uniformed officers suddenly fell away, propelling the protesters forward into the waiting ranks. Mark was thrown past her, and she saw the swing of a police baton and heard a crack as he went down.

'Shit.'

She dragged him back, out of the melee, knowing he had been hit but not knowing where. Only a sliver of his face was visible between the bandana and his cap. His skin was pale.

'That bastard broke my knee.'

He staggered to his feet, and to her surprise, lunged back towards the police, looking for revenge.

'Mark, stop!' She got in front of him. 'What are you doing? Save it.'

As she pulled him away from the front line, the cannons began to fire. She saw columns of water smacking into people a few feet away, felt the spray on her face. There was a crush of movement around them as people scrambled out of the way. The shouting became so loud it felt like white noise, and the air grew chill and wet. Arcs of water swept back and forth over their heads, and although some stayed under the cascade to dance their defiance, the riot police began their slow advance in two lines. Drenched and discouraged, the protestors fell back in disarray.

Mark leant on Katja's shoulder. It had been over an hour and the adrenaline must have been wearing off, because he was clearly in a lot of pain. They picked their way through the crowd. She had hoped they would find a bus stop or a taxi to get him somewhere safe, but even far from the main demonstration, the streets were closed off and there was no traffic in sight. They kept walking.

It was gone midnight by the time they got back to where they were staying. They considered taking Mark to hospital, but decided to keep away, just in case the police were stalking the waiting rooms looking for injured people to arrest. Mark went to bed with a bag of frozen peas strapped to his leg. The next morning it was a bit better: seemingly not broken, just badly bruised.

The news was filled with water cannons. Someone had bought the papers, and Katja and Mark were on the front page, masked faces in the line behind the banner. Mark was so pleased, he hobbled off to buy his own copy to frame.

At the warehouse, the Dublin Grassroots Network was writing press releases and doing interviews. But their march had stopped 200 yards from the police line. It was felt that the people who had defied the police should say something. Mindful that his knee needed resting, Mark and Katja offered to spend the morning drafting a statement, which would keep them away from places where they might be forced to run away.

From the Black Bloc statement 'Dublin Mayday: Why we pushed through police lines'
We did this to show that we will not be intimidated by a show of force and we will not allow state violence to silence us. Many of the people who stood and faced the police were ordinary women and men from Dublin. We would like to thank the solidarity of people, who despite their decision to stop and not confront the police, nonetheless waited for those who did, so that we would not become isolated, and so we could march back to town, as one.

At anti-summit demonstrations around the world, States have shown the extent of military force and violence they are prepared to use against people who question and confront their 'democratic' regimes. On Saturday the actions of the riot police using water cannons from the North of Ireland and baton charges to attack a demonstration, making indiscriminate arrests and refusing people bail for minor offences . . . shows that the Irish state is no different.

Mark and Katja read through the final text. It had been written in a hurry, and by committee, but it was all there: the meeting, the consensus decision to push through the police line, and the reasons why.

'Do you think people will get it?' Katja said when they had finished, 'That it wasn't just mindless violence, that it was a conscious act?'

'It's a good statement,' Mark said. 'People will understand.'

They printed five hundred copies. In the city centre, the Reclaim the Streets party had closed a road to traffic. People were sunbathing on the tarmac. Some were dancing to a sound system playing from the back of a truck. Katja and Mark took the van to collect the flyers, still hot and smelling of ozone, and set off to hand them out.

They didn't get far.

'Oh, here we go.'

Katja looked up to see a police motorbike flagging them down. Mark pulled over and she stashed the wad of flyers under her seat. The officer took their vehicle papers. He still had his helmet on so she couldn't see his face. He pointed at her with a gloved hand.

'Annabelle Watson,' she said quickly.

Mark didn't even raise an eyebrow.

'What have you got in the back?'

Mark complained, but he got out and opened doors so the officer could take a look. Katja got out as well and stepped off to one side. Pretending she was calling friends to let them know they would be late, she dialled the legal support number. It was her and Mark. They had been stopped by the police in his van. She made sure she got all the details in. She looked around for a street name but couldn't see one.

Then the phone was snatched from her hand. The cop threw it into the road and barked something into a radio, she didn't hear the words. Suddenly cars were pulling up all around them. Plain-clothed officers, one riot van. They shoved Mark through the side door of the van, a glimpse of booted feet all around him as the door slid closed. Katja was dragged away into the back of an unmarked car.

'Annabelle, is it?' said one officer. 'Well, Annabelle, we're going to give you a taste of what Paddy got in London. What do you think about that?'

Her guts clenched. She had only vague and unpleasant notions about what had happened to 'Paddy' in London, but she supposed it wasn't going to be good.

'And your underwear,' the man ordered. Katja hugged her arms to her chest and shivered, looking at the floor.

She had been strip-searched, then moved to another police station, where they stripped her again before putting her in a cell. She thought it might be normal to search prisoners thoroughly on arrival, but they had just made her strip naked for a third time.

She glanced in the mirror. Her skin was pale under the fluorescent lights. Her shoulders hunched, like she was trying to make herself small.

She moved to straighten up, to gather her dignity. Then it struck her: why a mirror? This was a police station, not a dressing room. Picturing leering faces in the space behind her reflection, she drew her arms tight around herself and looked fixedly down at the ground.

The cell walls were painted with lumpy gloss paint that glistened like grey slime. She squeezed her eyes shut and tried to control her breathing, but when she looked around again she had a dizzying sensation that the paint was moving.

She had to hold it together. She couldn't have been there more than a few hours. Her last sighting of Mark, being thrown face down on the floor of the police van, and the fate of the couple from the squat who were still sitting on remand, kept playing through her mind. She had no doubt she was going to prison, at least until the summit was over, and who knew for how long after that? She lay on the hard bench thinking about all the prisoner defence campaigns she had taken part in over the years, reflecting on how easily you could go from picking up some flyers at the local print shop to becoming one of the 'Dublin Two'. The police would want to make an example of them. She felt a spark of defiance. It was the militarisation of Dublin's streets and the attacks on civil liberties that were the problem. Right was on her side, but it would be long months before they got to tell that to a judge. Let's face it, she had just been arrested two days after the demonstration, with five hundred copies of a flyer that said: 'We had a meeting, that made a decision, that started a riot.'

There were footsteps in the hallway. Keys rattled outside. An officer beckoned from the doorway and her hands automatically went to her sweatshirt, clutching it tight.

She stepped out into a narrow corridor. Heavy doors lined one side. Halfway down she saw Mark, leaning against a window. She hurried over.

'What's going on, are you OK? What are you doing here?'

'They've released me.'

'What?'

She looked him over. He seemed relaxed, cocky even.

'They'll release you too, but they think you've given a false name. If you give me your permission, I'll go back to the house and get your passport. They've said that if we give them your real name, they'll let you go.'

She glanced back towards the officer who had let her out of her cell, who was standing at a discreet distance. She would probably have to tell them her name eventually. If Mark was right, it sounded like she might even get out. Could he really have been released, as easy as that? Had the police put pressure on him to get her real identity? He seemed perfectly calm, but none of it made sense. If they were letting her out, maybe that didn't matter.

'Yes, OK,' she said. 'Get my passport. I want to go home.'

* * *

'I need to make a photocopy, and then you can go.'

Katja handed the passport over, avoiding the officer's eyes. She wondered whether he had been watching when they stripped her. It seemed that Mark had been right and she was being released, but she still didn't quite believe it. She felt empty.

'You've got no right to copy that,' Mark shouted after the retreating figure. 'She's told you who she is.'

She tried to make him stop but he was too furious.

'I'll sue the lot of you! You give that passport back or I'll see you out of a job.'

'Leave it, Mark, please. Let's just go.' She tugged at his sleeve. She couldn't understand his anger and entitlement. She was terrified that the police would change their mind and keep them in.

In the street she took a deep breath of free air. Mark shot back one last round of 'I'll have your job!' and her heart stopped as the station door swung back open. The desk officer came running out and she braced herself to be grabbed and taken back inside. Instead, he was waving a piece of paper.

'You're right,' he said. 'I shouldn't have taken a copy. Here, you can have it.'

He handed Mark the offending document, then trotted back to his post inside the station.

CHAPTER 2

The first time I encountered him, I didn't know he was there. It was summer 2003. Twenty or thirty of us sat in a marquee in a field, discussing the G8 summit that would be held in the UK two years later. That workshop was the beginning of the Dissent! Network. In the background, Mark was watching.

A child of the 1980s, I grew up supporting the miners, defending the Greater London Council, singing 'Free Nelson Mandela', marching to ban the bomb. The Berlin Wall came down in 1989. In 1990, Nelson Mandela was freed and the repeal of apartheid began. On 26 December 1991, the USSR dissolved. The Cold War between capitalism and communism was over. We were told it was the End of History. There was no longer any alternative: capitalism had won. Alternatives are hard to keep down, though, and all over the world new movements were already emerging, bringing a new kind of revolution. These burgeoning movements didn't want to seize power. They wanted to break it into small pieces that everyone could hold.

On New Year's Day 1994, the North American Free Trade Agreement came into effect. It was expected to destroy environmental protections, devastate Mexico's rural economy and fill the air with the 'giant sucking sound' of US jobs flooding across the border to more cost-effective (that is, poorer) places. The same day, indigenous Zapatista rebels emerged for the first time from the mists of the Mexican rainforest. They took control of seven cities and declared war on the policies they called *neoliberalismo*. Many of them were armed only with sticks and toy guns.

DISCLOSURE

The Zapatistas became a symbol for direct action movements all over the world, from the Indian farmers in Karnataka State who turned out in their hundreds of thousands to take down fast-food outlets, brick by brick, to the sans-papiers occupying churches across Europe against neo-colonialism and in defence of migrant rights. It is difficult to capture the power of that moment. In the words of the Notes from Nowhere collective, 'how does one begin to tell the history of a movement with no name, no manifesto, and no leaders?'

The year that Mandela walked free from Victor Verster Prison, Mark Kennedy followed in his father's footsteps and joined the City of London police. He was twenty-one. In the photos he looks younger, eager and clean-shaven with a short-back-and-sides. Four years later, just as the Zapatistas were capturing the imagination of rebels around the world, he transferred to the Met.

I had just turned sixteen.

On 9 October 1994, I joined a demonstration to defend the right to protest, challenging a new law known as the Criminal Justice Bill. I was sitting on the grass in Hyde Park, eating sandwiches with friends, when dark-blue-helmeted Metropolitan Police riot units began to move, using their little round shields to shove people back before they went in hard with the horses. Who knows? Perhaps my path crossed Mark's even earlier than I realise.

For me, those events of the mid-1990s marked a beginning. The Criminal Justice Bill targeted all kinds of resistance, from ravers to squatters to hunt saboteurs. The unexpected consequence was that it caused these disparate groups to recognise each other as allies and create hybrid movements that didn't quite fit the old models. In turn, those new UK groups linked up with the new political currents emerging around the world.

I was just a teenager, of course. That might be why I feel that this is where it began. Others, perhaps, would go further back:

to the poll tax campaigns that brought down Margaret Thatcher, or the Committee of 100 and the early Greenpeace groups, the peace camps at Greenham Common, the feminist movements of the 1970s, or the counterculture and anti-war protests of 1968.

The year 1968 is certainly where Mark's road started, although he would not be born until the following year. 1968 saw the establishment of the Special Demonstration Squad (SDS), a Metropolitan Police unit created to target protests against the Vietnam War. Officers were sent undercover to live as activists for years on end, participating in campaigns and instigating action. Their reports were filed with the Metropolitan Police Special Branch and the even more secretive 'Box 500' – a code name for MI5. As time went on, they would spy on the anti-apartheid movement, trade union organisers, the women's liberation movement and the Campaign for Nuclear Disarmament (CND). Indeed, the history of political spying by the Metropolitan Police reads a lot like a history of political dissent in the UK. Which isn't surprising: they were, quite literally, following us around.

In 1998, as I was getting more involved in political organising, the SDS, now three decades old, was sending undercover officers to infiltrate groups that had grown from opposition to the Criminal Justice Bill: groups like Reclaim the Streets, best known for its massive, party-like protests that transformed urban space.

In the summer of 1998, our campaigns against environmental destruction, road building, militarisation and social injustice were connecting with a global movement that declared its opposition to 'capitalism, imperialism and feudalism, and all trade agreements, institutions and governments that promote destructive globalisation'.* That resistance took many forms. In the UK, the 'McLibel' group was leading protests against McDonald's, showing the power

---

* From the Hallmarks of Peoples' Global Action, founded at an international conference in Geneva in 1998.

of global defiance against a monolithic corporation. Earth First! (EF) 'ecowarriors' were using direct action and acts of sabotage to confront environmental destruction at its source. Reclaim the Streets occupied roads and motorways, turning them into joyous, car-free zones. Elsewhere, Brazil's landless peasants, the Movimento dos Trabalhadores Rurais Sem Terra (MST), the Landless Workers' Movement, occupied hundreds of thousands of acres of land to turn it into farms. There were monumental sacrifices, such as the villagers of Narmada Bachao Andolan (NBA), who refused to leave their homes in India as the Narmada River valley was flooded by dams. On 4 January 1999, I was barricaded into an office at Shell Mex House in London, in a protest against oil extraction in Nigeria, when we heard that two small indigenous communities in the Niger Delta had been attacked and people killed by armed soldiers using boats and helicopters contracted by Chevron Oil.

Those international links were extremely powerful. Yet the media only really took notice of them when they led to big moments of confrontation in the richest countries of the world, such as at global economic summits, when the likes of the World Trade Organisation, the International Monetary Fund, the World Bank, the EU or the G8 held their high-profile meetings.

In London, in the late 1990s, we had long, earnest discussions about how to define our protests. We didn't want to be pigeon-holed. We debated whether to call ourselves 'anti-capitalists', afraid that it would sound like a throwback to the Cold War days. But anti-capitalists is what we were. (A radical position, at least until bankers crashed the economy in 2008.) In 1999, we wrote a pamphlet setting out the role of global finance in our struggles. We called it 'Squaring Up to the Square Mile':

Our planet is controlled by a few financial centres – principally London, New York, Chicago, Tokyo, Hong Kong, Singapore and Frankfurt. Here shares, bonds, commodities and currencies

– lives, in effect – are traded like chips at the roulette table. The game is played over linked-up computers by people who have little conception of what life is like for those at the other end of the chain, whose lives and livelihoods are made or broken at their hands. A hiccup in the markets can close a business and put thousands out of work; a lack of 'confidence' can bring a government to its knees.

Capital (and the profit it demands), lies at the root of the world's social and ecological crises. Whether it's casualisation in the Merseyside docks or rising sea levels in Bangladesh, a path can be traced back to the City of London.

We took our inspiration from ecology, from the struggles of indigenous communities, and from the intelligence of the swarm. We valued diversity and subjectivity, because we believed that personal stories had as much to teach us as any manifesto. Our biggest mobilisation wasn't even given a name: it was known only as 'J18', a reference to the date 18 June 1999, when a massive demonstration was scheduled to take place in the financial centre of London, to coincide with the twenty-fifth G8 summit in Köln. Thousands of flyers proclaimed that 'Our Resistance will be as Transnational as Capital'. On the day, there were protests in more than forty cities all over the world, networked and reported by independent media activists using then-new technologies such as email and the internet. It felt like the start of something powerful.

Mark's unit, the National Public Order Intelligence Unit (NPOIU), was also set up in 1999. The first NPOIU officers to go undercover joined those of the SDS in spying on the organising meetings for J18. Mark Kennedy himself started working for the NPOIU's highly classified operations in the first half of 2003.

On 3 February 2003, I joined more than a million people on a march through London to oppose the Iraq War. That was a defining memory. I turned eighteen in 1996 and voted for the first time on

DISCLOSURE

1 May 1997. It was the first election in my lifetime that actually changed the party in power. Yet New Labour quickly proved a disappointment, cosying up to bankers, tabling 'anti-terror' legislation that targeted peaceful protest, and lying about Weapons of Mass Destruction to defend their decision to wage war in Iraq. So, we marched. I remember passing posters and graffiti along the route. The image of a war plane dropping depleted uranium bombs under the slogan 'Democracy, we deliver'. That march was possibly the largest political demonstration in UK history, yet the British government pressed on with their war regardless. The lessons of that day were not new, but they were clear: political change would not come about through voting, or even demonstrating. For protests to be effective they needed to be impossible to ignore.

We already knew then that the G8 summit would be hosted in Britain in 2005. Tony Blair chose 'climate change' to top the agenda, an ironic choice, since the Group of 8 was set up partly in response to the oil crises of the 1970s, with a remit to secure access to energy reserves for the most industrialised economies. The G8 was the epitome of the rationale driving both climate change and the oil wars raging across the world.

So, in the early summer of 2003, I packed a bag to travel to the Earth First! Summer Gathering, where hundreds of activists would come together to share skills, discuss ideas and plan future campaigns. And as I was preparing my notes for that workshop about resisting the G8 summit, the NPOIU were giving Mark Kennedy his orders. They issued him with a false driving licence and passport bearing his new, fictitious identity: 'Mark Stone'.

CHAPTER 3

21 October 2010 – Barcelona, Spain

Nine missed calls. A UK number, and not in my contacts. In the shade of a mulberry tree in the middle of the yard, I called back and listened to the English ring tone.

'Hello, Katja? I'm sorry to call you like this, but we thought you shouldn't find out from the internet. Mark's police, Katja. He's a cop. Always was. We have proof. We're going public this afternoon.'

Greg. A long-time comrade from Earth First! and a good friend. He sounded exhausted.

After a pause, I said 'OK.' I couldn't think of anything else. When he rang off, I was left standing on the patio, suddenly aware of sounds all around me: someone clattering pots in the kitchen; Italian punk music coming from one of the rooms upstairs; the blood rushing in my ears. What happened now? I thought of all the people I had introduced Mark to; the bright social scene we had been a part of, and the daredevil things we had done together over the years.

I dropped all my plans and booked tickets to fly to London for the annual Anarchist Bookfair that weekend. It was a key moment on the campaigning calendar, and many of Mark's former comrades would be there. Speakers that year included John Pilger and *Newsnight*'s Paul Mason, but, for those of us who knew Mark, there was only one event that mattered. I picked my way across a hall filled with trestle tables piled high with books and posters. My face burnt as I searched for the classroom where the crisis meeting would take place. I tried not to meet anyone's eye.

Hard chairs were arranged in a circle. No one else was there yet, but I couldn't go back into the crowded hall, so I sat near the back of the room. Soon there were more people than seats. People were crammed onto tables that had been pushed to the walls, and I was hemmed in.

Greg and some of the others who uncovered Mark's identity sat opposite, looking drained. They briefly explained what had happened: someone had found a passport suggesting that Mark was not who he claimed. Suspicions were raised, leading to searches on the register of births, marriages and deaths that revealed his real name to be Mark Kennedy. Mark Kennedy was police. They had confronted him on Wednesday night. He admitted it.

'We're holding this meeting to pass on what we know to the movements he spied on.'

I glanced around the room. There were people I knew there from all over the country, from direct action networks like Earth First!, Climate Camp, Dissent! and the W.O.M.B.L.E.S.; from the Social Centres Network, the Radical Routes housing co-ops and the London squats.

The discussion came to life, and I saw Greg sit back slightly, clearly relieved to have handed over the burden. People shared their recollections of the man we had thought we knew. I realised that I had been one of the first people to befriend him. I picked at the skin on my knuckles as the talk moved on to the backstory we had been given: Mark Stone. A working-class boy from a broken home in Battersea. One brother in America. An elderly mother in Ireland. Left school early to work as a cycle courier in the City, and later a delivery driver with his own van. An ex-girlfriend from Chelsea, bit of a 'Sloane Ranger'. He loved climbing, had spent time in Pakistan. In the shady jargon of undercover policing that

I would come to know so well, this was his 'legend'. Set out like this, it didn't feel like a lot to account for thirty-four years. People wondered aloud how he had ever managed to seem like a real person, and I felt a growing unease. Mark hadn't liked talking about his past. He claimed to have his reasons.

I raised my hand.

'When I first met him, he told me he had been involved in smuggling drugs. He sort of implied that he was running away from that life, and that some pretty dangerous people might want to know where he was.'

The absurdity of it hit me as I spoke the words. Was I stupid enough to fall for that? But what else could I have done? It's not the kind of story you can check.

The meeting went on, but I heard little of what was said, lost in an internal argument. I only noticed that the meeting was over when everyone stood up. The conversation went on, in couples and small groups, rippling out of the room as people headed towards the stairs.

Those ripples would soon spread across Europe and the conversation would continue for many months to come.

A small group gathered at the Nottingham housing co-operative where I used to live – Neds, after the folk legend Ned Ludd, a tribute to the city's history of Luddite resistance. My old friend, Eleanor, embraced me at the door and we stood there holding each other for a long while: the first thing I had really felt for days. When we met at university in 1996, we were Town Mouse and Country Mouse. I was coming up from London to study modern history, full of enthusiasm for student politics, throwing myself into campaigning, signing up to support migrants at the local detention centre. Eleanor was from a small village in Hampshire, bringing her love of the natural world to the study of biology. Chance made us roommates in our first year, and our respective interests in social justice and ecology eventually brought us together on the same environmental protests. We became best friends, living together first in Oxford, then Manchester, and finally Nottingham, where we shared a house with Mark Stone.

'He had a wife,' Eleanor whispered as we walked into the hall. 'He had children. Our lives, our memories, our friendship: we were just his work.'

Feeling unsteady, I reached out to touch her again.

We spent those days in Nottingham going over our memories, reminding ourselves who we were, trying and failing to make sense of it all. I remember there being no daylight. Perhaps it was the grey English autumn, or perhaps we just kept the curtains closed.

'Do you think he really was in Thailand?' Lisa asked one evening.

A small group of us were sitting around her on a bed. We had all lost something, but Lisa had lost most of all. She was Mark's partner after me, for six years. She was the first person to discover he was not who he said he was, and, with the help of Greg and the others, she had begun the awful process of exposing his lies.

I thought about her question. Mark told us he was going to Thailand during Christmas of 2004. On Boxing Day the news broke that a tsunami had hit the region. I was terrified, checking for texts, a call, an email, watching the news, thinking he might be dead. On his return he seemed so damaged. It had all seemed very real. I realised with a start that he had probably never been there. Far more likely that he spent that Christmas with his family.

I didn't know it at the time, but those late October days of closeness and mourning in Nottingham marked an ending. The changes were almost imperceptible: a growing discomfort around people; an almost unconscious avoidance of the places and situations that reminded me of him; a festering anger; and a sensitivity I had never felt before. The slightest conflict would lead to dark thoughts that went far beyond the scope of any real disagreement. An argument about taking the bins out would, in the confines of my head, become a vague but overwhelming fear that the other person wished me ill. The changes were subtle, and it took time for the shifts in my thinking to make themselves felt.

The panic attacks were different. They were impossible to ignore. Two months after the discovery, I was back in Nottingham to celebrate New Year. I walked through the rooms of the same co-operative feeling jarred by the festivities. No longer in mourning, the house was full of people and lights. A couple stumbled towards me in the hallway like they didn't see me, and I pressed my back against the wall to let them pass. I could hear my own breathing, so loud it drowned out the music. There was a tremor in my chest, tiny and frantic, like a small animal scrabbling to escape.

I need air.

I pushed through the front door, tripping over a pair of wellingtons on the porch, and recoiled at the sight of my old caravan looming on the drive. I rushed out, trying not to look at it, and stood in the street with my back to the house, hands on my knees, breathing in deep gulps of night air. The sounds of revelry continued behind me, but I wasn't going back in. I got in my car and drove away. It would be eight years before I set foot in Nottingham again.

I entered 2011 pulling into the fast lane, somewhere on the M1. My gaze was fixed on the wheels of the heavy goods vehicle pounding the tarmac a few feet to my left. Holding my breath, hands tense on the steering wheel, the truck inching closer to the line between our lanes.

'Lift your vision.'

I hit the brakes. The car swerved towards the central reservation and then righted itself as I pulled back in behind the truck. I could hear his voice like he was sitting in the car beside me. The memory was visceral:

DISCLOSURE

'When you're overtaking, lift your vision,' Mark explained gently. 'Don't look at the truck, look beyond it, to where you're going.'

I am losing my mind.

In the silence of my parents' empty flat, my head rattled with questions. On impulse, I fired up my laptop and began to write.

From: Kate Wilson
Date: Sun, 02 Jan 2011 21:23:40
To: Mark Kennedy
Subject: 'the desert's quiet, and cleveland's cold and so the story ends, we're told . . .'

i saw a documentary, about thailand.

and i was wondering.

about all of it.

about the time we lived together, about the weeks after you came back from thailand (i assume you did really go to thailand?), about all the times i had your back when the cops beat you up. about the years i was your . . . what? . . . meal ticket??

i have a lot of questions.

you know where i am. as always, you have the advantage on me there. in fact, i guess you know just about everything there is to know about me.

but if you have anything worth saying to say for yourself, i'd be interested to hear it.

i wonder what you make of it now . . .

katja

It had been an old joke of ours, writing without capital letters: anti-capitalism. I meant it as a wink, a signal – *whatever my words say, I am still the person you knew, still think of you as a friend.*

As soon as I hit send, I regretted it. I didn't really expect him to respond, but I got a reply just a few hours later.

From: Mark Kennedy
Date: Sun, 02 Jan 2011 23:10:26
To: Kate Wilson
Subject: RE: 'the desert's quiet, and cleveland's cold and so the story ends, we're told . . .'
The cold is every where Katja.

It was a cryptic first line. The subject was a line from a favourite song of mine: 'Pancho and Lefty'. It's about an outlaw whose sidekick snitches to the FBI. In the end, Pancho is killed, and Lefty runs away to Cleveland to live off the money he was paid for his treachery. It was meant as a dig – Lefty cuts a pathetic character by the end – but it was also a question, as I had a feeling Mark was also in Cleveland at the time. His answer made clear that he wasn't giving anything away.

He thanked me for writing, though, and wrote about our relationship as though it had been something beautiful.

> You showed me something those many years ago. More
> than I think you realised. I am grateful for that and grate-
> ful for the times we spent together and the experiences
> and love that we shared and your care in times of difficul-
> ties. In return all i shared with you was from deep within.
> You were and still are very important to me . . . In the past
> I expressed how I felt many times to you in different ways.
> I wrote a poem about you if you remember. That was not
> about trying to fool you or anyone else.

He talked about his feelings of loneliness and despair, and the hatred people must feel for him, and then he said this:

30

DISCLOSURE

I know you knew me better than most. So I hope you will understand when I say that so many many things never went anywhere. You and others were never mentioned by me ever. Make of that what you will. There is no black and white only a huge grey area in which I was trapped. If I left then the people I cared about would get more attention by others like me and to stay just compounded the situation.

I'd had visions of faceless police officers leafing through reams of files about the most intimate details of my life, and lurid canteen banter about Mark and me. But here he was saying that he hadn't told them about us at all. Had he really loved me? Is that what he meant? I was hit by a wave of relief, followed by one of nausea. Just by talking to him, I was betraying all the people he had betrayed. Why should I expect anything from him but more lies? His poor-me tone was sickening. He hadn't even answered my direct question about Thailand. Had he said anything of substance at all?

I shot back an angry reply at 1 a.m. telling him it was all bullshit, and then, in a fit of remorse, another telling him to take care. At that point I realised I had to stop. I crawled into bed, my stomach churning.

A couple of months later, Lisa came to see me in Barcelona. She had lost weight and looked faded, her red hair tightly bound in plaits. 'The news coverage has been awful,' she explained.

I was surprised. The initial stories had filled me with hope. The *Guardian* and the BBC led with Mark's role in the trial of a group of activists. They quite clearly implied that he had 'gone native' and supported the protesters, causing the prosecution case to collapse. That quickly degenerated when reporters discovered he had been having sex, but I hadn't realised how bad it got.

Lisa read aloud from one of the articles:

'The wine was chilling in the cooler on the plastic camp table alongside the white Transit van in which the couple had spent the hours locked in embrace. But for undercover police officer Mark Kennedy, it was a day that was to blow his cover. For his girlfriend, a shapely red-headed Welsh activist, was about to make a startling discovery . . .'

She put it down.

'That's from an interview *he* gave to the tabloids,' she said. 'He's hired Max Clifford to be his publicist. There were reporters going up and down the tow-path, looking for an exclusive from Mark's "shapely redhead"'. Her voice shook. 'I'm being hunted.'

It baffled me that Mark had chosen to engage Clifford's services. In his email to me he had implied that he wanted to 'recount everything' in order to ensure that the situation could never happen again. Yet now he had signed up with a publicist notorious for selling kiss-and-tell stories to tabloids. Anger welled.

'We should sue the police,' I said.

'Some people are already suggesting some kind of class action,' Lisa replied. 'I'm not sure I can imagine anything worse right now. Getting together with everyone he slept with would just encourage this focus on Mark and his sexual behaviour. I can't bear it. It's too raw.'

We sat in silence. After a while, she spoke: 'You should do what you feel is right. But do you think you could wait until I've had time to figure out what I want to do myself?'

I was angry at myself that she might have felt I was pushing her.

She left the next morning, and I didn't think about legal action again for a long time. I went back to university, to face, and ultimately fail, my end-of-year exams. Summer turned to autumn. I tried to forget what had happened, but every few weeks Mark would reappear in the British media, giving gut-twisting interviews about his life as a police spy.

CHAPTER 4

Almost a year to the day after I received the news about Mark, I found myself out on the patio, under the same mulberry tree, taking another call.

'We're going to sue them,' Lisa said. 'I know you said you wanted to, and I asked you to wait, but things have changed.'

I stood with the phone pressed to my ear, pushing a piece of twig around with my toe.

'It's not only about Mark any more,' she said. 'There are five officers implicated, which means it was a tactic, not just a one-off. I've spoken to Naomi. She's going to be involved. This whole process is so hard for me, but you, me, Naomi, we're all friends, so it should be easier. The lawyer is nice. Her name is Harriet. Have you got a pen?'

I realised I had been holding my breath.

'Yes, go on.'

'The thing is, there's a deadline. We only have until 21 October.'

Trapping the phone against my shoulder, I wrote down the date and began drawing circles around it. Round and round. The approaching anniversary was no coincidence, then.

'Take down this number. She knows you might call, but you need to hurry. You've only got a few days left to prepare your claim.'

After we said our goodbyes, I sat looking at the note. I drew a box around the phone number, turned it into a cube and began shading the sides. I had vague and unpleasant notions of what happens to women who bring charges against men involving sex. In this case the men were police. From the corners of the cube, I drew lines to the circle around the date. Seven days.

I hadn't slept through the night for almost a year. I would wake before dawn, paralysed by the mass of questions boiling in my mind. Mornings started with fear, followed by a mental scan of my body and my reality, in search of the source of my unease. Minutes would go by. Hours. I missed my classes. As the sun crept higher, the light hit my face, sending patterns across the backs of my eyelids, like the purple-tinted cells I should have been studying under a microscope in the histology lab. My studies had foundered until it was impossible to catch up and I lost my place at the university. I had to move on, but I spent my days obsessing about what had happened.

This was an opportunity to do something, and it sounded like if I didn't do it soon I might lose that chance.

I picked up the phone and dialled.

Harriet was friendly, but sounded cautious. Her voice went up at the end of her sentences, turning them into questions, as though she was worried that she might upset me if she were too definite. She explained I would have to make a formal statement, and that the Human Rights Act placed limits on the time available: you only have one year after the event to make a claim. She was a little unclear how that might apply in this case. My sexual relationship with Mark ended eight years ago, but we remained friends for years after that. However, she was very sure that the clock had started ticking on 21 October, when I found out he was a police officer. We only had a week left. I explained it was impossible for me to get to London, so we would have to do it all by email or phone. I was nervous, convinced that our communications would be intercepted, but I answered her questions as best I could, about my relationship with Mark, and the impact that discovering his deceit had had on me.

DISCLOSURE

The one-year deadline imposed by the Human Rights Act felt impossible. The last twelve months had gone by like scenery past a moving car. I didn't feel I had even begun to understand what had happened, or what the full impact would be. And yet, we did it: a collective claim was issued on 20 October 2011, less than twenty-four hours before we ran out of time.

* * *

'I had to have sex with eco-warriors to keep my cover'
                    31 December 2011 – Daily Mail

I stared at the headline, blinking occasionally to check it was real. Two weeks before, we had released a statement announcing that we were suing the police. It took weeks of back and forth by email with Harriet and the seven other women, who I hadn't even met in person yet. It was terrifying going public, but we knew it was coming.

This, however, was unexpected.

'An undercover police officer has defended having sexual relationships with unsuspecting eco-activists, saying they were "essential" to maintaining a convincing cover story. Mark Kennedy, who spent eight years posing as eco-warrior Mark "Flash" Stone, has spoken out after learning that three women plan to sue the Metropolitan Police for emotional distress, saying he "duped" them into sex.'

People used to call him 'Flash'. I had forgotten that. He obviously liked the nickname enough to tell the papers about it.

'"I never conned anyone into having sex," he says. "I lived undercover for eight years and if I hadn't had sex, I would have blown my cover."'

I scanned my way down the article.

'"I am not the first man to give a false name to a woman . . ."'

My eyes narrowed. Everything he told me about himself, from his life story to his moral beliefs, had been a fiction he was paid to tell. Did he think it was normal for men to lie to women to get them into bed?

I couldn't recognise the person I had known and loved. He claimed that he had been 'celibate' for the first year of his operation. I did the maths: less than five months after he first went undercover he was already sleeping with me. He also claimed that Mark Stone only slept with two women. I knew that was untrue. Our life together had been one set of lies and now he was creating another, weaving a new legend from the fragments of the old: Mark Kennedy, ex-undercover cop, telling his story to the *Daily Mail*.

He even gave them his wife's name, the ages of his children and intimate details about the state of their family life. I wondered if his family were reading it too. Would they also struggle to recognise this man?

'*"I talked to my cover officer dozens of times a day. There is no way he could not have known about a relationship. I told him where I was going and with whom. He knew where I spent my nights. I didn't have to spell it out to him. I couldn't go to the loo without him knowing."*'

My heart beat faster. Mark told me he had never mentioned me. Senior police in charge of undercover operations had made statements saying sexual relationships while undercover would never be permitted 'under any circumstances'. But now Mark was saying his handler knew everything he did. I thought back. He was the original phone addict, constantly texting on his BlackBerry at a time when many of us didn't even have mobiles. Had he been talking to his cover officer right in front of my face?

'*Kennedy says that his first sexual encounter came with a woman who "seduced" him at a party in Leeds in 2003. He believes she is one of his lawsuit accusers, although the women's identities are not being disclosed.*

'*"She came up and planted a huge kiss on me," he says. "One thing led to another and we ended up in bed. We had an on–off sexual relationship for two years. The lawsuit makes it sound as if I was predatory but I treated the women lovingly.*

DISCLOSURE

"I am surprised she states we were in a relationship from 2003 to 2005. She had multiple lovers and I didn't consider her a proper girlfriend."'

I went hollow inside.

There was a photograph with the article: Mark, but not my Mark, with his long hair, wrap-around shades and aura of rebellion. This man was visibly older, dressed in a flat cap and khaki jacket like he was about to go grouse shooting, facing the camera, looking stern.

My skin crawled. Those eyes saw me naked.

I had thought the worst thing about this was the unknowns, but now I realised that the answers I got might be worse. I felt cold and my legs shook as I climbed onto the bed and turned towards the wall, pulling the duvet tight around me, curling into a ball.

When I woke, I felt different. Memories of Mark, my friend and my lover, were still there, but they were shattered, I couldn't make them fit. The understanding that I had been used and taken advantage of took shape while I slept. It swept aside any sweetness left in those recollections like so much dust and broken glass. I was smaller, but also wound tight with anger, and determined in a way that I hadn't felt before.

We had been exchanging emails for over two months, sometimes dozens a day, and now here we were, sitting at a long dining table in the conservatory–restaurant of a hotel in west Wales. Harriet made the introductions. Lisa and Naomi I knew; we'd been friends for years, and all three of us had had relationships with Mark. Next around the table was Rosa. Her face was familiar. I raised an eyebrow and she nodded.

'I think we made banners together in a squatted church in North London back in the late 1990s,' she said.

I remembered her then, and her boyfriend Jim, from the many Tuesday-night meetings of Reclaim the Streets. Jim was a cop, it turned out. His real name was Jim Boyling. I tried that idea in my mind, poking at it like a sore tooth. I wasn't close to him, but I must have seen him once or twice a week at meetings for over a year. He and Rosa were among the cooler, older members of the group, when I was still new on the scene, green and enthusiastic. I had looked up to him.

'Hi, I'm Alison.'

Alison was a down-to-earth socialist. She had a wicked sense of humour that was quick and merciless towards wishy-washy anarcho-ecologist types like me. She explained that she had been involved in anti-racist campaigning and she had been in a relationship for five years with a man she knew as Mark Cassidy, until he suddenly appeared to have a breakdown and disappeared. She searched for him for years, and she now knew his real name was Mark Jenner, and he was a spy for the Metropolitan Police.

I liked Alison immediately. She felt provocative and outside my comfort zone. Somehow the fact that she came from beyond our activist scene made everything seem more real.

The last woman at the table was Belinda. As she told her story I realised with horror that the undercover officer she had been with – Bob Lambert – met her at a party, lied to her about who he was, started a relationship with her and moved into her flat, even though she hadn't been involved in any political groups at all. At the time, she worked in accounting. There was simply no conceivable reason for Lambert to target Belinda, except to shore up his own backstory.

Harriet explained that Ruth and Helen were not able to attend. I knew Helen already though. Everyone knew Helen Steel: she took on McDonald's in the longest civil trial in UK history, and I had been a little in awe of her ever since we first met in 1998. Lisa told me later that she was part of the group because, years before I met her, she had a relationship with a man called 'John Barker'. Like Mark Cassidy, 'John' seemed to suffer a long, traumatic emotional breakdown, then disappeared. Like Alison, Helen spent years searching. She discovered that the real John Barker had died in 1968, at the age of eight. The man she knew was called John Dines. For his work as a Special Branch spy, he had stolen the identity of a dead child.

Ruth, like Rosa, Helen and I, had been part of Reclaim the Streets. She went out with Jim before Rosa did, and we must have met once or twice in the 1990s. Working with her on the case, she impressed me, coming across as intelligent and reserved, speaking quietly and rarely. I tend to talk too much, nervously blurting out ideas before passing them through my brain. Not so Ruth: when she decided to say something, it was always thoughtful and deep.

We were eight women in all, with an all-women legal team. We came from different backgrounds and different political groups; we had relationships with five different officers, from two different units, and between us those relationships spanned around thirty years.

We cautiously felt our way around each other, on gentle country walks, and over long dinners, during the breaks between legal meetings. We built trust and shared our stories, and as we did, it became clear that the relationships we had were not one-offs, and they were not just personal betrayals. These men repeated patterns. They used similar techniques to manipulate and groom us. They must have been trained to do what they did.

Harriet, our solicitor, explained the details of bringing legal claims for civil damages. The claims would focus on the torts of Deceit, Misfeasance in Public Office, Negligence and Assault.

The assault claim caused us some unease. We talked about it for a long time. What had happened to us was hard to define, and none of us felt totally comfortable labelling ourselves victims of sexual assault. Eventually we did include it though. Ruth eloquently expressed why:

'Assault says: he never should have touched me. In some ways this cuts across the emotional difficulties, the ambiguities of love, betrayal, failure, anger, confusion – all those things that are hard to get your head round – and says quite categorically, in no uncertain terms – he shouldn't have touched me. And the moment he did touch me, he was breaking the law.'

Having read Mark describing our relationship to the tabloids, I felt less ambiguous than some of the other women there.

'The man is a complete narcissist!' Alison exclaimed, reading the article.

I glanced around the table. Lisa was fiddling with a fork, looking uncomfortable. I wondered if this latest dispatch from the Kennedy media operation had affected her memories as much as it had mine. Our eyes met for a moment, then she put the fork down.

'This isn't about a man who lied in a relationship,' she said. 'It's bigger than that. Our personal relationships were being controlled by the state without our knowledge. The press are making it all about him, but *they* made the decisions – whether I would go to dinner with my boyfriend, whether he would come to family events. Every time they mention Mark Kennedy we should mention his bosses and talk about culpability higher up the chain.'

At that point Harriet cut in to ask us what we were hoping to achieve by bringing the case. Although we were a diverse group of women, on that we spoke as one voice.

'We want answers. We want our files. We want to know the truth about what happened; and we want to make sure that this doesn't happen to any other woman ever again.'

CHAPTER 5

'The Claimants have no real prospects of succeeding on any of the claims or issues.'

We read the letter from the police solicitors with dismay. They had responded to our claim by informing us they would be applying for 'summary judgment', asking the judges to throw the case out without a trial. Harriet assured us that, although she was surprised, she wasn't worried by their unhelpful and combative tone. They refused to respond to our accusations, which would have been the normal course of events. Instead, they insisted we set out the details of what we thought we knew. Then, in April 2012, they wrote again:

'The intimate and sexual relationship which it is claimed Mark Kennedy formed with your client was a "personal or other relationship" covered by the [Regulation of Investigatory Powers Act 2000 (RIPA)] Authorisations and his conduct was therefore "lawful for all purposes" by virtue of s.27(1) of RIPA . . . As the Commissioner of Police of the Metropolis would, potentially, be vicariously liable only for unlawful conduct (under s.88 of the Police Act 1988), it would seem that your clients cannot succeed with their claims.'

Having publicly stated it could never be permitted, were they now saying Mark was officially authorised to sleep with us? They seemed to think that would be the end of it for our claim, but I was reassured by Harriet's response.

'It just gets madder and madder. Unless they are playing some very clever, convoluted game, I think we are dealing with a complete idiot.'

The police did get rid of that solicitor, and quickly dropped any suggestion that they might have authorised Mark to have sex with the women he was spying on. I never forgot though. It was their first real response to our claim, and it hinted at a dark world of operational back rooms, hidden behind layers of acronyms, authorities and command structures, and peopled by the nameless, faceless men who sent Mark into my life, gave him his orders and ran him the whole time he was there.

Their next step was to apply for the claims lodged by Lisa, Naomi and me to be 'struck out' and sent to a shadowy offshoot of the Home Office known as the Investigatory Powers Tribunal, or IPT. Our High Court claim was stopped in its tracks while the judges considered whether it should be heard behind closed doors by this obscure Tribunal, a court so secret that at the time it wouldn't even say how many cases it dealt with, let alone what it had decided.

The other five claims, where the events in question took place before the IPT was created, continued in the High Court. However, they fared no better. The police argued that because of a supposed policy of 'neither confirm nor deny', they would be unable to offer any defence. It would therefore be 'unfair' to take them to trial. They failed to provide any evidence that such a policy existed, and eventually they withdrew the application, but it would not be the last we heard of 'NCND'.

Those early applications for strike outs and secrecy set the tone for what was to become a stream of delaying and bullying tactics. For years, we were required to hand over seemingly endless details about our intimate personal lives, while the police gave us nothing at all.

In the spring of 2012, six of us were in a Greek café–restaurant in London, somewhere near the Inns of Court. Things always got a bit tense when choosing restaurants: we wandered around trying to accommodate everyone's preferences, and as people got hungrier, tempers began to fray. Once we were comfortably settled around a table, however, and the waiter brought dolmas, falafel, dips, flatbreads and salads, peace returned, and the conversation turned to what was on all our minds: the psych reports.

The interviews with the psychologist were upsetting and strange. We were asked about the men who deceived us, and about our darkest thoughts and fears. We were asked how it was affecting our health, our sleep patterns, our sex lives and our relationships, and how we were coping in our day-to-day lives. It was not therapy. There was no sense that we were there to heal the damage done. We were simply documenting our madness, our failures and our inability to move on, because it was a legal requirement that we reveal our suffering and weakness to the court. If there was no damages claim, we had no case. Yet to bring the case at all, to weather the intrusion of the experts, to bear reliving the experiences and exposing the intimate details of our private lives, we needed to be strong.

Back at home, the strain of that contradiction was tearing my relationships apart. It felt like the state was trying to take away my last coping mechanism by making me admit how broken I was. I was irritable and withdrawn with my partner, my friends and my housemates, prone to flashes of rage followed by tears that I only allowed to fall in private because I was terrified about revealing my vulnerability. Here, though, we were all going through the same thing.

'I'm finding this the most triggering thing yet,' Helen said with characteristic frankness. 'Why should we now have to give even more of our personal thoughts and experiences to a stranger who is going to compile a report to be handed to the police? Haven't they invaded our lives enough?'

I could see that the tensions I felt were weighing on all the women. I was flooded with anger that they, that we, were being put through this. But I also felt relief. Maybe I wasn't going crazy after all. If I was, at least I wasn't going it alone.

Almost a year into bringing our claim, we had provided the court (and through them, our abusers) with unimaginable quantities of private information about our lives, both before and after. Everything was exposed, from our financial circumstances to our medical records to our desperate feelings of confusion and loss. We were learning that the Civil Courts were not made for this. There was no place for complex emotions, unless we could give them a price. There had been a lot of talk about compensation, but we were yet to receive any answers at all.

'What the court doesn't seem to understand is that compensation here isn't about money, it's about closure,' Lisa complained, 'and closure can't happen without the truth.'

What we got instead was spy fiction, in the form of a Judgment from Justice Tugendhat, on 17 January 2013:

> James Bond is the most famous fictional example of a member of the intelligence services who used relationships with women to obtain information, or access to persons or property. Since he was writing a light entertainment, Ian Fleming did not dwell on the extent to which his hero used deception, still less upon the psychological harm he might have done to the women concerned. But fictional accounts (and there are others) lend credence to the view that the intelligence and police services have for many years deployed both men and women officers to form personal relationships of an intimate sexual nature (whether or not they were physical relationships) in order to obtain information or access . . . In the 1980s and the 1990s, when the Regulation of Investigatory Powers Act and other statutes were passing through Parliament, everyone in public life would, in my view, have assumed, whether rightly or wrongly, that the intelligence services and the police did from time to time deploy officers . . . in this way.

44

What the ruling meant in practice was that the police had won their application for secrecy. It all hung on whether Parliament intended the phrase 'personal and other relationships' to include undercover police having sex. Informed by his reading of James Bond, Justice Tugendhat concluded that it had.

We knew almost nothing about the Investigatory Powers Tribunal. We tried to find information, but it proved almost impossible, and as far as we could tell, it had seemingly unlimited discretionary powers to hear claims in secret, and a track record of almost never ruling against the Secret State. We appealed the decision to send our human rights claims there, but lost again in November of 2013. The ruling on that occasion was equally disturbing. The judges stated, 'there is no doubt that, in enacting the Regulation of Investigatory Powers Act, Parliament intended to override fundamental human rights.'

We had been fighting through the courts for three years and we were still no closer to getting any answers from the police. We hadn't even heard from Mark Kennedy's media machine in almost a year. In December 2012, Max Clifford was arrested on suspicion of sexual offences against teenage girls. With that, Mark's career as a B-list celebrity appeared to end. He had given his last media interview in November of that year, after which there was silence. The very last we heard was when the Home Affairs Select Committee published transcripts of evidence he had given in secret, *in camera* hearings, at the end of February 2013.

From The Home Affairs Select Committee Review of Undercover Policing, Interim Report
Michael Ellis: You feel the other party fully gave her consent?
Mark Kennedy: Correct.
Michael Ellis: You accept there was deception in the

relationship in that she did not know your true identity, do you?
Mark Kennedy: No, I disagree with that.

Even reading it in a dry and lifeless transcript, I could sense that his answer created confusion in the room.

Michael Ellis: You disagree with the concept that there was deception in the relationship?
Mark Kennedy: Yes.
Michael Ellis: Can you elaborate? Can you explain why?
Mark Kennedy: Because the person that I was seeing, the person that I was sleeping with, was sleeping with Mark Stone.
Chair: With Mark Stone? That is you.

This was Mark Kennedy speaking about Mark Stone in the third person, like he was someone else. Were the cracks beginning to show?

Michael Ellis: So you are saying that because she knew you as an individual called Mark Stone there was no deception that she did not know that your other job was a police officer?
Mark Kennedy: In the sense that I was an undercover police officer, I accept your point, but in the world that I was working in then for all intents and purposes I was Mark Stone.

He seemed to see no contradiction. He believed he had been two different people at once.

It was to be Mark Kennedy's last public act for years to come. For a while, I re-read the interviews. I even watched the documentary he made, *Confessions of an Undercover Cop* (2011). I wanted to understand how he had gone from the dweeby-looking young bobby photographed in his uniform the day he joined the City of London Police to the charismatic man I fell in love with.

The most striking thing about his film was how empty it was. Not one of the people he spied on agreed to talk to the documentary team, and the result was a resounding and dignified silence from the activist community, that the producers tried to fill using actors, to poor effect. Mark himself cut a pathetic figure. He was described by the *Guardian*'s Simon Hattenstone as a very confused man with 'no job, no friends and no idea who he really is'. His attempts to recreate himself as some kind of romantic hero in the public eye appeared to have failed. Meanwhile the police hierarchy were closing ranks. Relationships could never have been authorised: Mark Kennedy was a bad apple, an officer gone rogue.

CHAPTER 6

I have heard it said you can tell how worried the British state is about something by the number of official inquiries it creates. By 2014, revelations about undercover policing had sparked no less than eighteen separate investigations, and the litany of scandals kept mounting. It emerged that undercover officers had given false testimony to the courts, fathered children while undercover, stolen the identities of dead children to create their fake back stories, and maintained illegal blacklists of trade union agitators and environmental campaigners to prevent them from getting work in industry. The drop that really overflowed the bucket, however, was the Ellison Review.

I watched on the news as the Secretary of State for the Home Office, Theresa May, stepped up to the podium, to address the House of Commons.

'With permission, Mr Speaker, I would like to make a statement about the Mark Ellison Review . . .'

Almost two years earlier, Mark Ellison QC had been commissioned to investigate allegations of police corruption in their handling of the murder of black teenager Stephen Lawrence, in 1993.

'The totality of what the report shows is deeply troubling . . .'

It was.

'It will be of grave concern to everyone in the House and beyond . . .'

In fact, Ellison's investigation had been well underway when an ex-undercover officer, Peter Francis, blew the whistle on the fact that the police had sent spies to report on and discredit the Lawrence family campaign. Despite already being under investigation for withholding evidence, the Metropolitan Police had chosen not to volunteer that information themselves.

'My permanent secretary has therefore commissioned a forensic external review in order to establish the full extent of the Home Office's knowledge . . .'

Theresa May went on to announce a full-blown, judge-led public inquiry into undercover policing. It would bring dozens – eventually hundreds – of people together in an incredibly diverse group. More and more groups discovered that they had been reported on, from large, mainstream organisations such as Greenpeace, the Labour Party and the Young Liberals, to small local campaigns like the Battersea Redevelopment Action Group, Uist Hedgehog Rescue, School Kids Against the Nazis and Eat Out Vegan Wales. As our co-ordinated campaigns grew, it became apparent that dozens more women had been deceived into long-term intimate relationships. Every time we thought we had a handle on what we were dealing with, something else would emerge.

'Happy Birthday, darling.'

My parents were waiting to greet me in the hall. Dad was wearing an apron and I could smell cooking. Garlic, maybe aubergine. Mum had prepared a little pile of gifts for me, beautifully wrapped in pink tissue paper.

A news programme was playing on the TV, but Dad turned off the sound while I opened my presents. The last parcel was a flat rectangle. I turned it over and weighed it in my hands before tearing back the wrapping. It was a book. The cover showed a close-up from behind of a man on a demonstration, wearing a *V for Vendetta* mask on the back of his head.

Undercover: The True Story of Britain's Secret Police. The authors were two *Guardian* journalists who had worked with activists and a whistle-blower to break the police's veil of silence about their spies.

I flipped through, turning to Chapter 14: 'Birth of the Hound Dog'. It talked about Mark's life before I met him, how he had joined the police as a teenager and later worked undercover, buying cocaine in North London to catch drug dealers. I wondered about that. It wasn't unlike the story he told me about his drug-dealing past, only then he was the dealer, not the cop. Was that how it worked? Were all the lies he told some kind of fun-house-mirror distortion of things that were real?

I turned back to the beginning. The book opened with a scene from 1994: British undercover police officers sitting together in a safe house, watching the news from Germany, as people gained access to their *Stasi* files. The comparison was not just rhetorical. *Undercover* told story after shocking story of undercover operatives in the UK's secret political police units, going back to 1968. I had heard some of them before, but seeing them all together brought it home to me: this was far bigger than my personal feelings of loss and betrayal.

There are churches on both sides of the river at Putney, with almost matching, fifteenth-century towers. I like to stand in the middle of the bridge where they appear like reflections on either side, or perhaps rival positions. St Mary's, on the south side, is the more famous of the two. Cromwell's New Model Army hosted the revolutionary 'Putney Debates' there in 1647, during the English Civil War. These days it has a modern extension, with a light and airy café. Eleanor and I went there to eat cake. Around us, young mothers sported off-road buggies spattered with mud from the tow-path. Eleanor was filling me in on some of the latest revelations.

'Do you remember Rod Richardson?'

Rod had lived with my ex-boyfriend, John, at Neds housing co-op in Nottingham, back in 2001, just before I moved in. I remembered visiting, sharing dinners with all the housemates, and trooping across the road afterwards to the social centre bar, taking a shortcut through the fire exit at the back. I remembered Rod's bedroom too; it was dominated by bizarre cartoons he had painted across one wall.

'That eight-foot sperm-worm mural he did always weirded me out a bit,' I remarked. It seemed even weirder now, knowing he had been an on-duty police officer when he was seized by that creative urge.

There had been suspicions about Rod for some time. One day, he just disappeared. After Mark was outed, people delved deeper into his past and discovered that Rod had also stolen the identity of a child who had died.

Another person with questions hanging over her was Lynn Watson. When Mark was confronted, he named her as a fellow officer, adding that 'she hated you lot'. At the time there was no way of knowing whether he was just trying to distract from the allegations against him.

'Was it true then? Was Lynn a cop too?' I asked.

'Yeah. That's there, in the book. Chapter 13.'

Lynn had lived in Leeds and been a friend of friends. I met her a few times and we were both part of the 'Action Medics' first-aid collective in Scotland, in 2005. I recalled that she had also been part of the 'Clown Army', a group that trained in clowning and regularly showed up on demonstrations in full costume, complete with face paints, giant shoes, squirty flowers and bucket routines.

Had that been her choice? Or was she sent in under orders? It was a weirdly awful fate, after all. I imagined these officers' sense of self-importance and their superiority over the people they deceived, but how would that have fared when Lynn discovered her job was to run around squeaking, wearing a red nose?

'What about Marco from Cardiff, and Jason from Reclaim the Streets?' Eleanor asked, 'I thought you might have known them as well.'

I frowned. The names weren't familiar.

She pulled out her phone and searched for some photos online. Both were burly men, and Marco especially looked like a heavy drinker. I recognised Jason. Marco was harder to place. Yet as she read out details of his activities, I realised we must have been at a lot of the same events.

'I don't know. Maybe. But they're faces in the crowd.'

As I said it, I felt the hairs on my neck stand. I hadn't noticed those men. I couldn't tell you if we ever had a conversation, but that didn't mean they hadn't noticed me. Both had been around when I was with Mark. They must have known him, and my relationship with him was no secret. Were they reporting that back to their bosses? Did they have a pact of silence about each other's misdeeds? I looked at the people in the café. How could you guard against the fact that wherever you go, there might be undercover police watching in the background, propping up the bar?

I needed to be outside, so we paid the bill and stepped out onto Putney Bridge, where I breathed in the damp, dark-green smell of the Thames at low tide. It's not to everyone's taste, but it usually makes me feel at home. That day it provided little comfort. Instead, I was reminded of how Mark and I had walked together by the river. I even told him about the history of St Mary's Church. I thought about those other officers: Jim, Jason, Rod, Lynn and Marco. How close had they been? I couldn't really remember. Had there been others? Were they still following me?

CHAPTER 7

'Turn off the engine, place the keys on top of the car and step away from the vehicle.'

It was well after 11 p.m., and it had been a long drive, but I had got a second wind as we passed the border. Of course, it's not a real border any longer, just a blue sign with the EU stars to mark the passing from France into Spain, but it meant I was almost home. As I pulled up under the bright lights of the first toll booth on the Spanish side, I saw figures moving in the dark. I took a ticket, and as I drove through the barrier, a police officer flagged me down.

In the rear-view mirror, the red-and-white pole swung closed. It occurred to me that I was blocking the lane, but the road was empty. Up ahead, about ten men in blue coveralls fanned out across the tarmac. Some held big guns. Two were holding a vicious-looking stinger, ready to slash our tyres if we tried to escape. It was intimidating, but that kind of overkill on a roadblock was not unusual in Spain. What was strange was that rather than waving at us to pull over, we were being told to get out of the vehicle, at once.

I turned off the engine, reached through the open window to place the keys on the roof as they'd ordered me to do, then turned to my passengers, who had hitched a ride from Lyon.

'Sorry, guys, we'd better do what they say.'

We were led towards the central reservation. It was not a place to be walking. The road felt vast. I glanced back and saw an officer take the keys and drive my car away. A radio crackled and the man escorting us responded into his receiver.

'Don't worry, we've got them.'
Got them? I had a sinking feeling. Got who?

* * *

The court granted all eight of us women anonymity in the case, because of the sensitive and personal nature of the claims. We used pseudonyms. Mine was 'Lily'. My mum chose it, in a media interview: the name of my brother's first daughter, her granddaughter, born shortly before Mark was uncovered, and the first name that came into her head. As we stepped up our campaigning and I began to give public talks, I would be introduced to the room as 'Lily'. People would be asked not to film or take photographs to protect my identity, and the crowd would stare their unspoken questions: 'Who are you?'; 'What did you do to deserve this?'; 'What are you trying to hide?'.

Anonymity was supposed to protect us, but it was a constant strain. I would wake in a sweat at four in the morning from a dream where I had used the wrong name. I was afraid of the police, and the harassment I might suffer if the world knew my name; which was stupid, as it turned out, because if the police wanted to harass me, they already knew who I was.

* * *

They kept us for over an hour, shivering in the middle of the motorway. I repeatedly asked what was happening, and I was told it was a 'routine traffic stop', but nothing about this was routine. One officer eventually told me that someone had called ahead and they had been instructed to stop me. They were holding my car until their boss arrived.

The boss, when he came, wore John Lennon glasses and a ski mask. He didn't even glance at me as he walked past. Five minutes after his arrival, I was told we could go.

DISCLOSURE

The car was chaos. They had rifled through everything. A potted plant I had been given in London lay smashed on the back seat, surrounded by broken leaves. I started to clear up, but another officer with an automatic weapon told me I should leave or I would be arrested. I looked at the mess. Was this because of the case? To stop me speaking out? What had they been looking for? We got into the car in silence and drove away.

* * *

A short time later I was in Valencia to give a talk at an internet security conference. We were unloading our bags when a police car pulled up beside mine. At first I thought it was a parking violation, but this was my second 'routine traffic stop' in less than three weeks, and they were asking for ID papers from everyone nearby on the street.

'I'm not even driving, I'm unloading,' I protested 'And why on earth are you ID-ing these people? They're not travelling with me, they're just walking past.'

'Well, ma'am,' the officer began, then faltered, 'the window of the car is open, so we had to establish what was going on . . .' She trailed off. Even she was unconvinced.

After they left, I apologised to the bystanders then took my bag up to the room. There, I ran a Google search for 'vehicle tracking' and scrolled through images of GPS trackers hidden on cars.

A small group of us gathered in a back street around my grubby Opel Astra. A mechanic lay down in the gutter and pushed his head up into the grime of the driver's side wheel arch, prying at the plastic mudguard with a screwdriver.

'I'm sorry, this is ridiculous,' I said. 'I'm being paranoid.'

My friend was standing on the kerb, arms folded, watching with a grim face as the mechanic poked around. 'Do you think I'm losing it?' I asked.

They didn't get a chance to reply. The mechanic sat up, eyes wide.

'There's something here,' he said.

The *Guardian* website, 11 March 2015

One of the women who is suing the police after discovering that her former boyfriend was an undercover police officer has found a tracking device in her car ... The woman – known as Lily ... is part of a group taking legal action against the police for the emotional trauma they suffered after forming intimate relationships with men who were later revealed to be spies. This week, the German newspaper *Die Tageszeitung* reported that a tracking device – wrapped in tape – was found near a wheel of her car ... At the moment, it is not possible to establish who has attached the device to her car. Lily has made a complaint to the Spanish police.

* * *

Five months later, I was in Germany at a huge summer event hosted once every four years by Europe's largest association of hackers, the Chaos Computer Club. It was in the grounds of an abandoned East German brick factory. Everywhere I looked, rusty industrial ruins had been reclaimed as art installations, bristling with lights.

The marquee where our talk would take place was huge. I was told it had seating for eight hundred people, and it was standing room only, with people spilling out of the doors. The stage was hot, and the lights were blinding. This was by far the biggest talk I had ever done.

'Are you sure you want to do this?'

The answer was no, but the cameras were already rolling and

it was too late to back out. I couldn't see most of the audience, which was probably a good thing. A slide show was projected onto a huge screen above me, and my part of the talk opened with a photo from the media of 'Lily' and Mark together on holiday in Barcelona. Her face had been pixelated to obscure her identity.

I wondered if I was doing the right thing. Sometimes anonymity felt like a gagging order. It was ironic, pretending to be 'Lily' because Mark had pretended to be someone he was not. I often feared it made it harder to relate to our story, because it looked like I was lying, just like he had done.

That was about to change. I read from my notes, aware I was speaking far too fast.

'Privacy and anonymity were very dear to me, and I've spoken out before, but always under a pseudonym; I've avoided being videoed. But over the last five years there's been a lot more revelations about these undercover police officers. I now know that between 1998 and 2010 at least six people I knew and worked with, some of whom I considered friends, were actually undercover police officers. This year I went to the Circumvention Tech Festival in Valencia and after a pretty weird stop by the police we found this GPS tracker stuck under my car.'

The slide above me changed to show the tracker, in place on the wheel arch, then after we took it apart.

'So much for my privacy!'

I tried to say it lightly. It was meant to be a joke, but my voice was tight and the humour was lost.

'Finding that tracker was a wake-up call.'

I had first met Jim Boyling at RTS meetings in 1998, when he was going out with Rosa. By the time they put the GPS tracker under my car, they had been spying on me for sixteen years.

'I think people need to know that this happens to real people,' I said, my voice echoing over the PA system, 'So, hi, that's me.'

The slide changed again.

I wasn't expecting the applause. It probably only lasted thirty seconds, but it felt like an eternity, standing there, blinded by the lights with more than a thousand pairs of eyes on me, under a screen showing the same holiday picture of Mark and me. The pixelation over my face was gone, and the title had changed from 'Lily' to 'Kate Wilson'. That was it: the talk was being livestreamed. There was no taking it back.

CHAPTER 8

'They seem to have it in for you personally,' Harriet told me one day, after a frustrating phone call with the police solicitor. 'She basically said I should watch out for you, like maybe the other women are innocents, but you're a bad person, and I've been fooled into taking your side.'

I dug my nails into the palms of my hands.

'I was one of the first women targeted by Mark Kennedy. At one point they even said he was authorised to have sex with me. They must have convinced themselves I was a significant threat of some kind.'

We had been working with Harriet for four years by then. Quietly dressed, with short-cropped grey hair and grey eyes, her reputation as a feminist and human rights advocate was far more intimidating than her presence in person. In meetings she was serious, even severe, but the deadpan-lawyerly demeanour never lasted long before her face was transformed by a mischievous smile. I once saw a photograph of her jive dancing, radiating joy and energy, her suit jacket swinging out behind her, caught by the air.

On paper, my case was only about Mark, yet Harriet knew by then that the surveillance went beyond that. It spanned numerous undercover officers, and, with the discovery of the GPS tracker, was evidently ongoing, even as we were bringing the case. The question was, why? How did they justify it all, even to themselves?

I was introduced to protesting by my parents as a toddler, on rainbow-filled marches calling for nuclear disarmament; I made national news when I was eight years old, campaigning against sexism in under-elevens' football and calling for mixed-sex teams. I had only been twenty-three when I met Mark, but by then I was already an experienced political organiser. I didn't want to believe I was just an innocent victim. The police lawyers seemed to be implying I was a bad person though, which wasn't any better. I still knew nothing about why Mark had homed in on me. Was I an operational objective, targeted for my own political acts? Did he use me as a tool, to gain access to someone else? Or did he simply find me attractive and take advantage of his training to reel me in? Had I just been a perk of the job? Did any of my passion or convictions count for anything? Was I just a naive girl who slept with the wrong man?

'This is why disclosure of the secret files is so important,' I said. 'To see their version of who I am, and show them they are wrong.'

But our case was about to go to out-of-court mediation, and it was looking unlikely that I would ever get that chance.

What was discussed in those airless rooms is a secret. In any case, I don't remember much. I remember our nerves and our anger, and how we joked among ourselves while our lawyers went back and forth for days, negotiating with the police team across the hall.

Civil claims are not about truth. They are about money. Anything you cannot immediately put a price on, from the loss of a limb to the loss of a loved one, will ultimately be given a value by the court. Experts were deployed to tally up prices for what we had lost. When it came to the bottom line, emotional distress was priced relatively low. Losing the opportunity to become a mother was valued far lower than losing a potential career.

So it was that seven of the women were told they had to settle. If they refused and fought on for disclosure, they might become liable for the police's legal costs even if they won. They risked being bankrupted by the court for proving they'd been victimised.

For me, however, it seemed that might not be the case. Because I had been studying medicine at a prestigious university, the 'value' of my claim was relatively high. And so, when the police made their final offers, the lawyers told me I had a choice that the other women were denied. I could fight on if I wanted.

In November 2015, Assistant Commissioner Martin Hewitt live-streamed an apology on behalf of the Metropolitan Police.

'Thanks in large part to the courage and tenacity of these women in bringing these matters to light it has become apparent that some officers, acting undercover whilst seeking to infiltrate protest groups, entered into long-term intimate sexual relationships with women which were abusive, deceitful, manipulative and wrong. I acknowledge that these relationships were a violation of the women's human rights, an abuse of police power and caused significant trauma. I unreservedly apologise on behalf of the Metropolitan Police Service. I am aware that money alone cannot compensate the loss of time, their hurt or the feelings of abuse caused by these relationships . . .'

The apology was long and detailed, and ended with Hewitt gravely expressing his wish that the claimants would now feel able to move on with their lives with their heads held high. But only seven claims were settled, not eight. Neither his well-wishing nor his apology applied to me.

I took my place at the far end of the panel, my heart pounding. To my left, the other women were seated in a line. We had all done interviews over the years, but this was the only formal press conference we ever gave, and possibly the only time all eight of us were together in the same room. We were there to announce that the case was over and to showcase this historic apology. When the cameras turned to me, however, I would explain about disclosure.

Big as the apology was, it wasn't the answers we wanted. The police had not told us what happened, what went wrong, or why they were sorry. They didn't say who was responsible, nor how they would be held to account. Most importantly, they hadn't given us the files they kept on us or even explained why they kept them at all. Disclosure of those files was *our* bottom line. When I had to decide whether or not to walk away, that was what it came down to. I knew I couldn't live with the unanswered questions.

'It is a win, really,' Phillippa Kaufmann said brightly.

Tall and flamboyant, blonde hair cut in a steely bob around Kohl-rimmed eyes, Phillippa was the lead barrister on our case. She would often arrive at our hearings in Lycra on a racing bike, then do a twirl like Superwoman and reappear in her QC's wig and gown, ready for business, throwing us a wink like she was letting us in on the secret of her other self. As she spoke, her long, expressive fingers danced captivatingly.

'They are accepting all of your accusations: deceit, negligence, misfeasance and assault. All of that will be entered by the court.'

Harriet smiled and gave me a worried look. She knew I wasn't happy. For the past four years she'd had the unenviable job of mediating between the eight of us and our barristers. She once confided to me that she had never represented such a complicated group. Coming as we did from running our own campaigns, we insisted on having our say about every single step of the process. It never occurred to us that normal clients didn't demand complete control over everything their lawyers did.

'This is bullshit!'

It wasn't helpful or dignified, but it was all I could think of to say. That morning's hearing had lasted all of twenty minutes: enough time to establish that the police would be offering no defence to my claim.

I spent the next few days talking to the media, spinning it the way Phillippa had described. News reports called me 'the first woman tricked into a relationship with an undercover police officer to formally win her case'. However, deep down we all knew it was not a win. They were doing this to avoid the next stage of the process: disclosure. They hadn't admitted anything, they just refused to put up a defence, meaning that while there would be a ruling in my favour, there would be no answers, no evidence and no trial.

To add insult to injury, they were still fighting us on damages. The only issue left was the value of my claim. They didn't deny what happened, but they were disputing whether it really did me any harm. I still hoped I might get some disclosure, but the focus quickly turned to how deeply I was affected by what the police had done. The claim wasn't over, but now the person on trial was me.

In 2014, my relationship ended. After I found out about Mark, my boyfriend stood by me for four more years, but it changed everything. My deteriorating mental health and the disintegration of our sex life took their toll, and we decided we would be better apart.

A year later, in the summer of 2015, I completed my degree. Once it was clear there would be no catching up on my medicine course, I had applied to nursing school. It was the only way I could think of to avoid losing everything I had worked for. Nursing was less demanding, and I was able to keep up, but it took everything I had and left me empty. I never imagined that the case could drag on for so long, nor that, four years after we began, we would still have no answers. Starting work in a job where a moment of distraction could cost someone their life did not feel like an option, so there was no celebration when I finished. I didn't even go to my graduation ceremony. I just closed up my books and walked away.

I was in my late thirties. At a time when I was beginning to take stock of decisions and achievements, and evaluate what I was doing with my life, a string of experts – lawyers, psychologists, psychiatrists and employment specialists – were picking over my failures and struggles with mental health to determine whether they were my own fault or the result of police abuse. I was trapped in stasis by the endless delays and the police's attempts to avoid accountability; held hostage to an endless process of forensically examining my inability to move on. My stagnating career became another weight pressing on my chest in the early hours of the morning. The longer I left it without practising, the harder it would be to return. Another year dragged by. In the summer of 2016, I took a part-time job at a local hospital. I resolved to work a little, just enough to keep my skills up, until the case was done. My dreams of a career in healthcare had become so small.

One day I woke up to the realisation that I didn't have to take it anymore: I could give in, accept the money, walk away. I called Harriet and told her I wanted to end it.

Then suddenly it was over. The police agreed to settle, and the endless merry-go-round of examinations by forensic experts came to an end. I received a closed court order setting out the terms of our agreement and a bank transfer. After some insistence, I also received a letter, grudgingly extending the apology made to my seven co-claimants, to me.

In light of all this, it was with some surprise that I read the short, businesslike email from the Investigatory Powers Tribunal:

'The Tribunal now imposes a final deadline of 4.30pm on Friday 24 February 2017 for the service by the Claimant on the Respondent and lodgement with the Tribunal of the Claimant's fully pleaded case.'

I had all but forgotten that Justice Tugendhat's 'James Bond' ruling had sent part of my claim to languish in the Investigatory Powers Tribunal until the civil case was resolved. In the settlement we reached there was no clause demanding 'no future action', so the human rights claim reactivated as soon as my civil claim came to an end. The Tribunal was writing to inform us we had five weeks to present our case.

DISCLOSURE

'So,' Harriet said, when she had finished explaining the situation, 'the question is: do you want to go ahead with a claim in the IPT?'

Not an easy decision. I travelled to London to meet with the lawyers. Charlotte Kilroy would be leading the team. She was younger and even taller than Phillippa and had worked as the junior barrister on our civil case. Harriet was also there. Eleanor joined the meeting so that I wouldn't feel so outnumbered by legal brains.

My first concern was that I might have to endure more intrusive probing of the damage done to me. That was quickly assuaged: the focus in a human rights claim should not be on my life now, but on the police operations themselves.

There were other issues though. The IPT is what is called a 'costs-free Tribunal'. That meant that even if we won, the police would not be required to pay my legal costs, so we had to find a way to fund the case. I was shocked that I would have to foot the bill for proving the police had violated my human rights even if I won, but it cut both ways: if I lost, I wouldn't have to pay crippling costs to the other side. 'The "costs-free" system exists so that ordinary people can bring claims against the state without facing that risk.' Harriet explained.

'Bear in mind,' Charlotte added, 'the IPT is not an open tribunal – you lodge your case and then wait for them to investigate and reach a decision. The reality is we may not be granted much opportunity to input into the process.'

In other words, I shouldn't get my hopes up. An IPT claim was unlikely to get us any answers, but for the same reasons, the costs probably wouldn't be very high. I decided it was worth a try.

Our original human rights claim in 2011 was brief, referring only to my relationship with Mark Kennedy and its impact on my right to private and family life (Article 8 of the Human Rights Act), and my right to live free from inhuman and degrading treatment (Article 3). A lot had changed since then. The public inquiry announced by Theresa May in 2014 had begun, and 'Relationships' was now an entire category for its investigations. Because of deceitful intimate relationships they had with undercover police, dozens of women had been officially designated as 'core participants' in the inquiry process. Charlotte therefore proposed that we add a breach of Article 14 to our claim.

'Article 14 is a bit different,' she explained. 'It doesn't stand alone. It is the right to enjoy all your rights without discrimination, but it has to be read alongside a breach of your other rights.'

In my case we would be talking about sex discrimination. Our argument would be that the breaches of my Article 3 and 8 rights (the rights to freedom from inhuman or degrading treatment, and to privacy, which were already in the claim) occurred because of sexism in the police, which would make them a breach of Article 14.

The police often tried to spin the story as an officer gone rogue, rather than acknowledging a wider practice of officers forming deceitful intimate relationships. We were worried that, once I was bringing the case alone, the broader context might be lost. Article 14 was a way to keep attention on the systemic nature of the abuse even though I was the only woman left fighting the case.

I then explained how our understanding of the scale and political nature of undercover policing had changed since we filed our claim. I told Charlotte about the other undercover officers I had known, and the GPS tracker. 'It's not just about Mark now. It's about political persecution,' I said. 'I want our case to reflect that as well.'

That was where the meeting began to go wrong. I had expected the team to be excited at the implications. It turned out they weren't keen. The advice they gave is covered by legal professional privilege, but the upshot of the conversation was that they didn't see things my way at all.

DISCLOSURE

I met Charlotte's eyes briefly. They were intense and intelligent behind thick glasses. She and I hadn't had much direct contact before that meeting, but I sensed an unshakable faith in law and justice. Especially after our experiences with the civil claim, it wasn't a confidence I shared. I tried to explain why the political nature of the spying was so important. Charlotte glanced at Harriet. A tiny muscle in my lower left eyelid began to twitch.

'We're running out of time here,' Harriet said. I wondered if she had noticed my deteriorating state and was hurrying the meeting to an end, but she seemed sincere. We agreed that Charlotte would draft the arguments so we could see how big our difference of opinion was. Discussions continued via phone and email. I found them incredibly distressing. In the end, we had to ask the IPT for more time.

'I've sent you Charlotte's draft of the Grounds of Claim. You will see that she hasn't included the rights to freedom of expression and freedom of association.'

I listened sullenly as Harriet explained Charlotte's position, going over my own arguments in my mind. The relationship with Mark was important for sure, but he had been just one part of a massive operation that lasted decades. For a period of at least twelve years, probably more, I was exposed to fake people at meetings, demonstrations, actions and social events. I would never even have met Mark if they hadn't been targeting us all for our political beliefs.

'So, I need to know, can you live with the claim as it stands?' Harriet finished.

Articles 10 and 11 protect our right to protest. They said I was targeted because I was a campaigner and an activist. I wasn't just a woman who slept with the wrong man. Could I live with a ruling that ignored the violations of my political rights?

'I don't know, Harriet. I don't think I can. If we only talk about the sexual relationship, we miss the point that it's not just the depth of the intrusion that's a problem, but also the breadth of the operations.'

Harriet was silent for a long moment. I waited, listening to the buzzing of the line. Eventually she sighed.

'I'm trying to work out the extent to which you and Charlotte can reach an agreement, and if not, whether she's the right person to work on this. She is a superb lawyer, and she can be passionate and persuasive. But, well, no barrister likes to argue something they don't feel can work.'

Barristers are literally professionals at winning arguments. Charlotte understood far more about what we were getting ourselves into than I did. She was, as Harriet said, a brilliant lawyer. My eyelid started twitching again. I had every reason to doubt my own judgement. Conversations about legal submissions were turning into dreams about vampires, and I was barely functioning day to day. My encounters with the other spycops had been more than a decade ago, and my recollection of the details was sparse. Yet I was sure I was right. There was more to this case than a deceitful sexual relationship. Maybe I didn't have the evidence, but it had to exist.

I stood my ground.

From the Claimant's Statement of Grounds, 10 April 2017
In addition to the interference with her private life occasioned by Mark Kennedy's deceitful relationship with the Claimant, the Claimant's right to private life under Article 8 of the European Convention on Human Rights was also infringed by the excessive presence in her life, over a considerable period of time, of at least six Undercover Officers. Between at least 1999 and 2010, and possibly for longer, the Claimant had relationships, of varying types and degrees of intensity, with Mark Kennedy, Jim Boyling, 'Rod Richardson', 'Lynn Watson', 'Marco Jacobs' and 'Jason Bishop'. . .
In particular this level of interference cannot be justified as

necessary in a democratic society . . . Mark Kennedy and the other Undercover Officers' activities also amount to a violation of her rights to freedom of expression and/or the right to freedom of assembly and association under Articles 10 and 11 of the European Convention on Human Rights.

This short, simple statement expanded the case beyond the sexual relationship, to include the other undercover officers. It quickly became known to all parties as 'Paragraph 103', and it would change the course of the entire trial.

CHAPTER 9

The case in the IPT began as it had in the High Court, with an application from the police to have it struck out. A hearing was set for September 2017, only to be cancelled at the eleventh hour, after weeks of preparation, when their application was withdrawn.

In October we received their Grounds of Defence. There were some significant concessions. They admitted that the sexual relationship amounted to inhuman and degrading treatment that violated Article 3. They also admitted it violated my rights under Articles 8 and 10, the rights to privacy and freedom of expression. However, they refused to even plead to anything that took place outside the period when Mark and I were a couple (2003–2005), and apart from violations resulting from the sexual relationship, all other violations of my rights were denied. They said the allegation of sexism under Article 14 was 'unnecessary to address'. In relation to Paragraph 103, they said we had not provided enough information, and refused to respond, adding that they intended to neither confirm nor deny whether any of the individuals other than Mark Kennedy and Jim Boyling had even been police. In response to our claim that the operations were unlawful, they said nothing at all.

A pre-trial hearing was tabled for early December. Having used up all my available holiday time and good will at work for the aborted hearing in September, I was unable to attend. It should have been a simple pre-trial hearing, but three days before the court date they sent another strike-out attempt: 'Given the concessions that have been made in the Defendant's Defence in respect of the Claimant's case under ECHR Articles 3, 8, 10 and 11, [the Tribunal should decide whether] it remains necessary or proportionate for the remainder of the Claimant's case to proceed.'

I spent that day working in a clinic in Barcelona, pacing up and down like a caged animal, waiting to hear how it went. Was the case over? Would that be the last time I or my lawyers were allowed to be present in the courtroom? When I heard that Charlotte had convinced the Tribunal to hear the rest of the case, it was the first time I properly exhaled all day. I vowed that I wouldn't miss another hearing.

The year ended full of optimism. As I headed for London, where my mum was busy making home-made, personalised Christmas crackers and richly decorated fruitcake, and pulling box after box of decorations out of storage, I was looking forward to the year ahead, believing we only had a few months to go until the trial.

It had been the police who wanted to go to the secretive Investigatory Powers Tribunal. We resisted it every step of the way. So, they must have been as surprised as we were when the case didn't automatically disappear behind a wall of Official Secrets. Perhaps the Tribunal was on a drive to improve its draconian reputation. Perhaps they were used to working with 'national security' issues and could see from the outset that there was no national security at stake here. Whatever their reasons, right at the start, the Chair of the Tribunal informed us:

'We are almost entirely an open court . . . for national security it is absolutely vital that baddies shouldn't find out about how we operate our systems. But in this field, absent the particular names of the individuals, why should any of this be in closed?'

Directions were set for a trial in April 2018. The police were given deadlines. All their open evidence and a properly pleaded defence were due to be served by 19 February. If they wanted secret hearings they would have to make a formal application.

I felt a thrill: after seven years going nowhere, I was finally going to see those forbidden files.

The day after New Year's Day, my hopes were dashed. The police applied for their secret hearings. The February deadlines came and went without us receiving the first tranches of evidence, and progress was replaced by a string of confusing non-events.

Secret hearings meant there would be a new player in the proceedings: Counsel to the Tribunal, or CTT.

The position was to be filled by Sarah Hannett, QC. She arrived punctually to our meeting, laid out a notepad and pen, and introduced herself. Her role was to talk to both sides, then advise the Tribunal about what evidence I should and should not get to see.

It was clear that she would be reading all that secret material about me. I felt the colour in my face rise, and I interrupted her explanations.

'Do you have any idea how uncomfortable this is?'

'I'm sorry?'

'Talking to you. I don't know what the police have said about me. Maybe it's all lies, maybe it's full of really intimate things. I've been waiting years for these answers. You're a total stranger, yet somehow now you'll see them and I won't.'

Digging my nails into my palm to hold back tears I looked from Sarah to Charlotte and was struck by how alike they were. Both had blonde hair, cut just above their shoulders. Sarah's was curly, Charlotte's hung in gentle waves. Both wore glasses: Charlotte's were rounded and Sarah's were square. Charlotte wore little make-up and her face was serious while Sarah had a broad smile and daring red lipstick, but those differences only highlighted the underlying similarity. They were clearly from the same tribe. They shared the barrister's immaculate, understated style and confident professionalism. By comparison I felt frumpy, ragged and flustered. And outnumbered.

Sarah's smile became a little more awkward. She told me she

had received discs from the police, but she hadn't read any of them yet, and she did understand, and she wasn't there to judge. I knew it wasn't her fault. I was lucky that someone so approachable and human had been assigned, and even luckier to have Charlotte on my case. But all I could do was glare at the table.

When I got back to Putney, spring had arrived. The bulbs on my mother's balcony were pushing out fleshy spears that would soon become crocuses and daffodils. The trees were alight with tiny, budding leaves, flashing vibrant green against a pale grey sky. We should have been preparing for trial, but the April date had been pushed back to late September. I was facing another summer under the shadow, and those leaves would be faded and dying before we had our day in court.

CHAPTER 10

I let myself be talked into setting up an online dating profile, but the encounters I had were fleeting and disastrous. In the end I gave up. I was about to turn forty and I believed I was broken. My relationship days were done.

The dating account was still there, though. Occasionally it would send a notification, like a phantom itch from a severed limb.

'I feel like I already know you.'

I rolled my eyes, then clicked.

'Location: Guadeloupe, Eastern Caribbean.'

Very unlikely you do, matey.

He had posted eleven pictures. Shoulder-length, sun-bleached hair and friendly eyes. In some shots he appeared dressed as a pirate. Others showed him tanned and carefree, painting, swimming in waterfalls, or just hanging out on a tropical beach. I had to admit, he was cute.

The last shot was older. His hair was darker, his face more serious, and I realised with surprise that it was Ben. I had seen him around the activist scene in England since the mid-1990s, but we hadn't met properly until 2008, at an international squatters' convention in France, where we flirted a bit and exchanged emails.

I had vague memories of visiting him in London. He'd shown me round the building and we ended up in his room. I smiled. His bed had fake fur blankets on it, like a Viking lair. I looked at his message again. A genuine question then, not just an awful line.

DISCLOSURE

The scenery in the pictures looked amazing, and he really was easy on the eyes. I shot back a quick reply.

'Last seen in a squatted social centre in London, if I recall? What are you doing in Guadeloupe?'

Soon we were emailing every few days.

He told me how he left the UK in 2012, cycled to southern Spain and crewed on a sailboat across the Atlantic – Gibraltar to the Canaries, Cabo Verde and the Caribbean. There he'd bought a cheap, old boat of his own, with a broken engine. He'd been 'bumming around the Lesser Antilles' (his words) ever since.

He lived as an artist, selling his work to tourists on the beach, swimming with sea turtles, and hunting out hot springs and water-falls, until last September when he got caught in a hurricane. It sounded pretty wild. He told me about the storm surge, and the live power lines coming down, and how eerie and quiet it had been inside the eye of the storm. The island was devastated and most of the boats around him had sunk. His was missing a mast and his gearbox was stuck, but she was floating, and three months later he was back underway, en route to Martinique.

'Should you feel this year might provide you some time for a Caribbean getaway, please do let me know.'

I read his invitation a hundred times. Back when it looked like my case would soon be over, I had turned down a long-term contract at the health centre so that I could return to the UK at short notice and prepare for trial. Now the case was in limbo, I was unemployed and there was nowhere I had to be. Flights via Paris turned out to be cheaper than a train fare from London to Manchester. I couldn't come up with one good reason not to go.

When I stepped onto the runway in Martinique, the heat was like a blast furnace. Just a few weeks later, the hot and humid breeze felt comfortable on my skin. Ben slipped his arm around my shoulder. That felt comfortable too.

He had met me off the plane with an apology: he hadn't rented a car. Was I happy to hitch-hike? We hugged a greeting – one of those uncertain embraces that contain too many elbows – and set off, struggling with my suitcase, which seemed to have lost a wheel. We stopped beneath an improbable-looking palm tree and stuck out our thumbs.

It was dark when we got to the harbour. We manhandled my crippled suitcase through a hole in a fence, across a supermarket car park that backed onto the water, and into a slightly deflated dinghy. I climbed in and thought of joyful childhood weekends spent messing about in boats. Then I considered the dark water in all directions, the closeness of this man I hardly knew and hadn't seen in a decade, the impossibility of escape. The outboard engine seemed far louder than necessary: we were barely moving faster than walking pace. Conversation was impossible. We rode without speaking, watching the waves.

Home was a 39-foot fibreglass yacht covered in hurricane battle scars. Its interior was kitted out in dark veneer, with a tiny galley, a cluttered saloon table and a U-shaped bench, whose ill-fitting plastic cushions had clearly been made for a different boat. I could see what looked like bunks buried under piles of art materials. LED lights shone through grubby shades. The overall effect was cosy, and I smiled as I breathed in the heady smell of diesel fumes and damp. I love boats.

From the galley we went through a low-ceilinged walkway into the rear cabin.

'So, erm. That's the big bed,' Ben began. 'You can sleep there.' He paused. 'I can sleep wherever you want. I can sleep up front if you want. Or. Erm. We could both stay in here.'

He delivered the last suggestion in a lilting voice, as if to say that it was, in his view, the best option, but that the choice would, of course, be mine. I stood absolutely still, studying him. His hazel eyes were wide in the dim light. His face was open, his posture relaxed.

DISCLOSURE

It seemed a little ungrateful to make him dig a sleeping space out from under the paints and canvases while I slept alone on the vast mattress, which had room for three or four. Then again, it was just us on his boat. I was thousands of miles from home. Offering to share seemed terribly forward. And would that be such a bad thing? The possibility of romance with an old comrade was part of what brought me here.

'You can sleep here with me if you like.' I hoped my delivery was casual enough. 'But do you mind if I turn in early?'

It was only eight o'clock, but in European time that meant 1 a.m. It felt like I had been in transit for a long, long time. I was more than ready for bed.

Ben proved to be laid back and easy to talk to. We spent our time stripping down his gearbox and fixing things on the boat, dealing with the occasional episode of sinking, and going ashore to camp or paint on the beach. He'd known Mark, which meant there were many things that didn't need to be explained. It was incredibly refreshing. There was even romance, of sorts. We kissed, and he opened up about how lonely it was on the boat, how much he had missed human contact. As we held each other, I realised how much I had, too.

Five weeks later, our long first date was coming to an end. The frame of my errant suitcase had seized up in the salt air; it wouldn't open, and I had to stoop to pull it along on its three remaining wheels. As we made our way into the airport, I had no idea where I stood or even if I would see him again. I reached for his hand.

'I had a great time, thank you.'

'Did you really?' He looked surprised and a little awkward. 'Well, if you come back, I'll take you sailing. We can go to Grenada, and swim with sea turtles on the way.'

77

CHAPTER 11

The email from the police lawyers came while I was still high over the Atlantic. There were sixteen attachments in total. Each had a cryptic alphanumeric name. When I sat down to read them, I still had sand in my hair. The attachments were a 'sample' of the documents I would eventually receive. The aim, the email explained, was to give me the opportunity to comment on the redactions the police had made.

This was it. After all this time, I was finally going to see some of what they wrote about me.

I opened the first document. Every single page was solid black. I scrolled through the second file. Blacked out page after blacked out page. About halfway through I found a tiny gap. Was this some kind of joke?

There was nothing else, just my name.

I did eventually find a page with some text on it. An authorisation of some kind.

UCO ███████████ will continue to portray themselves as a committed anarchist activist, fully supportive of any issues with an Extreme Left Wing (XLW)/Environmental bias and will support protest activity against the HMG viewpoint . . .

DISCLOSURE

Name: WILSON, Kate

There were so many acronyms. UCO was easy: undercover officer. XLW had been helpfully spelt out as Extreme Left Wing; but HMG? I was baffled for a moment. Then I realised: 'Her Majesty's Government'.

We were spied on because we disagreed with the government.

The authorisation went on to say that the UCO would provide intelligence on named individuals who were leading, planning or orchestrating such protests. There it was, in black and white. I was a 'named subject' of Mark's operation. His commanders had specifically targeted me.

There were 182 pages in the sample disclosure, but more than half of them had been redacted in full. Where words were visible it was often just a few sentences, taken out of context and impossible to understand.

Document DLS-0000008 was different. It contained photocopies from a police notebook, page after hand-written page.

DISCLOSURE

Eight years ago I almost burnt his letters, but something had held me back. I looked at the small, sad pile of notepaper and coloured card; relics from a more innocent life. Picking a page at random, I held it next to police notes on the screen. There it was: a poem he had left on my pillow more than sixteen years ago. The same rounded, slightly childish writing.

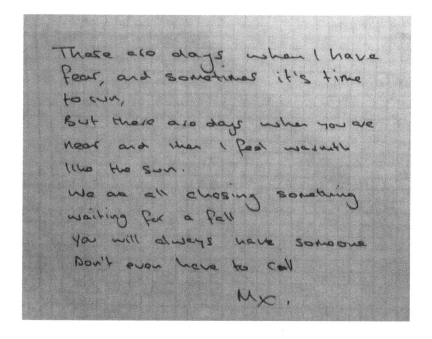

There was the Mark I thought I knew, author of endearingly awful poetry. And there was another Mark: an undercover policeman, sitting in a safehouse making notes. I thought back to the email he sent me in 2011: 'You and others were never mentioned by me ever.' But he had mentioned me. It was right there in his operational notes.

There was something heavy about the physical evidence. It crushed any lingering vestiges of denial.

The documents came with a timetable for the remaining disclosure: in total there were 9,600 pages to be redacted. I would receive

500–1,000 pages every week for the coming ten weeks, and the process would be completed by 13 June 2018. The sample I had was a tiny, confusing fraction of what we were to receive, but the rest would be coming soon.

Then, nothing. The deadlines came and went, and there was no word. In light of the failure to make any progress, on 8 June, the Tribunal cancelled the September trial. No new dates were proposed.

On 18 June, we finally received word from the police. It came from a new barrister. During their weeks of silence, they had completely changed their lawyers, and, using the excuse of new representation, they were once again applying for the disclosure exercise to be abandoned.

That meant more pre-trial hearings. The first was on 28 June 2018.

The IPT doesn't have its own courtrooms, so they borrowed a court for the day at the Employment Tribunal. We met outside its building in Salisbury Square. Travel guides would have called it 'secluded'. It was certainly no place for a demonstration. We wondered if it was even worth getting our banners out of the bag, and whether they had avoided the Royal Courts of Justice on purpose, to keep us hidden away.

We got to the courtroom to discover that the Chair of the Tribunal had retired. A new judge, Lord Justice Singh, sat in his place. This would also be Sarah Hannett's first hearing as Counsel to the Tribunal, and the police had their new lawyers. Almost everyone in the courtroom was new. The only people who had been slogging at it since the beginning were me and my team.

The Tribunal ruled that the police should have the opportunity to make their application. In the meantime, the disclosure exercise would stop. I could see the Chair felt this was fair and reasonable: all parties should be heard. But the next available date for a hearing was in October. By then my case would have been going on for seven years. Never mind that uprooting myself for hearings every three or four months made it impossible to have a career. Never mind that at every hearing so far, the Tribunal had ordered disclosure yet I never received it. Never mind that our team had already heard and defeated versions of the same application several times. Never mind my anxiety and anger as I waited in limbo, wondering whether all the time I had spent on this case would be wasted.

Back in the waiting room I lashed out, aiming a kick at a chair, hoping to send it sailing. I may not have been the first person to take it out on the furniture though: all the chairs were bolted to the floor. Wincing, I hobbled out into the hall.

When it came, the police application seemed perverse even for them. They asked the Tribunal not to investigate what had happened, not to order disclosure, and not to bother with evidence. Instead, they suggested, a ruling should be made based on hypothetical 'assumed facts'. As they pointed out, if I ever found evidence that those 'facts' were false, I would always be able to reapply to the court.

We had kept a low profile since closing my civil claim, but the time had come to go public. The police had admitted that the relationship Mark had had with me was a form of torture, and that his handlers and line managers knew about it. Yet, at the hearing in October, they would be asking the Tribunal to sweep it all under the carpet and make a ruling based on fiction.

I was visiting Ben at the time, but we put together a statement and the BBC agreed to run the story, but they wanted an interview. We went ashore in Kingstown, Saint Vincent, found a jaunty pirate-themed bar that had Wi-Fi, and set up a laptop for a call.

Then the music began. The sound was bassy and hollow in the empty bar. It seemed to be coming from the kitchens. Each track was worse than the last: Marvin Gaye's 'Sexual Healing', followed by Tom Jones's 'She's a Lady', and then The Police's 'Every Breath

You Take': *Every smile you fake, I'll be watching you.* There was no way I could talk about Mark with that on in the background, but it was the only place I could get online, and they were waiting to start.

In desperation, I took the laptop into the toilet, locked myself in a cubicle and climbed onto the cistern. I hoped that it wouldn't be obvious to BBC viewers that I was balanced on a loo. The technicians were being very understanding.

'Hey, sorry, how's the sound now? Can you still hear the music?'

'No, that's much better.'

'What about the plumbing? Can you see the plumbing?'

'What?'

'Never mind.'

I was shaking by the end: partly from the stress of talking about the case, but mostly from the muscular strain of keeping my balance with the pipes out of shot.

It paid off. In London, the story caught the media's attention and there was a flurry of news. On the day of the hearing, Eleanor and I were picked up at dawn and driven to ITV studios, where I gave a live interview before we even got to the court. This time, the IPT was sitting in the Royal Courts of Justice. The scene was nothing like Salisbury Square. A crowd of cameras and campaigners was waiting on the Strand as we arrived. Police Spies Out of Lives, the campaign group we had set up, pulled out all the stops, bringing banners, stylish masks for the women who wished to remain anonymous, and their own photographer to document the event.

Over and over, I was asked to pose. In one picture I stand centre stage, in a #MeToo T-shirt, holding a strand of blue-and-white incident tape that reads 'Police Have Crossed the Line'. Behind me there's a rally of supporters and behind them stands the doorway to the Royal Courts of Justice. I usually look cross-eyed and demented in photographs, but somehow, thanks to the skills of the photographer and the make-up artist at ITV, I look great: a force to be reckoned with. For months afterwards, I would sneak glances at it, unable to believe that this woman was me.

That absurdly flattering photo was the only good thing to come out of the day.

The police didn't win their application, but they didn't lose either. The Tribunal rejected the absurd notion of a ruling based on 'assumed facts' but they also cancelled the order for disclosure. It was replaced by a compromise: the defendants were to serve a sworn witness statement, in accordance with their duty of candour, setting out their version of the facts.

The 'duty of candour' is a legal concept: public authorities have a duty to give a full and accurate explanation of all the facts. Their objective should not be to win at all costs, but to assist the court by disclosing all relevant information, even when it harms their own case. I had read learned legal articles which said the principle's importance to the rule of law was 'impossible to overstate'. Yet it was clear that compliance was at best self-policing. In a case where the honesty of the police was precisely what was in doubt, that seemed like a fatal flaw.

Just days after the hearing, my fears were confirmed. The police served a list of the issues they intended to address. It contained only nine questions, many of which could be answered with a simple 'yes' or 'no'. Just two related to the wider issues of undercover policing beyond my relationship with Mark, and there were no questions at all about their interference with my political rights, or the role that institutional sexism had played in the case.

We sent a long letter to the Tribunal setting out our concerns. Some small changes were made, but the list of issues remained paltry. All we could do was wait.

CHAPTER 12

Dónal and I met at a protest camp in 2005, but didn't become close until after 2010, brought together by his work with the Undercover Research Group, whose investigations were vital in uncovering the spycops scandal. He had a strong Irish accent, and an unnerving habit of repeating the last words of your sentence as you talked to him. I once found him up early in my garden, reading mathematics research papers. It was what he did to relax, he said. He knew more about the structure and functioning of the secret political police units than anyone else I knew, and he visited me in Catalonia to help prepare for the police witness statement to the IPT.

'I bet they wheel out some doddery old cop, on the verge of retirement, maybe with a terminal disease or something. "Here, say this under oath, and then get a pat on the back and a golden handshake and go off to play golf."'

He delivered his prediction over lunch on the patio and at the time, I laughed at his cynicism. But when the statement arrived, it turned out the witness wasn't even on the verge of retirement. He had already retired.

From the first witness statement of Sir Stephen House to the Investigatory Powers Tribunal, 18 January 2019
I am the Deputy Commissioner of Police of the Metropolis. I am authorised by the First and Second Defendants ("the Defendants") to make this witness statement . . . I have over 35 years' policing experience across a number of different police forces . . . I retired in December 2015

to work in the private sector. I re-joined the Metropolitan Police Service in March 2018 as an Assistant Commissioner for Met Operations before taking up my current post in January 2019.

The statement had been due on 3 January 2019, but the police requested a two-week delay. They didn't say it was because they were still getting their man in place. I looked him up.

His last policing job had been as Chief Constable of the Police in Scotland, and he didn't exactly retire. In August 2015 he announced his resignation, following a series of controversies and failures. It was clear from the press that it had not been a good time for the Scottish Police. One article noted that House was replaced by Philip Gormley, who seemingly did an even worse job, resigning after two years amid a flurry of allegations of gross misconduct. The hairs on my neck stood on end. Perhaps it was just a general sense of unscrupulous men in positions of power, but I had a feeling it was something more.

The statement itself was over a hundred pages plus annexes. It included a *Dramatis Personae*, as though it were a stage play, rather than my life. It also contained tables listing the authorisation documents for some of the operations. Mark's table provided the most information, and the entry for 26 May 2005 stated, 'This is the first mention of Kate Wilson in any authorisation document.'

That was odd. The first mention of me was four months *after* my relationship with Mark ended. I scanned forward. My name appeared consistently after that, as a named subject in Mark's authorisations, until January 2007, when West Yorkshire Police took over the operation, and interest in me apparently disappeared.

As I read through the table I felt my skin prickle again. An authorisation for 2006 was described as 'signed off by Cmdr Gormley'. Philip Gormley, the man who took over from Sir Stephen House as head of Police Scotland, had been signing off on authorisations for Mark Kennedy in 2006 that targeted me by name.

Thirteen years later, House was back from disgrace and resignation, having been appointed Deputy Commissioner of the Metropolitan Police. Signing this witness statement about Gormley's operations must have been one of the first things he did in his new job. It was a small world.

Picking apart what the statement said was confusing and frustrating, and took weeks. The most obvious failing was that it was absurdly limited in scope. House himself admitted that he had 'never met Mark Kennedy or had any other contact or involvement with Mr Kennedy, professionally or otherwise'. There was no input from the officers who worked on the case, because they were 'unwilling to cooperate', so House was relying on the secret files alone.

Furthermore, the most important operational documents, covering the start of my relationship with Mark, were described as 'missing'. House didn't question the disappearance of these documents, nor did he draw any inference from their absence, except to speculate that they 'may never have existed'. With all his years of policing experience, he apparently saw nothing untoward about seven months of undercover deployment having produced no written records at all.

Even without that material, it was clear that they had kept extensive records about my life. The statement included many details of my movements, travelling with Mark between Nottingham and London and occasionally further afield. They knew that we were living together. They had accounts of us going to the cinema and out to dinner. They knew that Mark had met my family, and that he had named me his next of kin on an insurance form.

It seemed that no attempt had been made to critically analyse or cross-reference the material. House offered only short quotes and narrow, face-value interpretations. It was his opinion that 'Whilst the Claimant features significantly, in particular in 2004, there is no evidence in the cover officer logs of [his Principal Cover Officer], any other cover officer, or any other officer, having been notified in express terms that MK was having an intimate sexual relationship with the Claimant.' On the strength of this assertion, the police changed their defence.

Charlotte was outraged. 'Can you believe it? They now say other officers didn't know about the relationship, and only the principal cover officer "ought to have known". They say there was nothing wrong with training and guidance about intimate relationships. They're basically saying their previous defence was a dog's dinner! They don't even explain why they've changed their mind. It's not based on any new evidence, unless they're going to say that no one had looked at the evidence until now. Either way, they're on dodgy ground.'

At first glance the statement appeared to contain some answers, yet it was worded in such a way that no real conclusions could be drawn. The police refused to respond to any questions. We had spent many months negotiating with them and Counsel to the Tribunal to agree on a redactions protocol, but when it came to delivering their statement, they decided, unilaterally, at the last minute and without informing us, that instead of redacting the document by blacking out the sensitive sections, they would just give us a completely different version from the one they gave the Tribunal. On the face of it we appeared to have the full text. Only after careful reading did we realise that entire sections had simply been cut out. They eventually admitted that they had given the Tribunal a longer version in secret.

There was no way we could take the statement at face value. Unless we got access to the material that House had referred to, on the strength of which the Police had revised their admissions, we would not be able to properly challenge his claim that Mark Kennedy's training was perfectly adequate and that his supervisors had no idea what had been going on. For once, Charlotte and I were in complete agreement: disclosure was the only way we would get a fair trial.

CHAPTER 13

We pressed on in the hope that the final trial must be just round the corner, but the police kept coming up with new ways to resist disclosure. In May 2019, Sarah Hannett proposed a list of documents she thought they should disclose. Although it was less than I wanted, it would have been a start. But the end of the year came and we still hadn't seen a single page. The Tribunal had scheduled two further in-person pre-trial hearings, with more perhaps to follow. Our funding had run out months before. Because the IPT was cost-free, there was no hope of anyone in my legal team getting paid.

'You do understand, don't you?' said Charlotte. 'We can't go on like this.'

'So what happens now?' I asked, barely trusting myself to speak. We had been talking for over an hour. My ear was getting hot from the phone and I was getting dizzy. I wanted the conversation to end before my resolve cracked. They didn't need to hear how terrified I was, or to be made to feel any worse about this than they clearly already did.

'We will draft a letter to let the Tribunal know we are standing down, and you can take it from there.'

* * *

DISCLOSURE

litigant in person

noun countable legal UK /ˌlɪtɪɡənt ɪn ˈpɜː(r)s(ə)n/

1. someone who represents themselves in court instead of using a lawyer

It was the first of many legal terms I would have to look up.

'[W]e wish to remind the Tribunal that the Claimant is an acknowledged victim of a serious Article 3 ECHR breach at the hands of the Defendants. Now that she is representing herself it is especially important that sensitivity is employed . . . As a litigant in person the Claimant should be treated at least equally to the Defendants and should not be held to impossible standards.'

The lawyers' letter was powerful and articulate, and it was the last time anyone was going to speak for me for a long time. I was going to have to learn to represent myself.

'Are you police?'

There was no uniform and no introduction, but something about his manner – the way he stood, the way he spoke – gave him away.

'Off-duty,' he replied curtly. 'Just here to make this delivery.'

He handed over a heavy cardboard box, lid fastened with cable ties.

More than nine years after we decided to sue, and a month after I lost my legal team, the first disclosure arrived.

In my haste, I tried to open it with door keys. It was tougher than I expected. I twisted the hard plastic, cursing as it pinched my fingers, but just as I was about to give up and find a knife, it snapped.

Inside the box were two blue lever-arch folders containing almost two thousand pages. Swallowing, I lifted one out and opened it to a random page. It appeared to contain a record of communications – text messages, calls and in-person meetings. The sender of the messages was referred to as 'Source'.

> Source requested a meeting and debrief because of the issues arising
> . . . I travelled to London to meet with Source . . .
> 2015 Meet with Source at safe location. Account of debrief

The language was clipped and alien, the stuff of espionage, and it was broken up by black rectangular redactions. Some covered entire paragraphs, while others covered just one or two tantalising words. I flicked the pages back and forth.

> 1103 Text from Source 'going out in the van with Katja . . .'

My stomach dropped like I'd hit a pothole. Only my friends called me Katja. Of course, by then I knew I would be in there, that was the point, but it didn't prepare me for seeing the actual files. I tried to stay calm and read through systematically, but my anxiety to see what the other pages held was overwhelming and I couldn't stay focused. I found myself scanning back and forth looking for other mentions of my name.

> 0711 Text from Source 'In London all OK'
> 0800 Call from Source who has just left Katja's parent's house.
> Source is meeting up with Katja Friday evening for a curry.

The redactions made it difficult to follow the narrative. Spelling and grammar had clearly not been an operational priority. They hadn't even bothered to check people's names, often spelling them wrong, and not even consistently wrong, making it hard to fathom how it could ever have been useful as intelligence. Many entries were time-stamped, but the pages were mostly undated and didn't seem to be in chronological order. Some ended in the middle of a sentence, and the records appeared to be incomplete. Even so, between the redactions, and beneath the obscure references to

DISCLOSURE

'Source', 'debriefs' and 'safe locations', I felt a growing sense of familiarity: I was reading about my life.

I continued my erratic scanning until very late. There were dozens of mentions of my name, and it was clear I would find many more. I lay in bed for hours that night, going over scenes from my life, seen through someone else's eyes. It was strange, reading about myself in the third person, yet it felt somehow appropriate. The files were about the woman I had been before I knew.

PART TWO

PART TWO

CHAPTER 14

The caravan had a little built-in gas heater, but Katja had only tried it once. It created so much condensation that whatever warmth it put out was self-defeating. Instead, she slept under a big pile of duvets and blankets. She burrowed deep, pulled the covers around her face and, putting off the moment she would have to leave her warm cocoon, thought about the day ahead. She was back from Spain and had only been in Nottingham a few days, but she was planning on staying for a while. That morning she would write a CV and sign up with a temping agency, then go to Eleanor's for lunch. Later, there was a NASA meeting. NASA (no relation to the more famous space agency of the same name) was the 'Nottingham Assembly of Subversive Activists'; she suspected that the acronym had been chosen before the words.

Operation Penguin – Contact Log (2003)
Monday 3rd November
Source travelled to Nottingham.

. . .

Source received a call . . . re tonight's NASA meeting at the SUMAC Centre. Source will attend and the meeting starts at 1900.

The Assemblies were spaces where all kinds of environmental and social justice groups could come together, advertise events and put out calls for volunteers. Lots of cities had them: Manchester's 'Riotous Assembly', Brighton's 'Rebel Alliance', 'the London

Underground'. Katja was excited to find out what was going on.

The meeting that evening, however, turned out to be quite small. She already knew about most of the projects presented and was feeling a little bored. But the guy next to her was new. She looked him over: tall, skinny, dressed in black. Long brown hair, tied in a ponytail, and a neat goatee beard. He was a bit clean-cut, but definitely more interesting than organising coaches for a Stop the War demo.

He turned to face her. His right eye was looking right at her, clear and greyish-blue, but his left was skewed, looking off somewhere else. The effect was unnerving. She quickly averted her gaze, then felt guilty. He was sure to have noticed. She looked back, meeting his good eye and, in an attempt to cover her discomfort, offered her opinion on the discussion.

'Coaches will be an absolute drag,' she whispered. 'Bloody Socialists trying to sell us newspapers all the way to London? No thanks! I'd rather hitch-hike.'

He laughed.

'Won't even be big-city Socialists,' he joked. 'Provincial ones from the Midlands I expect.'

Was his accent London? Definitely not Nottingham or anywhere near. He leant in closer to whisper in her ear.

'You're from London too, aren't you? I can tell from your voice. I grew up in Battersea.'

She smiled. He had been thinking the same as her, about the accent. And Battersea was south of the river too, right next to Wandsworth, where she grew up.

They spent the rest of the meeting talking like that, in whispers, like the naughty kids at the back of the class.

Operation Penguin – Contact Log (2003)
Monday 3rd November
1915 Source arrived at the SUMAC Centre. The meeting was already

underway. There were 12 present ... Loukas and Katja had not been
to previous NASA meetings and were introduced as friends of Eleanor
... Katja is a white female who is staying at Neds. She has anarchist
connections ...

The Meeting

The Agenda began with discussions on what the Nottingham activists
were going to do as far as the visit of George Bush ... The consensus
was that they would want to travel to the demonstrationnstrations*
in London but not be tied to the 2 coaches being organised by the
Nottingham 'Stop The War' group.

The room still sported the same threadbare carpet and textured
wallpaper that had adorned its walls when it was a Ukrainian
social club. Now it was the Sumac Centre. They had toyed with
other names: the Makhno Centre had been her favourite, after
Nestor Makhno, commander of the Makhnovshchina Revolutionary Insurrectionary Army of Ukraine. But not everyone had
liked the reference to obscure anarchist history, so they had gone
with the safer, rare-botanicals option: it was named after a sumac
bush growing in the front yard.

When they had finished putting the chairs away, he was gone.
Eleanor and John were on stools, talking. Loukas had gone behind
the bar to serve drinks. Katja joined them, dropping 50p into a
collection tin at the end of the bar and helping herself to a snack
from a tray marked 'Samosas for Social Change'. She listened to
their gossip for a while before pitching in.

'Who's the new guy?'

She tried to sound casual, but it didn't work.

'We saw you two, whispering away,' John laughed.

---

* This bizarre spelling of 'demonstrations' inexplicably appears at least four
times within the 2003 contact logs. Spelling and grammar in the police files
has been left as it is in the original documents.

Eleanor said he had showed up a few months ago. 'Lives on his own, out in Sherwood.'

Operation Penguin – Contact Log (2003)
Monday 3rd November
Eleanor Katja, Ronnie and Lucas are looking to obtain and share a new accommodation together...
Policy decision. Should Source move in with the above?
Pro. Would give us knowledge of actions being planned as they develop both local and towards the G8 summits in 2004 and 2005 . . .
Against. No 'down time' for Source. No safe haven. They would know when Source was around and when not.
Source view. Believes it is a perfect opportunity to be centrally involved right at the beginning of all future plans of local activists, including the run up to the G8s. Is happy with the 'down time' ▓▓▓▓▓
▓▓▓▓▓▓▓▓▓▓▓▓▓▓▓▓▓▓▓▓▓▓▓▓▓▓▓▓▓▓
▓▓▓▓▓▓▓▓▓▓▓▓▓▓▓▓▓▓▓

Cover view. Agrees with Source on the major opportunities that living with these people will provide. Will monitor the stress and need for down time which this situation would generate ▓▓▓▓▓▓▓
▓▓▓▓▓▓▓▓▓▓▓▓▓▓▓▓▓▓▓▓▓▓▓▓▓▓▓▓▓▓
▓▓▓▓▓▓▓▓▓▓▓▓▓▓▓▓▓▓▓▓▓▓▓▓▓▓▓▓▓▓
▓▓▓▓▓▓▓▓▓▓▓▓▓▓▓▓▓▓▓▓▓▓▓▓▓▓▓▓▓▓
▓▓▓▓▓▓▓▓▓▓▓▓▓▓▓

This would be a major step in us achieving our objectives of infiltrating leading activists in both local and national arenas.

Katja found out his name was Mark. He'd been coming to the centre since the early summer, and he'd been to a few actions and events. She asked about his eye, and was told that as far as people knew, he wasn't blind.

'He told me he caught it on a staple while playing in a box when he was a toddler.' Eleanor said. 'The muscle was damaged.

So he can see from both, but his left doesn't move as well.'

Katja flinched at the thought of the accident, and then at what it must have been like to grow up with a wandering eye, how he must have been treated. She resolved not to even see it. She would look past it from then on.

In all, no one knew much, but the general feeling was he seemed nice, if a bit shy and awkward, and no, he didn't have a girlfriend.

'You're running the café on Friday, aren't you?' John said, 'If he comes in, why don't you invite him to come this weekend?'

Operation Penguin Intelligence Reports
[MK] 05/11/2003
Leeds activists have a cooperative in Leeds similar to Neds. They are holding a party on the 8th with bands. The Nottingham group plan to attend the party.

Operation Penguin – Contact Log (2003)
Wednesday 5th November
Source has been told that the party in Leeds is Rocker fancy dress so needs to get some clothing . . .
Saturday 8th November
0800. Call from Source.
Last night staying late at the Sumac centre were Katja, [others] and Eleanor . . . Katja does not use drugs or drink alcohol. Katja was brought up in Wandsworth and went to Elliott school . . .
Source travelling with others to Leeds for the party at the Cooperative 'Cornerstones'

* * *

Katja sat on the stairs, peering down through the wooden banisters. She picked at a chip in the paint and examined the woodgrain underneath. It was almost 3 a.m. The house party was in full swing, but she was sober, as always, and people were reaching levels of intoxication that made it harder for her to fit in.

She wandered into the living room. The music was so loud she felt it in her solar plexus before it reached her ears. Her organs were vibrating, and she paused for a moment while her eyes adjusted to the dark and the disco lighting. She scanned the room, packed with writhing dancers, and her eyes caught the new guy, standing quite still amid all the movement, his face lit up by the pale screen light of his mobile phone.

Operation Penguin – Contact Log (2003)
0306 Text from Source 'All is well . . .'

She watched as he slipped his phone into his pocket and leant against the wall. He looked out of place. She decided to take pity. She made her way over and leant in, moving his hair slightly so she could shout in his ear.

'You want to go hang out somewhere a bit quieter?'

He shook his head and indicated that the music was too loud to hear. She rolled her eyes and took his hand, pulling him out of the immediate blast radius of the speakers and into the hall.

'I said: "You wanna blow this joint and go somewhere you can hear yourself think?"'

He glanced around. 'Where?'

'Let's try upstairs. Maybe we can find a bedroom that's free?'

His eyes widened and she realised that he must have misunderstood her intentions. The bedrooms would be used as chill-out spaces, people smoking and chatting, taking a break from having the rhythms of DJ Shadow penetrate their spleens.

She looked him over. It wouldn't be the worst way to end the evening. She decided not to explain too much, and led the way upstairs.

DISCLOSURE

Operation Penguin – Contact Log (2003)
0317 Text from Source 'Relax, I'll be heading home soon.'

'Seriously? You live in a caravan? That is so cool.'

She thought about her pile of damp blankets. She had to break the ice on the glass of water by her bed the other morning and had taken to sleeping in the house whenever any housemates were away.

'Not just cool, bloody cold. I can't believe I've come back to the UK just in time for winter. I must've been mad.'

They had found a comfy spot in one of the chill-out rooms, just as she had hoped, and had been chatting away for hours. Other people came and went but she hardly noticed. Dawn was peeping through cracks in the heavy curtains. The party downstairs must have been winding down. She realised they were alone.

'I think it's awesome' he insisted. 'I've always wanted to live in a caravan, but I didn't think it was something you could do here. More like on a trailer park in the US. My email is "trailer trash hero". No, really, it is! I've always had a thing for redneck American culture.'

Her caravan was more budget holiday in Skegness than motorhome in the American desert, but she was enjoying how romantic he was making it seem. She snuggled into the pillows, and must have dozed off for a minute, because when she opened her eyes he was talking about how much he liked country music. She sat up. Nobody she knew liked country music. Her friends would wind her up about it whenever she subjected them to a burst of Emmylou Harris or Steve Earle & the Dukes.

'What are you doing after the party?' he asked.

'Oh man. I need to get to London tomorrow. I guess it's already tomorrow, isn't it? So I need to go to London today. I'm going to Paris with my mum the day after tomorrow. Er, that's actual tomorrow, not today tomorrow.'

He pulled away from her and climbed off the bed. 'Hold that thought. I've got to wee.'

Operation Penguin – Contact Log (2003)

Sunday 9th November

0945 call from Source who had remained at the party all night with no sleep. There had been a lot of Ecstasy pills taken during the night with the main exception being Katja and of course Source.

Katja told Source that she is travelling to France on Monday and needs to get to London. Source has indicated that Source may be able to give her a lift. I subsequently agreed this course with Source, as it will give Source 2-3 hours alone with Katja and endear Source to her.

She must have dozed off again and was disturbed by Mark climbing back onto the bed.

'I'll be driving to London tomorrow. I have to drop a parcel at Heathrow. That's tomorrow tomorrow, not today. I could take you, though, if you want a ride.'

This really was too good to be true. She had been dreading the hitch-hike down the M1 on no sleep. 'Oh wow, yes please. When do we leave?'

Eleanor and John stumbled into the room. 'What are you two up to?' they asked. From their stifled laughter, they evidently thought they already knew.

'Seriously,' said John. 'Mark, you're new here. We feel obliged to tell you what you're getting into.'

'She's wonderful,' said Eleanor, 'but she's a heartbreaker.'

'Just don't go falling for her, that's all we're saying.'

John was Katja's ex, and their break-up had been a bit abrupt: she just left the country one day and went on the road. He had been angry with her at the time, but distance made it easier. Here they were, two years later, good friends, and he was happy to barge in on this intimate moment to defend . . . well, she wasn't really sure what he was defending, but still.

'Heartbreaker?' she laughed. 'That's a bit unfair.' She turned to Mark. 'Don't listen to them. They're just jealous that I've got myself a ride to London.'

Emboldened by her boisterous friends, Katja leant over and kissed Mark, glancing at Eleanor over his shoulder and raising an eyebrow. Eleanor and John staggered out of the room, laughing, and Eleanor shouted back:

'She's dangerous! Don't say you weren't warned . . .'

Operation Penguin – Contact Log (2003)
Sunday 9th November
1615. Call from Source. Katja does want a lift to the west of London. Source has told her that Source needs to go to Heathrow Terminal 4 Cargo Village.

* * *

'I almost left without you. What's up with your phone?'

'It's old and, well, I might've accidentally dropped it in the loo. I'm amazed it works at all. These old Nokias are practically unkillable.' She held the ancient relic up to show it was lifeless.

They were hurtling down the M1 in his grey Ford Escort van with no windows in the back. A caged bulkhead separated the front seats from the box and it had a slam-lock door: once you closed it there was no way to open it, except from the outside, with a special security key.

They'd left late, but Mark was doing 90 miles an hour and they'd be in London much earlier than she had expected. He was a confident driver, and a great listener. All the way he asked her questions about her family, her opinions, her plans for Paris and when she was coming home. Could they meet up and hang out when she got back to Nottingham? Could he come and see her caravan?

She agreed that when she got back they should go on a date.

'Where shall I drop you?' he said. They were approaching the exit for the M25.

'Anywhere there's a Tube station would be awesome.'

'But where are you going? Maybe I can take you to the door?'

She told him Putney.

'That's on my way.'

He had said he was going to Heathrow to pick up a package. Putney wasn't on his way, but she was sure he knew that as well as she did, so it would be rude to point it out. They had stayed up all night at the party. Even though she hadn't been drinking she was feeling a bit worse for wear. If he wanted to drive her all the way to her parents' door, she wasn't going to complain.

* * *

Operation Penguin – Contact Log (2003)

Monday 10 November

Source went to the SUMAC centre and Neds in an effort to trace Katja. Found her on second visit ... Then Source and Katja travelled to Putney London with Source dropping Katja off at her parents address [the full address is recorded]. Her parents were out. Conversation in the vehicle covered many different political subjects and views ... Katja is travelling to Paris ...

1640 Debrief with source at safe London location.

Wednesday 19 November

2030 Text from Source saying that Source had given Katja an old mobile phone that Source no longer used. This gives Source the ability to establish Katjas ... location if and when necessary. The phone is 'clean' having been purchased for cash from Tesco some time ago and is a 'Pay as you go.'

CHAPTER 15

As soon as I lost my lawyers, everything changed. At the start of February 2020, I set myself up to work from home, in Catalonia. My first court appearance would be in just three weeks, and I had barely finished looking up my first bits of legal jargon on Google when the police solicitors sent an email reminding me that all the files I received would be 'subject to IPT rules'.

I spent days trying to find out what the IPT rules were. The only answer I found was that there were no clear answers. The Investigatory Powers Tribunal had the power to make its own rules, and as soon as I lost my lawyers, the police began asking them to do just that. They said that if I wanted anyone to help me with the evidence, I should have to give the police lawyers their names. Eleanor was appalled.

'How on earth is that supposed to work? I can't imagine anyone will want to help if it means their name being given to the cops.'

She was right. All my potential witnesses and most of the people who might offer me assistance had themselves been victims of intrusive police surveillance. What the police were asking was unfair, and it was almost certainly unworkable, so I had to respond.

Just reading the relevant conventions and regulations and drafting my response about that tiny side issue swallowed up days. I had less than two weeks to prepare written legal submissions, and at this rate I was never going to get it done.

The biggest issue for the upcoming hearing was that the police were refusing to disclose authorisation documents for the officers named in paragraph 103. I wasn't sure what an 'authorisation document' was, so I began by studying equivalent documents from Mark Kennedy's deployment, some of which I did have. By the time I reached the end of the third one, I was losing the will to live. The operation was reviewed or updated every three months, generating a lot of paperwork. It was dense, repetitive, procedural and very boring to read.

> Operational Objectives
> Includes the following:
> The Operational Objectives remain very much as the original application. The UCO will be tasked to continue with his infiltration of the groups referred to above . . .
> Recording of telephone communications PART II RIPA – Directed Surveillance granted ['yes' box ticked]. The interception of communications intended for, or sent by, the Undercover Officer(s) nominated, with their written consent, by means of monitoring, listening and recording of the communications by or with the assistance of an electronic device . . .
> [Authority is granted for the UCO to participate in criminal activity as outlined earlier in the form].

I realised I had read the same line four times. Yawning, I rubbed my eyes and took a deep breath. The authorisation was dated 24 September 2003.

> OPERATION NAME: PENGUIN
> Force seeking authorisation: Nottinghamshire Police
> RIPA update
> . . .
> Intelligence case:
> Includes the following:
> Since the granting of this authority the Undercover Officer has made contact with and been accepted by activists from the Sumac Centre.

This has progressed very quickly and he has been able to report accurately and pre emptively on the intentions of such persons to attend the Earth First summer gathering in Yorkshire, which he also attended. This was a useful exercise in as much as he was able to network and gather intelligence from other persons attending.

. . .

I sat up, remembering what he had said.

* * *

'I spotted you last summer, at the Earth First! Gathering, you know?' Mark moved a strand of Katja's hair on the pillow as he spoke. 'I was really happy when you showed up in Nottingham. But, I mean, I can't believe that you're here right now. I thought you were out of my league.'

She felt embarrassed. She wasn't used to this kind of attention, and he kept catching her off guard. She had been busy at the Gathering, organising the first workshop about the G8 summit. She hadn't noticed Mark, and he'd obviously been too shy to talk to her. He'd sat next to her at the NASA meeting though, perhaps that had been more than just happenstance?

He was quite forward now. He picked her up in London the day she got back from France and now he'd invited her back to his flat. It was spotlessly tidy and spartan. No books, no ornaments, almost no possessions at all. The only sign that it was someone's home was a hand-made quilt on the bed, made from patches of cloth printed with little flowers in shades of lilac. It was a lovely thing. His mother made it, he told her. They were lying on it now, and she traced the stitching with her finger. She had been telling him about Paris, and the European Social Forum (ESF). The next one would be in London in autumn 2004. She and a lot of other activists were worried because London was so expensive. Any big event would inevitably end up dominated by a few powerful groups with funds.

'There's going to be an organising meeting in London, at the Greater London Assembly. The GLA for pity's sake! It's like it's sponsored by the Mayor of London. You can already see where it's going. Big, rich trades unions and NGOs and totally London-centric. Social Forums should be about local grassroots organising not party politics. It's so frustrating.'

'Was there anything good about the Forum?' he asked. 'Did you eat any posh French food?'

The best thing had been the network of language interpreters, called 'Babels', whose mission was to help social movements from all over the world communicate. She had joined more than nine hundred volunteers, working in booths alongside professional interpreters.

'It was so amazing,' she said, her eyes shining at the memory, 'seeing people from totally different countries and cultures being able to share ideas and experiences. These are people who don't share a common language. They could only talk to each other because of the work we did.'

That was when he leant over and kissed her, and told her how he had noticed her all those months before. It was sweet, and romantic, and she didn't really know how to respond. She gave him a quick kiss back and pulled away.

'Where's the bathroom?' she said.

When she closed the door, she found one more personal touch: a framed picture of some boys in old-fashioned climbing gear. She studied it as she dried her hands: they were sitting at the base of a rock face around an older man wearing sky-blue polyester slacks. She thought one of the boys must be Mark. He was scrawny, with a bad haircut. He'd clearly grown into himself a bit since then. On her way back to the bedroom, she wondered again at how bare the place was. She was a traveller, sometimes living out of a backpack for months on end, but she still managed to accumulate stuff. This emptiness was unnerving.

'What's up, gorgeous?'

She hadn't heard him come out of the bedroom and was startled by his voice. He stood in the hallway watching her.

'It doesn't feel like a real person lives here. Where are all your things?'

He put his arm around her and pulled her back into the bedroom. 'I left most of my stuff when I moved. I wanted a clean break.'

She hovered just inside the door.

'A break from what?'

'Bad relationship.'

She must have reacted in some way because he reached out and took her hand. 'She was nothing like you. A proper Sloane Ranger, from Chelsea. Awful. I realised she was trying to trap me into marriage, and I got wise, ran away. I wanted out of London anyway, and I came here to be near the Peak District. I wanted to be close to Stanage Edge. Have you ever been? I could take you climbing. You'll love it. It's beautiful out there.'

'Is that you in the picture?' she asked. 'The one in the loo.'

He looked uncertain for a moment.

'Yeah,' he said slowly, 'that's me and my brother, at Harrison's Rocks.'

'Who's the older guy?'

'My dad.' He said it like a full stop. They stood there for a while, not speaking.

'There's this great deli in Sherwood,' he said at last. 'They do a muesli and blueberry breakfast. It's really good. Why don't you stay the night? I'll take you there in the morning.'

It was a long way back to her dismal caravan. He really did seem nice. She smiled, and he lifted the edge of the quilt, inviting her under.

* * *

The Operation Penguin contact logs for 16 November 2003 record that 'Source' would be picking Katja up in London. However, there is no entry at all for the following day.

Every minute he spent undercover, Mark was shadowed by a cover officer who kept a log of all telephone and text communications, providing a detailed record of where Mark was, and who he was with at all times. I wasn't given the cover officer's name, but he was referred to repeatedly in the disclosure and in police witness statements using the cipher 'EN31'. In his witness statement, Sir Stephen House noted that 'In the course of the review of the 10,000 pages, it has become clear that EN31 . . . "deleted and amended items" in the logs'.

That first night Mark and I spent alone together, 17–18 November 2003, is the only date I found where I know for sure that Mark was working undercover, and yet there is *nothing at all* recorded. Had EN31 felt it was necessary to delete two entire days?

Contact logs kept by EN31 were used at the time to write intelligence reports for wider dissemination. Intelligence reports were filed on 18 November, suggesting that contact logs did at some point exist, and offering a clue as to what the missing logs for the 17–18 November might have contained:

Operation Penguin Intelligence Reports
[MK] 18/11/2003

. . .

Katja says that the European Socialist Forum in Paris attracted 50,000 people. The next ESF is planned for September 2004 in London. Katja and Lukas are keen to start a local Socialist Forum in Nottingham . . . Katja stayed at her parents address, [full address recorded] prior to travelling to Paris for the European Socialist Forum where she worked as a Spanish / English interpreter. Her parents spend 6 months of the year in Spain . . .

Katja stayed the night of the 17/11/2003 at . . . Marshall Street Nottingham the home address of Mark Stone.

* * *

After that night it moved fast. Mark had a lot of free time, an income and a vehicle, and he was enthusiastic about everything. They saw each other almost every other day. He quickly made himself invaluable, while at the same time emphasising that he couldn't believe his luck to have landed a girl like her. He wasn't fazed by the political action she was involved in: he seemed to love it more than she did, and soon they were organising meetings and events together. People would talk to Mark to get messages to Katja and vice versa. She sometimes felt a little stifled by his public displays of affection, but it was who he was. He wrote her poems and gave her gifts, including a mobile phone, so they could be in touch all the time, even when he was out of town for work.

She chopped onions, carrots and flat green beans, a small piece of celery for flavour, and a potato to give texture to the sauce. Then she reached into a cupboard and pulled out a large, heavy-bottomed pan. Her first boyfriend's family taught her how to make curry, when she was just seventeen. She used whole seeds for the spices, not powders. She liked how simple, one-pot cookery could create such subtle flavours.

Living in a collective house like Neds meant cooking for up to a dozen people at a time. She was used to it now. She knew all the right quantities, and she had begun to find that cooking for one or two felt a little pointless. A good curry is at its best when the flavours have had time to blend. She had started early to let this one sit for a few hours before serving.

While the sauce was thickening, she read through Mark's texts again. He sent her three or four messages a day, little love notes, peppered with complaints about how boring life was as a delivery driver. She smiled. She quite liked the idea of driving work and had applied for some herself. But Mark had his heart set on a new career: he had just completed his training as a rope-access technician and had dreams of scaling the sides of skyscrapers, doing maintenance on wind farms, maybe even working on the oil rigs.

She was looking forward to seeing him. There had been a rush of meetings and actions recently and they were due for some downtime. Although she would never admit it, she was taking extra care with the cooking because she hoped he would be impressed.

Operation Penguin - Contact Log (2003)

Tuesday 2 December

Penguin meeting in Leicester HQ. Source attended so that Source could see the representatives of the 5 forces and they had an opportunity to see and question Source . . . Detective Inspector [O-31] issued Source with a PNB and read to Source the 1 to 7 instructions. On completion of the meeting Source travelled to Nottingham to meet up with Katja who has invited Source to dinner as it was her turn to cook.

After dinner, they moved out to her caravan to be alone. She lit the gas heater in his honour, knowing she would pay for it tomorrow. Gas combusts with oxygen to produce heat, but it also produces carbon dioxide and water, and already drops of condensation were forming on the window frames. In the morning everything would be wet, but for now it was cosy and warm. Mark lay back against the pillows, hands folded behind his head, and she propped herself up on one elbow so she could watch his face as she talked.

'People have to stand up to injustice. That's why I do it. And sure, sometimes our actions aren't all that effective, but they still count, because it matters that people stand up to injustice, even if we fail.'

She really wanted him to understand.

'When I was fourteen we studied the Nazis,' she said. 'Our history teachers had us reproduce the Milgram experiments in class. Not for real, obviously, just a role play. But it was really intense.'

He looked at her blankly. She explained that Stanley Milgram had conducted psychology experiments at Harvard in the 1970s. He studied how far people would go to hurt other people if they thought they were obeying authority. The researchers were shocked to find that over seventy per cent of people tested would do things they believed were seriously hurting a fellow human being, just because they were told to do so by an authority figure.

'We studied *The Banality of Evil*, and we studied resistance as well, the minority who didn't just go along with it, but stood up against the Nazis. I remember thinking then that whatever happens, whatever I do with my life, when fourteen-year-old history students are judging my generation in decades to come, I want to have been one of the people who did the right thing.'

'So you'll protest about absolutely anything?' he asked.

'Well, yes,' she said, 'if it feels important. I think we have a responsibility not to stand by and let unjust things happen.' She trailed off. She wasn't totally sure if he was winding her up, but she meant it. She decided to turn the question round.

'What about you? Why did you get involved in political action?'

'Me?' he laughed. 'I'm an adrenaline junkie. I just like the rush.'

He saw the look on her face and stopped laughing, pulling her in for a kiss. 'I'm only half joking,' he said, his face close to hers. 'I don't think about it as deeply as you do, but I do want to make a difference. I remember seeing those Greenpeace climbers hanging "Save the Whales" banners when I was a kid, and thinking that's what I want to be.'

She perked up.

'You totally could do that, you know,' she said. 'You're a trained climber. I know someone who works for Greenpeace. I could introduce you if you like.'

'You really think Greenpeace would have me as a climber?'

He stammered when he was nervous. It was cute.

'Honestly? I don't know. All the actions we do are . . .' she paused, 'unofficial, you know? Greenpeace would support a lot of them, like actions against genetic engineering, pulling up GM crops, but, well, I guess it would be kind of deniable if anything went wrong. If you really wanted to be an official Greenpeace climber, I am sure you could though.'

He wrapped his arm around her and pulled her head down onto his chest, stroking her hair.

'I love how you believe in me,' he said. 'Sometimes you even make me believe in myself.'

She snuggled up close.

'Why don't you come to my flat tomorrow?' he said, 'I could cook dinner for you.'

'I thought you were meeting Eleanor to talk about houses?'

'I'll just invite her too! She can bring her boyfriend. It'll be a double date. Let's say seven. But why don't you come early to make sure we get some time alone? I'm off on Thursday, working for my uncle again.'

'Oh, that reminds me,' she said. 'I got a delivery job, from that agency. Isn't that cute? We'll be in different parts of the country, but we'll both be getting paid to be stuck in traffic listening to the radio. I'll be thinking of you.'

DISCLOSURE

Wednesday 3rd December

0914. Call from Source. Katja will introduce Source to ███████. ███████ is described as a 'deniable' operative for Greenpeace. He carries out high profile actions including the climbing of buildings to drop banners. Katja has asked Source if Source would be interested in that sort of action. Source has shown enthusiasm . . . Katja works for a driving agency and tomorrow is collecting a Royal Mail van from Nottingham to deliver it to Maidstone . . .

2030. Katja, Eleanor and [Eleanor's boyfriend] visited Source at Home Address and stayed for evening meal cooked by Source. The evening involved general chit chat about life in general and music. No activism was discussed.

CHAPTER 16

From the second statement of Eleanor to the Investigatory Powers Tribunal

When Mark moved to Nottingham in the summer of 2003, I actively took him under my wing . . . even moving him into my house. Living together for almost two years, at the same time as taking political action together, made us very close friends. He always praised me a lot, saying things like 'I have never met anyone who is so clever at science, and so artistic at the same time'.

When we no longer lived together (i.e. after August 2005), we would regularly invite each other for dinner. He would also seek me out at my new home, or at the Sumac Centre, and would say things like 'You are like my contact in Nottingham – I know I am home when you are here.' I had an intense trust of Mark and, at a period in my life where I had hundreds of friends, he was probably among my top five closest friends.

Mark and his handlers began considering the decision to move into a house with Eleanor in November 2003. The discussions went on for several weeks. They recorded concerns about 'Source's welfare', 'risk assessments', possible 'exit strategies' and ways to manipulate his housemates' expectations of him. However, at no point did they consider the welfare of the people whose home he was about to invade. When it came to recording the official decision, they didn't even bother to correctly spell their names.

DISCLOSURE

Operation Penguin – Contact Log (2003)

Wednesday 12th November

1215 Source received a call from Eleanor saying that she had found a house for rent ... In line with previous policy decision Source has expressed an interest in order to save money on current rent whilst tempering it with being the first time for a long time that Source has lived with others. This provides an exit strategy if living with them does not work out ... they have asked Source to take on the responsibility [of 'Primary Renter']. I have told Source to avoid this if at all possible. Source has indicated that it would be a good idea for them to review the situation after about 6 months. This again assists our exit strategy ... Source says that on a welfare front those involved are not a stressful group of individuals to share with.

Operation Pegasus Decision Logs

Decision Number 9

DECISION:

For the Operative to live in joint accommodation with

- 'Lukas'
- 'Ronnie'
- 'Elenour'

REASON:

To ensure integration with individuals holding an anarchist perspective. To provide greater credibility and access to the leading activist circle.

* * *

Katja stepped up to Mark's flat and rang the doorbell. He opened the door and kissed her before pulling her inside. Up close, he smelt of soap and something else, and her stomach gave a little flip as she was reminded of how they had been the night before. Maybe he was thinking the same, because he lingered with his lips against hers for a long moment, before pulling back.

'Gimme a minute. I'm just finishing something and then I'm all yours.'

He disappeared into the next room and she looked around, and was struck, once again, by the sparseness. The flat would barely look any different after he was gone. Mark wandered back into the room and her stomach twisted. Who was this man she had become so close to so fast?

'What's your story?' she blurted out.

Mark looked startled. 'What do you mean?'

'Your house has no personality. You and me, we've got pretty cosy these past weeks.' She blushed. 'But I know nothing about who you are.'

Mark was silent for a moment, and then he took a step towards her.

'What if I told you I was in hiding?'

'It's not funny Mark, I'm here all alone with you, and I still know nothing about you. You could be a fucking axe murderer, for all I know.'

'Hey, calm down,' he said, more serious this time. 'I'm not a serial killer.' He paused. 'I am kind of running away though.'

She saw his expression and sat down.

He told her he had got involved with a bad crowd while working as a courier in London. They would pay him to drive a van to Granada and bring it back full of cocaine. He had made a lot of money and had savings squirrelled away, but it was a risky business and it couldn't last. That world was filled with some very nasty people, and some of them would not be happy that he had just upped and gone.

As they packed the boxes into his van her head was buzzing. She had a thousand questions she wanted to ask him about his former gangland life, but she was worried she would come across as silly or naive. He swore her to secrecy. He was trusting her with information that could put him, even her, in danger. She felt a thrill.

DISCLOSURE

As he reached down to put the van into gear, she placed her hand on top of his. Then they drove to Foxhall Road and began moving him and his secrets into a new home with her closest friends.

Operation Penguin – Contact Log (2003)
Wednesday 10th December
2109 Source moved into new premises and spent first night there.

* * *

I got up and filled the kettle. Disturbed dreams lingered, leaving me on edge. I packed bitter green yerba mate leaves into a small bamboo cup, then gradually added hot (not boiling) water. I picked up the habit when I was living in a squat in Barcelona with some Argentinians. Mate is drunk through a special filter on the end of a stainless-steel straw, and packs a punch like coffee, but it's more than just a drink; it's a whole ritual. It is meant to be drunk socially, a single cup passed around. But I had no one to share it with.

I thought back to the day ten years before, when I stood on the patio first absorbing the shock that Mark was police. If you had told me then that I would end up living alone, I wouldn't have believed you. But betrayal destroys your ability to trust.

I used to say that easily, like I was stating the obvious. I had learnt my lesson: I was no longer so trusting. I wouldn't get caught out again. It took me a long time to realise that, if you don't let people in, you can't have community. When every tiny conflict hides a deeper, more threatening wrong, you end up watching all the time, waiting for people to reveal how they're going to hurt you. It grinds away at your relationships. By the time I realised that not trusting was a bad thing, I was living alone.

I looked out over the valley of umbrella pines, letting the rising Mediterranean sun warm me. Then I turned back to my desk, sipped my mate, and resumed preparations for the hearing.

CHAPTER 17

It was rush hour on the Peripherique and six lanes of traffic had crammed themselves into what should have been a four-lane section of road. Cars spread across the white lines and onto the hard shoulder, filling every available inch of space. Nothing was moving. Horns blared and occasionally a frustrated driver added to the chaos by trying to change lanes.

I flipped down the sun visor to check my reflection in the mirror. For the hundredth time, I wondered if I was overdressed. Calf-high boots, thick woollen tights with a diamond pattern, a fluffy, black knitted dress and a touch of make-up. I wanted to look my best, but perhaps I had overdone it. It was the tights: I had found them while packing and thought what the hell, why not show off my legs? Now I felt awkward and exposed.

I checked my phone. Ben's flight into Orly would be landing in twenty minutes. I was late as it was.

We had seen each other a few times since that first trip to Martinique. He visited me in the UK and Spain, and we went travelling. We even swam with sea turtles, like he promised. Whenever there was a pause in the case, we tried to meet. Then I lost my lawyers, and I had to explain that I no longer had time for anything else.

Ben seemed undeterred. He had declared that he was flying into Paris to accompany me to London and help prepare for my first solo hearing. As I pulled off the Peripherique onto the airport road I felt a bit giddy. Ben hated winter, and I knew February in the UK was not where he wanted to be. He wanted his own back at the police, and the operations that targeted our movements; but I couldn't help but think that he was coming, at least in part, because he was into me. It was a big gesture, after all. Hence the decision to dress up. I cringed at that thought and tried to pull the dress down towards my knees.

When I reached the terminal, he was already through customs and standing by the road. Over six foot tall, he stood out from the crowd, with a tiny-looking carry-on suitcase and shabby, sun-bleached clothes. He glanced my way, I flashed my lights, and he jogged over and jumped in, leaning over to kiss me as I pulled out onto the road to Calais.

'Nice tights.'

At my parent's flat in London, we got to work on the blue folders straight away. We pulled out all the pages and attempted to sort them by document type and date. Soon we had occupied every inch of the dining table and parts of the floor. Everywhere you looked there were piles of paper and handwritten notes.

I was scatter-brained and unable to focus on any one thing for more than a few minutes, but Ben turned out to be single-minded to a fault. He would immerse himself in a task or set of documents so completely that he lost sight of everything else, including the people around him. The intensity of his concentration helped me to keep working, but the atmosphere in the flat was tense.

'We can't live like this,' Mum said, after a few days. 'You need to keep your work in the study. This is driving me mad.' She swept an arm out to indicate the mess.

I had just five days to complete my submissions for the hearing, but she had a point. I looked at the teetering piles of paper.

'He's doing my head in,' said Dad. 'He's staying in our house, but it's like he doesn't even notice we're here!'

My heart sank. I really wanted them to like Ben, but I should have realised this would be a stressful enough time without me bringing a new boyfriend along.

'Ben.'

He was on the sofa, hunched over a page of contact logs. He didn't seem to hear me.

'Ben! We need to move all this upstairs.'

He looked up slowly, and it was clearly an effort to drag his attention away.

* * *

Operation Penguin - Contact Log (2003)

Sunday 14th December

Call from Source having been to the ESF and been introduced to several notable individuals by Katja. Further information when we meet for debrief. Source has also been invited for a meal to Katja's parents house.

'Mum? Dad? This is Mark.'

Her dad waved from the kitchen, and her mum stuck out a hand.

'I'm Pauline, that's Dave. Welcome, would you like a drink?'

'Are you vegetarian too?' her dad asked, wiping his hands on a tea towel. 'Don't worry, I'm making a veggie option for madam here, but we're having roast beef.'

Mark looked a little panicked.

'I'll just have what Katja's having, thanks.'

Her mum poured him a glass of red wine and turned to Katja as she lowered the volume on *Channel 4 News*.

'How was your meeting? What's the GLA building like inside? I was at CAAT today, and people there were talking about the Social Forum,' she said.

'What's CAAT?' Mark asked.

'Campaign Against the Arms Trade.'

'Do you work there?' he asked.

'No, no I just volunteer. I was stuffing envelopes today. I like to do my bit. I used to be a probation officer, but I stopped taking clients a while ago. I do training now, for the probation service and the Metropolitan Police.'

Katja winced a little. She was never sure how her activist friends would react when they heard her mum worked for the Met.

'She's a freelancer,' she said quickly, 'not a cop.'

'I do diversity training,' her mum explained. 'I'm not sure it does any good.'

Katja got up to help her dad bring the food through. Mark followed. 'What do you do, Dave?' he asked. She smiled. Mark was charming, attentive and inquisitive. He really seemed to want to get to know them.

'I'm a land surveyor. Freelance as well, these days.'

'Dad used to work for Thames Water, but it got deregulated,' Katja said. 'He had to apply to get his job back with each sell-off. He went from being a civil servant to an employee for a private contractor, to eventually setting up as a sole trader and doing the contracting himself. He could probably write the book on why privatisation is shit.'

Operation Penguin – Contact Log (2003)
Tuesday 16th December
1000. Debrief with Source at safe location.
Source had visited the home address of Katja's parents after the ESF meeting yesterday. Mrs Wilson is a researcher for the Campaign Against the Arms Trade (CAAT). Mr Wilson is a surveyor.

'So what about you Mark, what do you do?'

'I'm a delivery driver, mostly. But I've just qualified as a rope access technician. I'm looking for work now. I'll be cleaning windows on skyscrapers in the City soon.'

'Mark grew up in Battersea,' Katja said, and then turned to Mark. 'That's where my parents lived when they first came to London, back in the seventies. You must have been living there at the same time.'

'We had a flat in Lurline Gardens,' her dad offered. 'We used to drink in The Eagle, do you know it?'

Mark gave a non-committal shrug and shook his head, before turning to ask Katja's brother if he would pass the salad. 'This is delicious,' he said. She wondered if she had touched a nerve by bringing up his childhood.

Operation Penguin – Contact Log (2003)

Friday 19th December

Afternoon and evening visiting areas of London that Source needed to refamiliarise with because of developments with Katja's relatives knowing the area.

Mark was heading back to Nottingham. Katja leant through the window of his van to give him a last goodbye kiss before he left. She was staying on in London to spend Christmas with her family.

'What are you going to do?'

'I'll go to Ireland, to be with my mum. My brother is coming over from Cleveland.'

'Will you tell your mum about me? I'd really like to meet her. Maybe we can call each other on Christmas Day?'

'Maybe. I might not get a signal.'

They kissed again. He opened the driver's door to reverse, leaning out and looking behind. She felt a pang of sympathy: his damaged eye meant that he had no depth perception, and judging distances in the mirror was hard. Then he closed the door and spun the wheel with the heel of one hand in that way that, try as she might, she could never master, and he was gone. She wondered why he hadn't been more enthusiastic about introducing her to his mother. He had made such an effort with her family, but it felt one-sided. Watching the road, she shivered and turned back up the steps to her parents' flat.

* * *

'When the documents talk about "Source" being in Putney, does that mean Mark was here, in this flat?'

Ben and I had set ourselves up in the study, and he was organising the piles of paper in a line along one wall. He had stopped to read the top page of a set of contact logs.

'Yeah. He stayed here all the time. The worst thing is, they got on really well.'

A lot better than they are with you.

I didn't voice the thought out loud. Mark was trained to put us at our ease and worm his way into our lives. He used common interests to build complicity. He feigned vulnerability over his abandoned childhood to create intimacy, not only with me, but with my parents as well, calling them the family he never had. He drew us all in. He was a fictional character.

'It must be weird for them, having me here,' Ben said.

I swallowed, blinking back tears.

Ben and I were living like recluses. We ate at the desk while we worked, or simply forgot to eat at all. But suddenly there was a lull. I had sent the draft of my submissions to Eleanor, Dónal, Helen and Charlotte, because they had all offered to comment. The papers had to be served by 4 p.m. the following day. There was nothing more we could do until we heard back. We emerged from the study, blinking like moles.

'Dare we ask how it's going?' my parents asked at dinner.

'Getting there, I guess. It feels like the last night before a big exam.'

'Well, you couldn't have worked any harder, that's for sure.'

Dad had made goulash topped with baked yogurt and cheese, and it was delicious. I realised I hadn't tasted my food in days. Some of the tension seemed to finally be lifting. I wished I could make it easier on my parents, and for Ben.

'Mark, could you pass the wine?' someone said.

The words hung in the air.

My dad moved first, muttering that he was going to bed. Ben stayed quiet and I sat on the sofa hugging my knees. Mum tried to salvage the evening, switching on a re-run of *Silent Witness*, but I couldn't concentrate. One by one we drifted out of the room.

* * *

Operation Penguin – Contact Log (2004)
Saturday 17th January.
Source in London for tonight's WOMBLES meeting. Currently unknown what to expect.

'W.O.M.B.L.E.S.' was another acronym undoubtedly chosen before the name. It stood for 'White Overalls Movement Building Libertarian Effective Struggles'. The group was made up of anti-capitalist activists who united around a tactic originally from Italy. They would dress up in thickly padded white overalls, evoking the popular children's TV characters the Wombles of Wimbledon. The padding was to protect them from police violence, making them much more difficult to disperse, and their trademark tactic was standing their ground to show that demonstrations should not be bowed by threatening behaviour from the police. They protested a range of different issues, bringing an anti-capitalist flavour to anything from migrant rights to May Day demonstrations. A couple of years previously Katja had been involved in an action they organised in Oxford against immigration detention, and she had good friends in the group. Now they were mobilising around the G8, and she was going to their meeting to link them with the Dissent! Network. Mark wanted to come too.

Operation Penguin – Contact Log (2004)
Sunday 18th January.
0111. Text from Source. 'At Putney loads of info, safe!

. . .

1347.
Debrief Source.
The meeting of the WOMBLES took place last night . . . Source was accepted into all the groups present and Source puts this down to being so closely associated to Katja.

Katja had passed her driving test about a year ago, but she didn't own a car. When they went to London together, he would let her drive and give her pointers: 'Lift your vision when you're overtaking. Don't look at the truck, look past it, to where you're going.'

She was gaining confidence, but she didn't have his stamina, and after an hour or so on the motorway she pulled off at the services. He got out.

'I'm going for a wee. Fancy a pasty?'

'Yes, please, I'm starving.'

She unwrapped the pale pastry squares as Mark pulled back out onto the motorway. They were undercooked. Mark threw his out of the window.

'Mark!'

'It's all right, I'll get us a takeaway when we get home. Did you see the emails from the W.O.M.B.L.E.S? They seem like an interesting group.'

She laughed. 'The police certainly think so.'

The van veered slightly, growling along the rumble strip. Mark pulled the steering wheel and straightened up.

'Why do you say that?'

'They just seem to get way more stress than other groups. They kicked a guy out recently for being an infiltrator. Special Branch showed up on someone else's doorstep, making veiled threats. They wanted him to inform on the group. They do that, you know? They pick on vulnerable people. Like if you get arrested, for drug offences and stuff, they use it as leverage to get you to be an informant.'

She trailed off, wondering if Mark was also thinking about his past. She decided to use a different example.

'Have you heard of McLibel?'

He nodded, eyes on the road.

'Well, McDonald's paid infiltrators to spy on that campaign. I've heard there were times when there were more spies at London Greenpeace meetings than genuine activists. Maybe it's just a London thing, I don't know. We should probably be more careful, but it's hard, isn't it? The Sumac Centre is a social project. We want it to be a welcoming place.'

Mark flicked the indicator and pulled out to overtake a caravan that was doing sixty in the middle lane. Once they were past it, he stayed in the fast lane, picking up speed.

'So, what do you do?' he asked carefully, eyes firmly on the road.

'I don't know. Get to know people, I guess. Meet their family, look at baby pics.' She paused. 'I'd love to see your baby pics,' she said.

Operation Penguin – Contact Log (2004)
Friday 30th January
2013 Text from Source. 'Just spent a horrible hour with Katja talking about police informers. She hopes I am not one'

DISCLOSURE

I asked Source for a meet

2025 Text from Source. 'Can't I'm with them until Sunday but thanks.
This 'meet your mum' thing came up again. Got to go.'

Mark was in America and Katja missed him more than she cared
to admit. She found herself fantasising about adventures they
could have together. She looked through her photos from the
demonstration the previous weekend, outside the Lindholme
immigration prison, where he had used his climbing skills to scale
the fence. He looked so intrepid.

He hadn't replied to the message she sent yesterday. In less
than ten days he would be back, but it felt like forever. Valentine's
Day was coming up. What if she were the soppy one for a change?

She gathered coloured paper, old postcards, magazines and
glue, and got to work.

They were driving along the M62 in the dark. Mark was explaining that it was the highest motorway in Britain, snaking its way
across the Pennine ridge. She listened, gazing out of the window
at the broken white line flashing past in the headlights, playing
with his hair while he drove. She stroked the back of his neck
with her fingertips and he rolled his eyes, taking her hand from
his neck and pressing it against his inner thigh.

'Easy,' she said, laughing. 'Watch the road!'

Soon after, he pulled the van off the motorway and drove
out onto the moor. He switched off the headlights and they sat,
looking out over the dark, frosty expanse of lonely granite and
heather. It felt like they were the only people in the world.

'Why don't we stay here tonight?' he said. 'I've got my camping
stuff in the back.'

The ice crunched under their feet as they put the tent up,
and their breath lingered in frozen clouds in front of their faces.
Cold seeped into their earlobes, fingers and toes. Soon, though,

they were close, noses almost touching, wrapped in the warm, slippery fabric of his down sleeping bag, limbs entwined, cold fingers exploring warm untravelled places on each other's skin. She inhaled and he smelt musky, like crushed geranium leaves.

Past the soft rustling of their bodies as they settled, she could just make out a whispering noise. It seemed to surround them, coming from all directions at once. At first she thought it must be an animal, but it was too vast. Mark laughed and turned on his torch. The beam illuminated snowflakes through the canvas as they slid across the roof of the tent, each one making a tiny, silky hiss as it settled into place.

They held each other then, listening to the snowstorm as it gently fell around them, turning their fragile cocoon into an igloo. 'This is incredible,' she sighed.

'Do you mean that?' he said. 'You really like it?'

'It's magical, don't you think?'

'I mean, yeah. I love it.' He sat up a little, as if to really look at her. 'But I expected you to be mad at me for making you sleep out in the snow. I never thought I'd meet a girl who would love it too.'

She laid her head against his chest and said nothing. He was such a strange mix. Despite his action-man antics, he seemed so innocent and awed by their relationship. Even with the shadows cast by his past, or perhaps because he had lived through those things, he made her feel safe. He switched off the torch and they lay in silence. She listened to the whisper of the snow on the tent, and the beating of his heart, and wondered what he was thinking. She didn't dare to ask.

Sunday 15th February
1937 Call from Source who has received a Valentines card from Katja. This has put Source's mind at rest re the challenges about being an undercover/informant.

CHAPTER 18

The architecture of the Royal Courts of Justice is designed to make you feel small. Great arches and vaulted ceilings tower over a chequered floor of black and white tiles that stretch endlessly away. I held my head high as I walked through the atrium in my ill-fitting suit jacket and a pair of my mother's shoes. The night before, I had re-dyed my hair, and that morning, when Eleanor, Ben, Mum, Dad and I crammed ourselves and the boxes of evidence into a taxi for my first solo court appearance, I was wearing my blue dreadlocks like war paint. As the taxi navigated its way through the rush-hour traffic, Ben said: 'You know the saying, the person who represents themselves has a fool for a lawyer?'

We arrived to find all our campaign groups at the court, and the crowd lifted my spirits just enough to laugh at Ben's jokes. Alison held a campaign banner proclaiming 'Police Spies Out of Our Lives'. Helen Steel was handing out flyers.

She came with us when we went into court, her reputation for representing herself in the McLibel trial adding gravitas to our side of the room. Even so, we were a motley crew. I glanced at the other side. Sharp-suited barristers, solicitors, balding men with serious faces. Plain-clothed police, I assumed.

There isn't much pomp or theatrics in the Investigatory Powers Tribunal. It was a relief to find that no one was wearing wigs or gowns. Nevertheless, the bench, with its three-judge Tribunal, was high above me, and my friends and family were behind, in the public gallery. I was sitting alone.

'Court rise!'

I got to my feet, clasping my hands in front of me as the judges filed in. How should I address them? Did I have to say, 'Your Honour'? I couldn't remember. Charlotte had always done the talking. My lawyers had sat between me and the court. I just watched from the public gallery, surrounded by friends. I wished I had paid more attention.

We sat, and the Chair of the Tribunal looked down at me and smiled. At least they seemed friendly. I looked at my notes and started working through the arguments in my mind.

Over the past few weeks, I had logged more than four hundred hours, writing, reading and reworking those arguments. The blue lever-arch folders were laid out on the table in front of me. I had only read a fraction of what was in them, but maybe it didn't matter. I had plenty to say. I explained why I was requesting the disclosure of the disputed authorisation documents, for the deployments of Jim, Jason, Rod, Marco and Lynn, and why the police ought to comply. Then it was the police lawyer's turn to speak.

'May I just say at the outset that this is not in any sense a delaying tactic,' he began.

My grip on my pen tightened in irritation. Of course it was a delaying tactic. Their entire approach was one big delaying tactic.

I looked over at the man talking: David Perry, QC. He led the defendants' sixth legal team. Six different teams in as many years. They all blurred to me – faceless people in suits doing the bureaucracy of evil – but as a litigant in person I would have to deal with their lawyers directly. I needed to focus.

People seemed to think that hiring Perry was a sign the police were worried. A Google search informed me that he was 'phenomenally impressive, consistently viewed by peers as one of the hardest working and most committed silks at the Bar'. It also revealed he had acted for the Security Services and advised foreign governments. I looked across the courtroom. I wasn't sure what to make of him. He didn't seem all that impressive. I was struggling to hear what he said.

'. . . the position in relation to the other undercover officers and the authorisations is that it is not possible to move to disclosure of that material without undertaking a comprehensive risk assessment . . . The point that is being made – and it is one that has vexed the Inquiry – is even the most trivial detail, when placed alongside other information, can lead to a risk of harm.'

Risk of harm. I wrote the words in my notes, underlining them so hard that my pen tore the page. The police had presented no specific evidence for any 'risk of harm' that could result from giving me the files. It was entirely hypothetical. It was clear from what Perry was saying that they hadn't even done a risk assessment. I explained to the Tribunal that Mark's supervisors had conducted risk assessments and consistently concluded the risk was 'low', with 'no concerns at this time for the UCOs safety'. It had been their view that 'these persons do not show any propensity for violence when a suspected source is identified'.

Then we were ejected from the room so that the Tribunal could sweep for bugs before they and the police continued in secret. For hours, the doors remained closed, with us on the outside. The Tribunal eventually decided they would put off their final decision until the following June.

Yet another trial date was set, for October, but it was quickly clear that it was not to be. We emerged from that strange bubble of court preparations into a changing world.

CHAPTER 19

'The World Health Organization have just declared it a pandemic.'

I heaved my suitcase onto the check-in conveyor belt. It was several kilos overweight. The hearing was over and Ben was anxious to get back to the Caribbean. I was going too. It was intended to be a holiday, just for a few weeks, but events were progressing fast: Italy was closed, and it was touch-and-go whether we would be able to take our flight. At the last minute, I decided to pack the court papers in case I couldn't get home. More than two thirds of my luggage was secret police files.

Mark's deployment was originally called 'Operation Penguin'. It began in the summer of 2003, headed by Nottinghamshire Police, and ended on 15 February 2004, a few hours after I gave Mark that Valentine's card. I didn't have much material relating to that time (the logs relating to Operation Penguin would not be disclosed until 2022).

On 16 February 2004, operational management was transferred to London, to be run by the London Metropolitan Police, although Mark continued to be based in Nottingham. It was the Met who changed the name to the more vainglorious 'Operation Pegasus', leading me to wonder what operation names had to say about the people in charge. Jason Bishop's operation was code-named 'Red Herring' and, more worryingly, Jim Boyling's was 'Psycho Dream'. If those were selected at random, the universe has a dark sense of humour.

DISCLOSURE

All the documents in my suitcase were from 'Operation Pegasus'. The Met inherited an operation in which Mark and I were already an item and he was living in a house with a group of my closest friends. Pegasus began with a series of signed policy decisions setting out Mark Kennedy's command structure and establishing the living arrangements for Mark Stone. The names of all the officers involved were kept hidden, replaced with ciphers, such as Disclosure Officer, 'O-72', Deputy Deployment Manager, 'O-42', Deployment Manager, 'EN59' and Cover Officer or handler, 'EN31'.

It turned out that Mark had the same cover officer for the entire time he was undercover. EN31 was Mark's handler throughout Operation Penguin, and he (we were told it was a he) stayed in the role when it became Pegasus, remaining there until the deployment ended in 2010. He spent his days collecting Mark's calls and text messages and logging what 'Source' was doing. Those logs revealed that he was often physically close to Mark, sometimes just round the corner, watching us, for almost seven years. His was the voice in most of the documents. I wondered if I had ever seen him: a man in a car, a stranger walking past us in the street. Had I met him?

Forced to shelter on the boat, out at anchor, Ben and I were truly isolated. We collected rainwater to drink and wash, and swam in the sea for exercise. Internet came from 'Captain Wifi', a marine wireless service in the bay. Weeks went by without seeing anyone.

As we waited for news from the IPT, Eleanor and I spoke regularly on Zoom. One day she organised a surprise 'housemates reunion'. She, Ronny, Loukas and I gathered to reminisce and catch up on the last ten years.

'We used to use your dictionary as an oracle, do you remember?'

'I've still got it,' Loukas said. 'Would you like a reading?'

They went off screen for a moment, then reappeared. 'You first, Katja.'

Questions to the Oracle were secret, between you and the book, so I silently asked, 'Why am I doing this? Should I still be pursuing this case after so many years, while the world is falling to bits around our ears?'

Eyes closed, Loukas opened the dictionary at random, placed a finger on the page, and read aloud: 'Tribe! Noun: a group or class of people with strong common traits, customs, values, or interests. How's that?'

'The Oracle never fails us,' I said with a smile. In truth I was a little spooked. I hadn't heard from Ronny or Loukas in years, but I was reading every day about the time when we lived together. Obviously, things had changed: both Eleanor and Loukas had children, who would occasionally interrupt in search of snacks or arbitration in some sibling row. Ronny was staying in a castle; I was thousands of miles away, on a boat. Mark wasn't there. Nevertheless, it felt surprisingly normal to be chatting again. It also gave me a chance to tap into our collective memories. When it came to interpreting the files, that would prove vital.

* * *

From the witness statement of Loukas to the Investigatory Powers Tribunal, October 2020
From around May 2003 to July 2005 I lived in Nottingham, UK. In that time I lived at an address in Foxhall Road with three other people, including the man I now know to be former police officer Mark Kennedy . . . One night, in late 2003 or early 2004, I came home to find that Mark had brought round some people he introduced to me as 'childhood friends'. . .

The three men, who I now believe were probably all police officers, were grouped nearest the door. I believe 'Ed' was sat in an armchair like mine, facing me . . . Mark was next to him on some other kind of chair, maybe a kitchen chair, half facing him and half facing me. The third man, who I think was called 'Vinny' remained standing at the back. I don't remember him saying a word all evening.

I remember both 'Ed' and 'Vinny' having a lot of hair and being dressed in low quality or old clothes. Ed had golden-ginger hair and Vinny had a shock of dark hair, maybe black. I don't remember either being bearded. It is possible they wore wigs. I recall mentally dubbing Vinny as 'Phineas' after his physical resemblance to the character in the comic strip the *Fabulous Furry Freak Brothers*. He seemed to have a similarly long nose and thin lips and to be skinny. I assumed the reason he was silent all night was because he was in some way damaged from too much drugs or had some kind of social anxiety; it is of course possible that he was actually terrified during this mission and was therefore always ready to flee for the exit.

Ed did enough talking for all three of them . . . I named him in my head 'the cowardly lion' after the portrayal in the 1930s film *The Wizard of Oz* . . . I remember being struck by the way that Mark deferred to him, with closed body language like knees together, arms wrapped around himself and torso leaning towards him, and I remember Mark's nervous laughter at Ed's lame witticisms. Based on what they said and from my observations of them I assumed that Ed had been some kind of leading figure in their boy gang . . . The patter from Ed seemed to be mostly about the things they'd done as young lads. I don't remember any details. My other housemates returned at various points throughout the evening and Kate Wilson was also present. She and Mark had been in a romantic relationship since early November 2003 and she was keen for a first opportunity to meet people from his childhood . . .

From the first witness statement of Eleanor to the Investigatory Powers Tribunal, October 2020
At some point, early on in living in the first house we lived in together, Mark brought up some 'friends from London'. He told us they were people he used to know – not activists. I remember Mark told us Vinny worked on a market. A day or so after they left, Mark said to me, when we were on our own in the kitchen, that Vinny had really fancied me, and asked if I liked him. Luckily, I said no. I found the episode curious, as I had noticed no spark at all between me and Vinny.

Since Mark was revealed to be an undercover officer, I have concluded that these men had to be police – he would not have invited real friends from his past, it would have been too risky and unprofessional. I have assumed that Vinny was some kind of undercover officer in training . . . our other female housemate from the time, has also since told me that Mark told her [Ed] was interested romantically in her as well at the same time.

With hindsight, I am forced to assume that either Mark was trying to procure sex for his police mates, or he was trying to provide [Ed and] Vinny with an entrance into the activist scene via having a romantic engagement with me or my housemate.

* * *

I asked the Tribunal to investigate whether 'Ed' and 'Vinny' had been police officers, but the police responded that they could neither confirm nor deny.

I was introduced to these men as Mark's girlfriend. I remember sitting on the arm of Mark's chair in the living room, listening to their conversation, noticing how his accent got more Cockney in their presence. Mark and I slept together in his bed that night. I scoured the documents for references to the visit. 'Ed' and 'Vinny' must have known exactly what kind of relationship we had, yet we received no disclosure about what they reported back. I did find one strange entry from March 2004, however. EN31 appears to be the author, and he describes *himself* going to Nottingham. The entry then describes 'redacted individuals' hanging out in Nottingham over several days:

Friday 19th March
1200 (Me) To Grantham area to recce Railway station

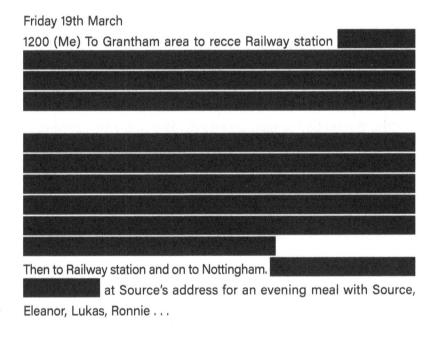

Then to Railway station and on to Nottingham.
at Source's address for an evening meal with Source, Eleanor, Lukas, Ronnie . . .

Saturday 20th March
1030

SUMAC centre for breakfast and mixed with the locals. They then walked to Nottingham city centre and visited various locations including the vegetarian café that Ronny works in . . . ate an evening meal with Source and the other flatmates.
2130
To the SUMAC centre and socialised with those present . . .

Returned to the house and had general conversation with all those present until 0200.

The redactions were unusual, and it certainly seemed that some-one whose identity was being concealed (and not even ciphered) was spending time socialising with Mark and his housemates and 'mixing with the locals'. It wasn't conclusive. I had been on a teaching course in Spain that weekend, so that wasn't when I met them. However, Eleanor and Loukas assured me that 'Ed' and 'Vinny' visited their house more than once. Who were they? Was one of them EN31? What role did they play in the operation?

The news coming out of Europe was frightening, and my co-workers at the health centre were preparing for the worst. They needed nurses, but no flights were going into Spain, so I was stuck watch-ing the disaster unfold online.

It was difficult to concentrate. In April 2020 the court case was officially postponed. Reading the police disclosure was punishingly boring, for the most part, but it was stressful too. From time to time, I encountered little details that would trip me up and trigger emotional responses that were a physical ordeal.

Operation Pegasus – Contact Log (2004)
18th February 2004
Katja (not present) is having a farewell get together in Oxford on the week end 28/29 prior to going to Spain. She has invited Source. GOOD THING TO ATTEND

I could hear my own heartbeat, and the blood pounding in my ears. I closed my eyes. Adrenaline; anger; sadness; breathlessness; and an empty sensation in my chest. I set the folder aside and tried to focus on nearby sounds until my heart rate had slowed to a more manageable pace.

DISCLOSURE

The Oxford trip revealed the workings of the faceless backroom men. I invited Mark and he told his cover officer, 'EN31'. In turn, EN31 flagged it in the logs in capital letters, for the attention of the Deployment Manager, Detective Chief Inspector 'EN59'. These were the men who gave the orders. They even recorded it in a log.

Operation Pegasus Decision Log

Decision number 31 – February 2004

DECISION: Social evening + following day Sat 28/Sun 29 Oxford . . .

REASON: Oxford – identified centre for activists surrounding which coverage needs improving.

The document itself was handwritten. I stared at it for a long time, trying to imagine the man who wrote it, whose name and face were a state secret, and whose job it had been to decide whether my boyfriend and I would spend the weekend away.

* * *

When they came to Broad Street, Katja stopped by a small patch of cobblestones.

'This is the place where Cranmer, Latimer and Ridley were burnt at the stake for their beliefs.'

The stones formed a cross, and she traced the shape of it with her foot.

'Back then, Catholics and Protestants were all about burning each other alive. If you didn't know it, you could walk past this spot without a glance, but once you know, it's kind of fascinating, imagining the burning pyre right here.'

Oxford University was a piece of her past she didn't share with everyone. She came from an inner-city comprehensive and had kicked against this bastion of British privilege when she arrived. In 1998, she took part in protests against a new business school that was to be funded by an arms-broker. That put her at odds with the university authorities and she ended up taking a year out, returning for her finals in 2000. She never really got back into the spirit of student life, but left with a decent degree, and still felt passionate and conflicted about the city. She was pretty sure the cobblestone cross didn't mark the exact spot where the Oxford Martyrs died, but she was enjoying her role as Mark's tour guide, and she was adding a bit of drama because she wanted him to feel something of the magnitude of the place.

The night before, she had taken him to the local housing co-operative where old friends cooked for them.

'Mark, this is everybody. Everybody, this is Mark.'

About a dozen people had shown up: friends Katja had studied, campaigned or lived with. It turned into a party. Later, when they were alone together in bed, Mark had joked about 'high-achieving Oxford brainiacs', but in truth he had been his usual attentive and charming self. He seemed to fit right in.

She took him to Blackwell's, the tiny, quaint shopfront that hid a vast literary emporium; and walked him round the square surrounding the Radcliffe Camera, where heavy metal grilles in the pavement exhale the smell of old books. From there they took back lanes, past the observatory where Edmund Halley first saw his comet ('Eleanor and I lived together in that house for a while, in our second year') and into New College itself. Once inside, they walked in silence. She wanted the gothic beauty of the quads, college gardens and cloisters to speak for itself.

When they left to find lunch, she thought Mark seemed subdued.

* * *

DISCLOSURE

Operation Pegasus – Contact Log (2004)

Sunday 29th February

Source spent the day . . . doing the 'visitors' tour of Oxford colleges and museums. They also visited Katja's old college 'for old times sake.'

Monday 1st March

1830 – 1935 Debrief Source re the weekend's events.

███

███

███

████████████████████████████████

I read the lengthy report on our romantic weekend in Oxford. It was filled with personal information about all the kind, friendly people I had introduced Mark to, including their families, employment, campaigning activity and interests. My friends had made him welcome, never guessing what I was bringing into their lives. The debrief ended with the triumphant observation that, 'Source has an open invitation to return at any time.'

Ben and I had been alone together for forty days and counting: a full quarantine. We had no income, so we would row to shore at night to rifle through the bins at the back of the supermarket. We never had any trouble finding supplies. There was always an abundance: rice, pasta, flour, cheese, fresh vegetables. Even packets of toilet rolls occasionally got thrown away, despite news stories about panic-buying and empty shelves.

By day, I spent my time analysing the disclosure. This was made much harder by its disorganisation. I had to study time stamps and context to place stray pages and establish whether documents were missing or just misplaced. Coming as it did from a police institution dedicated to observing, recording, indexing and filing information, I could only assume that it had been done badly on purpose. The

Tribunal ordered that it be rectified, but the correctly redacted files wouldn't come until mid-August. In the meantime, making sense of it felt impossible. I had almost two thousand pages to digest, but I was paralysed by low-level, concentration-killing anxiety.

'I need a searchable index.'

'A what?' said Ben.

'A way of listing the documents so that I can go back and find key information when I need it. Otherwise, it just crashes through my brain wreaking havoc, and when I want to find stuff again, I don't know where to look.'

I didn't know how to approach it, but it was increasingly clear that any kind of system would be a start. We spent the rest of the day designing an indexing project.

'This is going to be a mammoth undertaking,' Ben said. Then he smiled. 'But it's not like we don't have time on our hands.'

I posted a call to all my friends: 'More free time than usual? I need people to help analyse & index 1500+ pages of evidence for my case! PM me xxx'

The game was afoot.

CHAPTER 20

'Disaster Commander is inviting you to a scheduled Zoom meeting.'

Disaster Commander was Alison, who was working for Police Spies Out of Lives. She helped me set up a Zoom meeting, and one by one people joined, their faces appearing in little rectangles on my screen. After the obligatory sound checks and false starts, we got down to business. I explained the problem and the plan to make a searchable index of the evidence. Ben, Dónal, Eleanor and I had gone over ways to organise the data, and we had settled on a keep-it-simple-stupid approach.

'We're going to make a timeline, and sort the evidence by date.'

This sort of project would normally be done by solicitors and paralegals who are professionals at reading and cataloguing evidence, but we were on our own, so it was going to be very DIY. We had a LibreOffice spreadsheet and a plan to extract the relevant information, page by page, and enter it in the appropriate field. Ben explained the details.

'It's important to get the date format right – year, month, day – so the entries will sort properly.'

The other fields were type of document, locations, mentions of me, my family, or anyone else, and any reference to police officers.

'The officers are almost all cyphered in the disclosure, so we will mostly be recording cypher numbers in this column, not names. The last column is all yours, for you to add a summary of the evidence and any other comments. Does anyone have any questions?' There were none, so I took over.

'We'll start with the contact logs, because they are mostly already organised by date. We have more or less complete logs for the period between February 2004 and March 2005. After that, it's just extracts, but it goes right up to 2009. There's around five hundred pages in all, so I'll send you about fifty pages each, and a blank copy of the spreadsheet to fill in.'

'We should make a WhatsApp group,' Eleanor suggested, 'in case we have any questions. We can flag up any issues and work them out together.'

It was good to be working as a team. Things were beginning to move. France relaxed lockdown restrictions, which in practice changed very little for us, but it felt different. We had a new sense of purpose and direction, and we stopped counting the days.

Our second Zoom meeting was even more animated. Everyone had encountered things in the files that made them furious. Some had recognised references to themselves behind the redacted text. All had emotions they wanted to vent. The spreadsheet was steadily growing. More than a dozen people worked on it, but by far the most prolific turned out to be my mum. She spent hours entering hundreds of pages into the index, which very quickly became a useful tool: a searchable, at-a-glance reference of the documents we did or did not have for each day. It was a vital first step towards joining the dots.

I realised I could also incorporate my own evidence and con-trast it with the police files. I took my memories, diary entries, photographs and other records, and began adding them to the index. It was scarce pickings. My diary-keeping habits were erratic, and many of my one-word calendar entries – 'TPD', 'pamph-let', 'Wimpy Way', 'Manc' – were meaningless to me, twenty years on.

Some of my recollections coincided with the police's version, albeit with subtle differences. My planner for the week starting 2 February 2004 recorded 'Mark to Cleveland'. His contact logs more accurately stated: 'Annual Leave'. However, I did find one interesting discrepancy.

According to my diary, Mark Stone visited me in Barcelona on 8 April 2004. He arrived on easyJet flight EZ5131 at 10.30 a.m. and stayed for at least four days. I looked for the corresponding contact log entry. It just said, 'Thursday 8th April to 16th April OFF.' Not 'Annual Leave', or 'Rest Day', just 'Off'. That term didn't seem to be used anywhere else.

I looked through my photographs. There we were, sightseeing in Barcelona, playing with children in the square where I used to live, visiting squatted social centre projects, sunning ourselves on a beach and eating ice cream in the Plaça del Pi. There was no question that Mark Stone had been undercover in Barcelona that week, yet there were no operational logs, and no authorisation for him to take the deployment abroad. It was proof that the documents could not be taken at face-value. The operation clearly wasn't as by-the-book as the police would have us believe: sending an undercover operative into a foreign country without the necessary protocols sounded very dodgy indeed.

CHAPTER 21

Operation Pegasus – Contact Log (2004)
Tuesday 27th April
0304 Text from Source 'On ferry. Bit of an epic journey . . . Stopped by
Customs but managed to talk our way around things. Arrive 0645 . . .
We ran out of diesel on the way up but I managed to get it very slowly
to right outside the only garage that was open in Wales.'

I had reached the files about Dublin. So many things about that trip, from the motorbike helmets to our arrest and subsequent release, and the contrast between my fear and Mark's fury, had never quite made sense. It was only many years later, when I found out that he was an undercover police officer, that things began to fall into place. I was anxious to find out what had been going on behind the scenes.

The first thing that struck me was that it was (discounting Barcelona) Mark's first official overseas deployment. His management team evidently took it very seriously. Decisions relating to the planned deployment were made as early as February 2004.

Operation Pegasus – Contact Log (2004)
Monday 23rd February.
0900.
Call from Source.
Weekend debrief.

. . .

DISCLOSURE

EU Summit Dublin.

Source was tasked with attending the May Day EU Summit in Dublin

As soon as Mark had persuaded me to go with him, his handler booked our tickets, and the purchase was recorded by the Senior Investigating Officer (SIO) as policy decision number 39:

23rd March 2004
Decision number 39
DECISION:
Op Travel 0200 – 27/4
Fishguard – Rosslare (Katja)
Awaiting arrangement for accommodation.
Cover on 26/4.
Returning Op – 2150 4/5 arriving 0230
(Notts 0600 ish)
Cover returning 5/5 1230-1345

As we got nearer the time of travel, however, and the extent of the security operation in Ireland became evident, I began to feel unsure whether I wanted to go. Now I could see just how much of a spanner that must have thrown in the works.

Operation Pegasus – Contact Log (2004)

Friday 23rd April

0900 Call from Source re the Gardai having water canons that they have borrowed from the PSNI (RUC)

Saturday 24th April

Source believes that [Katja] is suffering from 'Post Traumatic Stress Syndrome' brought on from her previous actions and protests around the world. She is questioning her own need to be present at protests putting herself in the way of danger. 'Once you are there you can't say no' this concerns her. With this on her mind she is questioning Source as to 'why' Source is going to Ireland and what is Source's political reason for going ... Source and Katja were engaged in these discussions until 0300 this morning.

* * *

Mark had become deeply involved with the padded, white-overall-clad anti-capitalist group, the W.O.M.B.L.E.S. He was at their social centre almost every week, making friends, attending meetings, printing T-shirts and collecting shipments of the fair-trade Zapatista coffee they imported. He would deliver the coffee around the country on his travels, to social centres like the Sumac, where it was sold in support of the Zapatista cause. His latest thing was the May Day protests against the EU Summit in Dublin, and he talked Katja into going with him.

'It's not exactly going to be a holiday though, is it, Mark? Have you ever been on a demo that kicked off? It's no joke.'

'I just want to do this together,' he cajoled. 'I thought it would be your kind of thing.' They could even visit his mum while they were in Ireland, he said.

That had swung it: she agreed to go. Now, however, she was having second thoughts. The press were spinning the event as a massacre. It was rumoured that water cannons were being shipped down from Northern Ireland, and the authorities were priming for a fight.

'Answer me, Mark, do you have any idea what these things can be like when they go bad? People get hurt. Why do you even want to go?'

'Come on! Gorgeous! You're overthinking it. Lighten up. It'll be fun!'

'Gung-ho, macho posturing might make you look cool at a W.O.M.B.L.E.S. meeting, Mark. But it's bullshit if you don't even know why you are doing it.'

She said it quietly, almost to herself, but she was sure that he heard.

He reached over and caressed her neck, trying to pull her into an embrace. Her whole body stiffened. Was he using sex to change the subject? Her skin crawled as he stroked her back and she closed her eyes, wishing she had spikes, like a porcupine, that she could shoot out to make him keep his distance.

'Don't touch me.'

He took his hand away.

Source believes that last night Katja was suffering from a panic attack brought on by her susceptibility to suffering from anxiety.

Sunday 25th April
1755. Debrief of [MK]

. . .

Katja questions Source as to why Source is going to Dublin. What source's motivation and political beliefs are. She is doing this because she is not sure why she is going. Katja is very despondent about the whole activist scene.

The redacted text refers to a specific request by MK for a briefing

* * *

'He never should have touched me.'

I had said it before, but I shuddered at the memory of that night. Reading Mark's comments to his handler the following morning, and thinking about what happened next, really brought it home. All the sleepless nights since I discovered the truth; the days when my 'susceptibility to suffering from anxiety' had left me stripped down to my raw nerve endings, with nothing to protect me from the world; the moments when even the touch of the air was too much on my skin.

The cajoling man who had caressed my neck was an on-duty police officer, in my bed, in my parents' home, at 3 a.m. He unashamedly reported it all back to EN31, and to another officer, EN30. He requested a specific briefing, the details of which were redacted, but which looked unpleasantly like it might have been about my mental health. He used intimacy and lies to manipulate a 25-year-old woman he knew to be vulnerable and afraid.

I wanted to reach out and comfort my former self. I knew she was going to blame herself. She thought her fear and weakness would drive a wedge between her and her lover. I wanted to tell her she should trust her instincts: it wasn't just emotional instability making her feel something was off. But I couldn't, and I knew she was about to let feelings of guilt cloud her judgement and allow herself to be persuaded to go to Dublin, to try and make amends.

* * *

Operation Pegasus – Contact Log (2004)
Saturday 24th April
0955
Call from Source. Source still in London with Katja . . .
I instructed Source that if Katja was reluctant to travel to Manchester or Ireland to not put any pressure on and that she must make her own mind up but that Source must travel to Manchester.

She stared out of the van window feeling edgy and wrung out. Their discussions had continued all morning, going nowhere, until suddenly Mark put his foot down.

She felt that if she continued to push it, something irrevocable might break, so she backed down and agreed to go.

By the time they arrived in Manchester it was gone 5 p.m., and the day's meeting was almost over. Everyone went quiet as they walked into the room. Katja pulled up a chair next to John, who looked unusually dapper, in dark green, corduroy trousers and a checked shirt. He was wearing his trademark, geek-chic NHS glasses and had trimmed his moustache, which tickled as he kissed her 'hello' on the cheek and whispered in her ear. His voice had a barely perceptible Midlands lilt. He used to exaggerate it, when they were a couple, to wind her up, and he did that now.

'All right, duck?'

She nodded, but he frowned and nodded towards Mark.

'What's the matter? Are you guys OK?'

Her cheeks flushed and she shushed him with her hand.

The tension lifted a little on the drive back to Nottingham. The trip was going ahead as planned, after all. When they reached the Foxhall Road house, Mark opened the door, then barred the way so she couldn't go in.

'Close your eyes. I've got a present for you.'

Eyes obediently shut, she heard him moving things around inside.

'Ta da!'

He wheeled a purple mountain bike down the hall.

'A bicycle!'

'Yeah, it used to belong to Vinny. He wanted you to have it. I thought it would be good for Dublin. We can leave the van and cycle around together.'

She threw her arms around his neck.

'It's perfect. Can I take it for a spin?'

'Don't be too long,' he said. 'We need to be in Fishguard by midnight.'

* * *

Operation Pegasus Policy Decision Log
16th April 2004
Decision Number 45 DECISION: To purchase a used mountain bicycle
for the use of Katya within Dublin and subsequently to facilitate ease
of travel around and also maintain contact.
Limit £80
REASON: Ease of transport within Dublin. Provide facility for quality
time to reinforce bond/relationship. Provide joint interest.

That gift, which Mark told me came from 'Vinny', was actually
bought on the instructions of his DCI. The purchase was signed off
by EN59, the 'Officer in Charge', and I realised I needed to know
more about him.

The disclosure contained redacted correspondence from 2018,
between several of Mark's managers and the police legal team.
EN59 was asked what he knew about me, and the nature of my
relationship with Mark. I read his reply aloud to Ben:

'I can confirm that I was the Senior Investigating Officer (SIO)
for Operation Pegasus from February 2004 to March 2005 . . .
During my time as SIO I had no knowledge of the sexual relationship between Mark Kennedy and the Claimant . . .'

I hadn't expected anything other than outright denials, but it
was still infuriating. About the bicycle, he had this to say:

'My rationale was that by riding bicycles together then they
would have opportunity to discuss issues, and not being surrounded
by others, the discussion may well extend into areas pertaining to
protest where Katja may be more open with her knowledge . . .'

Ben laughed out loud. 'There's a man who has never tried to
have a conversation while riding a bicycle in city traffic.'

I read on.

'At this time, my understanding was that Katja was an individual within the identified grouping, but not a specific person of interest and consequently I did not seek to glean a greater understanding of the individual in any material manner.'

The language was absurd. Mark and I had been sleeping together for seven months by the time we went to Dublin. Could EN59 really have been ignorant of my role in Mark's legend? Would they really have paid for a ferry ticket in my name without knowing who I was? And a bicycle, to 'increase the bond' between us?

We weren't alone when we travelled. A police team travelled ahead, dealt with the Gardaí on our behalf and kept detailed records of everything we did while we were there.

Operation Pegasus – Contact Log (2004)
Tuesday 27th April
1530 Call from Source . . . Source believes that the Leeson Street Lower address is 'too hot' to stay at so will stay elsewhere.
1634. Text from Source 'Helmets and stuff now at Leeson'

Wednesday 28th April
0933 Text from Source.

██

████████████████████████ Redacted text refers to the raid of the
squat
██

████████████████████████

0937 Text from Source '. . . things just got a level harder having just dropped off all the stuff an hour before.' . . .
██

████████████████████████ Redacted text refers to the raid of the
squat
██

████████████████████

0947 I spoke with EN59 . . . we briefly discussed what had happened. EN59 then broke off from the conversation to speak with O-73 of the Garda.

1002

████████████████████████████████████

████████████████████ Redacted text refers to the raid of the squat

████████████████████████████████████

████████████████████

Risk Assessment

Source had commented that the address was too hot to stay in earlier in the day when invited to stay there.

████████████████████████████████████

████████████████████ Redacted text refers to the raid of the squat

████████████████████████████████████

████████████████████

Welfare work re ███████████████████

. . .

1340 Call from Source. 'Apparently the squat was raided . . . They have been remanded in custody for a week. A bit awkward because the police made a big thing about the item I brought over . . .' ████████████

████████████████████████████████████

████████████████

1359 Text from Source 'We nearly stayed there last night. That would have tied our hands for the week. It was only at the last minute that we went to the [other] address.'

Thursday 29 April
1033 Text from Source. 'Ok Ta. Good or bad I'm seen as a player . . .'
1408 Text from Source 'Houses being raided. Is mine OK? All my travel docs are there'

DISCLOSURE

I thought back. Those days before the demonstrations were chaos. Mark described himself as 'a player' who was in with the 'Top Boys' but, in reality, everyone was doing their best, in the face of constant harassment, to make sure the weekend of actions went ahead. Demonstrators were arriving in the city to protest against the cruelty of Fortress Europe, only to find themselves all but sleeping on the streets. Mark and I spent hours going through the bins behind the supermarkets to find food for the communal kitchen and looking at buildings for new squats. All the while, Mark was feeding advice back to his handlers about how best to stop us assembling and organising.

Operation Pegasus – Contact Log (2004)
Friday 30th April
1806 Text from Source. '. . . The key as I see it is the disruption of accommodation, it's causing turmoil and confusion.'
1820 EN107 updated

And yet, the protests went ahead. At 6 p.m. on the day of the big demonstration, EN31 went to the O'Connell Street meeting point to observe the start of the march. The documents show him trying to keep in contact throughout the evening, as Mark clashed with the Gardaí riot squads.

Operation Pegasus – Contact Log (2004)
Saturday 1 May
1848

████████████████
████████████████

Unable to make contact with Source.
Called EN107 re above ██████████████ May well be that only

the five or so people at the front know where they are taking the march.
2012 Text from Source. 'Going for it'
2054 Text from Source. 'Taken a hit. Ok. Am in the middle.'
2141

██████████████████████████████
██████████████████████████████

2142 Text to Source re above
2146

██████████████████
██████████████████

2147 Called Source who was unable to speak or hear anything I said (there was tremendous noise in the background and it was obvious that Source was very busy.)

I was astounded by Mark's audacity: hooded and masked, texting and even calling his handler from the middle of the melee.

Sunday 2 May
1255
Source thought that sources right leg was broken when a Gardai hit sources knee cap with his baton.

. . .

Source says a good lesson for the future is ████████████
████████████████████████████
██████████████
████████████████████████████
██████████████

Press releases are being prepared today and Source and Katja have been asked to prepare an article for the Indymedia web . . . This may also be presented as a flyer . . .

I paused in my reading. That was the flyer we were bringing back from the printers when we were arrested. I went back to read it again.

DISCLOSURE

'Dublin Mayday: Why we pushed through police lines'

... around the world, States have shown the extent of military force and violence they are prepared to use against people who question and confront their 'democratic' regimes.

It was so strange to think of Mark Kennedy writing those lines. Even stranger to realise that his managers knew that was how he spent his morning. By evening, we were under arrest.

Monday 3 May
2010
Call from Source who has been arrested and taken to the Bridewell Police Station. Source is with Katja who has also been arrested. Source was unable to say why the arrest had taken place other than for Road Traffic Offences but the Garda would not explain.

██████████████████████████████████████
██████████████████████████████████████

Together with EN107 and EN30 we carried out certain calls and actions in order to try to establish the situation as far as charges etc.
2110
I telephoned the Bridewell Garda Station as the person previously informed of the arrest of Source but after eventually being allowed to speak to the Garda officer in the case [O-74] he would not talk to me because I refused to tell him where I lived.
2150
Call from Source who had been released without charge. Source is trying to establish the whereabouts of the vehicle because the Garda are holding on to Katja until Source returns with her Passport ... Source says that Katja is very annoyed and will complain about the unlawful arrest.
2205 Source called again. Discussion re the feasibility of sources involvement in a complaint against the Garda and the possibility of suing them ...

It was clear from the contact logs that Mark genuinely wanted to sue the Gardaí. He pushed the issue with his handler several times.

Tuesday 4th May
1050
Call from Source . . . Discussed the unlawful arrest situation. The Irish Grass Roots organisation are talking about getting a good solicitor to sue the Garda for all the assaults and stops.

How could a British police officer working undercover in Ireland be involved in a court case against the Irish police, in the Irish courts, under a false name? Perhaps Mark's grip on reality was growing tenuous even then.

He originally told his handlers that the lawsuit was my idea. It wasn't; the phone call when he first raised it was made at 9.50 p.m., while I was still in custody, watching the walls move. I don't believe I ever considered suing the Irish police. Dublin had left me very shaken, and it was a shock to discover that Mark's handlers knew that as well.

Operation Pegasus – Contact Log (2004)
Wednesday 5th May
0800 call from Source who has just left Katja's parents house . . .
Katja was totally 'freaked' about being arrested. She has been previously arrested for actions . . . but this was a different experience. She was strip searched 3 times and 2 plain clothes officers put pressure on her.

Reading the disclosure, it was clear that they knew everything. EN59 received briefings every few hours. He was the one who dealt with Mark and me being arrested by a foreign police force. It's hard to see how he could possibly have avoided knowing who I was.

Nor was he the only officer involved. EN107 and EN30 appeared frequently in the Dublin logs, so I turned to their correspondence with the police legal team. EN107's answers were partly in the third person, and appeared to be notes of a conversation on the phone. It said only this:

'EN107 had no role or responsibility in Operation Pegasus prior to his/her involvement as Officer in Charge [in March 2005] other than some limited exposure to the intelligence generated by Mark Kennedy (MK) from the roles EN107 held in the NPOIU.'

The NPOIU was the National Public Order Intelligence Unit. It was the secret police unit that employed Mark and ran his operation. EN107 worked for that unit, but claimed to have no involvement in Operation Pegasus. However, during the five days that Mark was in Dublin in 2004, EN107 was named in the contact logs twenty-three times. Updates were recorded as being sent to EN107 every three to four hours. There were questions, tasking requests and calls to the Garda while Mark and I were under arrest. EN31's last contact with EN107 on the night of 3 May was at 2.33 a.m. It certainly seemed a stretch to describe that as 'no role or responsibility at all'.

EN30 declined to respond to correspondence. A solicitor replied instead:

'We are instructed on behalf of EN30 to respond to your letter . . . Our client wishes to make clear that he/she only ever spoke to MK on two or three occasions over the telephone whilst operational. He/she did not meet him personally on any of his deployments . . .'

I pursed my lips. That wasn't true. During the weekend before we left for Dublin, when Mark requested that special briefing from his handlers about my mental health, EN30 had been involved. House's statement cited contact logs for 25 April 2004 stating: 'Arrangements already in hand for Source to meet up with EN30 tomorrow.'

The logs also recorded a second meeting after Dublin, on 16 July 2004:

'1830 Met with Source and EN30 at a safe location . . . tactical briefing for EN30 . . . EN30 carried out a recce of the areas and premises frequented by Source in order that EN30 could take over cover duties whilst I am on annual.' EN30 clearly did meet Mark Kennedy in person, and even acted as his cover officer while EN31 was on leave. So, EN30 lied.

They were probably all lying. All these officers were hidden behind ciphers upon ciphers, they were protected by anonymity orders, and none of them would be giving evidence under oath.

CHAPTER 22

I stared at the horizon. The heat was sketching hazy lines over the palm trees on the shore. Reading the police account of Dublin left me numb. I used to be brilliant, sharp and insightful. These days I could barely pull myself together to make lunch. Hearings were cancelled at the last minute then rescheduled with less than two weeks' notice. Long before the pandemic, I had stopped making plans. At some point I stopped listening to music. When did that happen? I avoided movies that might make me emotional. I hadn't read a book in more than three years. I had been working on the case for almost a decade, far longer than the seven years I was friends with Mark Stone. In a few weeks I would turn forty-two.

We were living in a cloud of Saharan dust, brought across the Atlantic by the relentless wind. The sky was a muggy yellow and there was a thin film of dirt over everything. We hadn't seen the sun for days, and the rhythmic thumping of the water desalinator was making me feverish. I sifted through the files like an archaeologist, dusting off interesting fragments, and putting each piece into context, hoping it would make sense in the end.

In the confines of the boat there was nowhere to spread my thoughts, so I imagined a wall instead, where each detail could be arranged and connected to the others with pieces of imaginary string. I was supposed to be building a case, but I longed to weave something else from those colourful threads; to take the whole tangled mess and turn it into a coherent story.

I thought about how Mark manipulated my life choices. The trip to Dublin was a key moment emotionally, but also politically. Mark was out on the Saturday, drumming up support for the banned march. He wrote communiqués on behalf of other activists to be posted online and handed out in the streets. I hadn't wanted to be involved, and although his superiors said, 'don't force her', the dynamic of our relationship meant that it was always going to be hard for me to say no.

At the time, Mark and I shared almost everything. It was impossible to extricate our personal lives from our political organising, and from the operation itself. Mark was my partner, and I consulted him about every big decision. In turn, he was passing those questions to his management team for operational consideration.

Operation Pegasus – Contact Log (2004)
Tuesday 4 May
1220 Call from Source. Katja has asked Source to help her buy a car. Katja would like a Peugeot Diesel Estate for about £1000 . . .

Friday 2 June
1100 Call from Source. Sources vehicle is in the garage for a new fuel tank. The vehicle has been making a 'clunking' noise from the front near side and the garage has found that it needs a new lower wishbone . . .

Saturday 19 June
Source and I discussed the disposal of the current vehicle when I am able to obtain a new one. 1850 Call to EN59 to discuss the sale of the current vehicle . . .

Tuesday 13 July
1545
Call from Source.

DISCLOSURE

Katja says she cant afford the insurance on sources vehicle so may not buy it. She was quoted £520. Discussions about the pro's and con's of her having a vehicle of her own. I feel that if she has transport separate to source's it will relieve Source of giving her a lift everywhere, whilst needing to accompany her to actions and meetings. Source felt that Katja having her own transport would not impede the operation and that Source would still be able to accompany her when the operation required it.

1820

Discussed the above with DCI who agreed the gradual negotiating of the sale of source's vehicle to Katja in stages down to £1000 if necessary. I will instruct Source to suggest Katja gets a quote from Elephant.co.uk who seem to be the cheapest for new drivers.

Saturday 21 August

Me Rest Day

Source in London

[Discussion regarding a vehicle for MK's use on deployment]

1628

Text from Source

'Katja says she is 97% certain she will have the vehicle off of me. I'll explain when I have more time . . .'

I text back that she must be told that Source needs the money for the new vehicle and that we must not let it drag on or she will change her mind a few more times. Source will not let that happen. I also told Source that she must understand that she does not keep coming back if things go wrong with it. Source said that she understood that . . .

Tuesday 24th August

Katja has agreed to purchase the old vehicle for £1100. This vehicle is already booked into a Nottingham garage for service prior to it being sold (duty of care).

It took Mark two months to persuade me to buy his van. It wasn't really what I wanted. I wanted an estate car, which would take more passengers, and he was asking more than I could afford (which made it even more galling to see that he held out for that extra hundred quid). Conversations about selling me his clapped-out old Escort went right up to policy level, with Detective Chief Inspector EN59 setting the price.

CHAPTER 23

Mark made a grand gesture as he opened the door. The hallway smelt of paint. 'Welcome to your new home!'

'Have people chosen rooms yet?' she said.

'Kind of,' he said. 'Mine is on the top floor.'

He led her up the stairs, covering her eyes with his hands. When he took them away she saw a room with bare floorboards and very little furniture. There was a chest of drawers in one corner and, in the middle of the room, a giant cube made from scaffold poles.

Chains ran from the top four corners of the cube to a plywood platform and a double mattress, suspended in mid-air.

'I can't believe you really did it,' Katja said.

Mark had been talking about building a four-poster bed out of scaffolding ever since his rope-access course. The real thing was altogether larger and more imposing than she had imagined. He had strung fairy lights and gauze curtains from the poles to tone down the austerity of the construction, and the mattress was neatly made up with the lilac quilt his mother had made, but the effect was still more BDSM than fairytale.

She laughed and jumped up onto the mattress, which lurched alarmingly. He climbed up next to her, a little more cautiously, and took her in his arms. Their lovemaking made her slightly seasick: the slightest motion set the bed oscillating on its chains and the pillows all ended up on the floor, but she didn't say anything. He was clearly very proud of his creation.

Afterwards, they lay as still as possible.

'It's a bit unstable, isn't it?' he said.

'Yeah, it is.' She laughed.

'I think we may need to modify the design.'

It was clear that they would be sleeping in his room, so she had no qualms about taking the worst one, on the ground floor, between the kitchen and the living room. It had a sash window in one corner that looked onto a narrow passage down the side of the house. She furnished it as a study, with a sofa-bed that only got used when they had guests.

Sunday 13 June

On Monday Source will travel to London with Katja to assist with transporting furniture from Ikea for Katja's brother having been put on the spot by Mrs Wilson.

Katja's whole family was going shopping, and they had asked Mark if he could help with his van.

'This is exactly the kind of thing my ex would make me do,' he complained.

'Yeah, right, one shopping trip and I'll have trapped you into marriage.' she jibed, with a grin.

Katja was used to furnishing houses out of skips. She liked the eclectic mix of styles you got when interior decoration was left to chance. It was usually Mark who wanted nice, newly bought things, and she sometimes felt he was a little too conventional for her taste. She was surprised at how resistant he was to the idea of a day at IKEA, and although she was reassured by this sudden revolt against the symbolic commitment of buying soft furnishings together, she had promised her mum, so she pressed him.

'Come on. It's a favour to my family, and we can get some nice things for the new house.'

DISCLOSURE

He had eventually agreed, and they were on the way to Croydon, with her parents behind them, in her dad's car. As they turned onto Purley Way, the old chimneys from the Croydon B power station came into view, topped with IKEA's blue and yellow stripes.

'I can't believe I'm doing this.'

'You'll be OK. It's just kitchenware.' She put a hand on his thigh, and proclaimed, with mock seriousness, 'I solemnly swear that there are no strings attached.'

* * *

Monday 14th June

1855 Call from Source who has left Ikea with a vehicle full of furniture and mattresses on the roof. The Wilson family are in their vehicle in front of Source.

I laughed out loud. Once Mark and I moved in together our lives became so deeply intertwined it was all but impossible to pick apart the ways in which the needs of the undercover operation were influencing my life choices. I had been caught up in the horror of it, but in that moment I realised it was also absurd. What had they thought they were doing? A top-secret, multi-million-pound policing operation followed my family to IKEA. I imagined squad cars radioing our position as we wove our way back across London, snipers hiding on the rooftops, watching our convoy of mattresses drive by. Laughter shook my whole body in waves, until I was gasping, tears running down my face.

* * *

They woke to the sound of gulls.

'Happy birthday, gorgeous!' she murmured, curling into the

crook of his arm. 'I'm thinking: stroll to the beach for some clotted cream ice cream, then a birthday outing somewhere. What do you think?'

Their birthdays were just two days apart, and they had decided to celebrate with a few days in Devon. It turned out to be a typical English seaside break: the sky was ominous and the forecast grim. But inside the cottage it was cosy and warm, and they celebrated together, curled up in front of a roaring fire.

* * *

Wednesday 7th July
2231 Text from Source. 'All ok here except the major storms and flood warnings. Will call in the morning.'
Further text message conversation about Source calling home. ██████████ but Source had had no opportunity. I called home on Source's behalf.

I frowned. His handler called home?

It took me a moment to understand that EN31 had not called *our* home, the new house at Wiverton Road. He must have called Mark's family, where his wife and children would have been waiting to wish him Happy Birthday. His real home.

In his more vulnerable moments Mark talked about how his dad left his mum to raise two children alone. I watched him cry over the abandonment that had scarred him growing up. The emotion seemed genuine. The story was not.

As far as we know, Mark had a happy childhood. He grew up in Kent with both his parents. He became a police officer, just like his dad, and he continued to live with them until he got married. Then he and his wife moved to a house that was walking distance away.

At some point, however, while he was deployed undercover, his wife and children moved abroad. Mark did not grow up without a father, but perhaps his own children did. I believe those tears may have been for his own family, the emotion his own guilt.

In 2010, when I discovered Mark was married, it hit me just how completely he had deceived me; but it wasn't until I read that log entry from his birthday that I realised he must have lied to his family as well.

From the opening statements to the Public Inquiry, 4 November 2020

The Category M participants were some of the ex-wives of undercover officers (UCOs), the mothers of their children, the family they came home to . . . Those women fulfilled their role dutifully, towards both their husbands and the honourable causes they believed they were serving – the fight against crime, terror and violence. These sacrifices came with a heavy price for their own lives and their families, and they believed they were making them for all of us . . .

The Inquiry will hear from many whose most intimate lives have been affected by the practices of undercover policing, heart-rending stories of betrayal and deceit. But there has been little focus on the harm done to the wives of UCOs . . . [E]ach of these women were police wives. That was woven into their identity. At the outset, they saw themselves as part of the wider police service, investing in their husbands' careers, and also saw themselves as respectable members of the community . . . When their husbands went undercover, they provided the support, unwaveringly. They willingly made all the sacrifices that went with that. They took on the burden of secrecy, unable to talk about the impact on them or their husbands. They lived in fear of reprisal . . . but they believed that their sacrifices were worth it for the cause. They did so without any proper support from the Metropolitan Police Service . . .

Years later they found out that their marriages were based on lies, that their husbands' jobs – of which they had been so proud – had been vehicles for the worst kind of infidelity . . . None of them had any idea that in the name of policing their husbands were having sexual relationships with other women . . . All were left shocked and devastated by the media coverage as it unfolded . . . and the clear indication given to them that the groups to be targeted were serious and violent criminals or extremists, not protesters that posed no threat to the UCOs or their families . . . When the women found out the truth about the groups their husbands infiltrated, they were horrified . . . Whilst their husbands had fellow officers, managers and supervisors to share their experiences with, the women had no one. They had never met each other, never even knew the others existed, until this Inquiry was set up. Such was the secrecy, that there was no way of finding mutual support . . .

I don't know whether Mark's ex-wife was one of the women who wrote that statement. They, like so many of the women these officers betrayed, have opted to keep their real identities out of the public gaze.

CHAPTER 24

Katja set off towards a copse. The grass was springy beneath her feet and she could hear the bustle from the marquee where people were making dinner. A murmur of voices also came from various tents dotted around the field. The sun was shining and she felt good for the first time in ages. Her unease since Dublin had receded in the face of the camaraderie of the past few days.

Earth First! only really met twice a year – camping like this in the summer, and a more serious indoor event in the winter – but the result was a network of trust so solid that for the rest of the year, someone could propose an action and dozens of people, many hardly knowing each other, would come together, almost without question, to blockade an oil refinery, take out a genetically modified crop before it cross pollinated onto local organic farms, set up a squatted land camp, or throw a party to reclaim a street.

There were three or four hundred people at the camp that year. It felt like a music festival, but with workshops and political discussions instead of bands. Trust was built there, based on shared values. And it was a good value system, with no leaders and no party line. Everyone had some opinions most of the others would disagree with, making it impossible to represent the network as a whole. Yet it was politics that held it all together. Everyone pitched in, becoming their best selves, buoyed up by everyone around them being their best selves as well. They did life, limb and liberty-risking things together, and it bonded them like a little tribe. The rural gatherings in the summer were her favourite event of the year.

That year she had gravitated towards workshops on activist mental health. She didn't consciously associate that with how she had been feeling since Dublin, but the discussions about how political repression could result in post-traumatic stress disorder (PTSD) had made her think. She and John ran a presentation together about Dissent! and the upcoming mobilisation against the G8. She also joined the team teaching basic first aid on demonstrations. She had experience of large political demonstrations in mainland Europe, and she had helped run a session on dealing with CS gas. But that afternoon she was taking a break from intense discussions to join a practical tree-climbing workshop instead.

The trees were in a little hollow, and when she arrived, the workshop had already begun. She didn't know the guy leading it, but he immediately put her at ease, cracking silly jokes with a smile. He was burly and strong, but sweet, not domineering, and she thought she recognised him from yesterday's discussions about PTSD.

He demonstrated the knots and coiled the ropes with a dexterity and skill that made her think he was probably a tree surgeon, and when he moved in close she felt a flush of self-consciousness. She had been watching him move rather than listening to what he was saying. He checked the fastening on her climbing harness and she realised he was taller than he looked. When he put his arm around her to give the waistband a tug, he winked.

Katja had been clear with Mark from the beginning that she believed in open relationships, built on honesty and mutual trust. She liked her lovers to be free people and she wanted to be free herself. Mark had surprised her by being quite insecure about it. He had needed a lot of reassurance, but had eventually embraced the idea, in theory. In practice, they had become so involved with each other over the past ten months that neither of them had thought about seeing anyone else. Until now.

She watched as the workshop leader moved away to help someone else with their equipment. Mark was in Ireland, supposedly visiting his mum, and they had agreed they were both free to see other people if they wanted. There wasn't any reason not to just go with the flow.

She was honest with Owen, explaining that she had a boyfriend back in Nottingham, and that was fine. He had a girlfriend who wasn't at the camp either, and they were open to seeing other people as well. When the gathering was over, they said their goodbyes, with plans to meet at his squat the next time she was in London. It all felt so uncomplicated, but she feared it was going to be a big deal for Mark.

EN31 debriefing Source on 17th August
Saturday 14 August
Source attended a 'garden party' at Cornerstone, Leeds . . . on sources return from leave . . .
The feedback during the evening concerned the 'EF gathering' in Lincoln that Source did not attend. Those that attended were very upbeat about the event, they said it was very positive with many practical workshops.

'Where I come from, a guy will punch you for looking at his pint, let alone his girl.'

Mark raised his pint glass to emphasise his point.

They were sitting side by side on a sofa in the lounge bar. Hers was an orange juice and soda. She sipped it nervously, wondering how best to respond. He had taken the news about Owen better than expected. She drove to London to pick him up when he got back from Ireland, and told him straight away, in the van on the way up the M1.

They spent the weekend at a garden party in Leeds, followed by rock climbing with friends on Ilkley Moor. Things felt really close between them, but she sensed there were layers of feeling beneath the surface.

'For me it's the opposite of cheating,' she explained. 'It's about honesty, and trust.'

She set her drink on the low table in front of them and turned to look him in the eye. She didn't separate love from politics. Wasn't it their politics that had brought them together?

'The way I see it, society gives us this rule book about relationships, and it doesn't matter what you want, you're expected to follow the rules. But we're anarchists, right? So we question those rules. It doesn't mean we can't have any, but they should be the ones we write ourselves. We don't just blindly accept someone else's.'

She touched his hand.

'The thing is, it's actually a lot harder than just doing what you're told. To make an open relationship work, you have to be really open about who you are and what you want.'

She paused. This was an important conversation, but maybe political theory wasn't what he needed right now.

'I love you. You know that, right?'

He smiled then. She kissed him, and asked if there was anything he needed from her to make it work.

* * *

EN31 debriefing Source on 17th August (continued)
Sunday 15th August
Source went climbing at Ilkley all day with people from Leeds and Nottingham . . . Katja, Eleanor [and eight others]. Source raised an issue with me that [one of the women there] really fancies Source and this has upset her boyfriend.

Four days after I told Mark about Owen, he told his handler that there was a woman who was attracted to him, and that it was causing trouble with her boyfriend. That was odd. It was one of only a tiny handful of occasions in the reporting where there is any reference to the possibility of intimate relations with the opposite sex.

At the time, Mark and I were working through a major shift in our relationship. We were being careful with each other, talking about our emotions, feeling our way. He sometimes seemed uncomfortable, and I assumed that his reluctance came from a place of jealousy or insecurity. It never occurred to me that he was already dealing with a complex web of secrets, or that he might simply be unable to contemplate a relationship based on trust.

* * *

From the first witness statement of 'Lisa' to the Investigatory Powers Tribunal

Mark was also quite flirtatious with me in 2004. Friends commented that they thought Mark was attracted to me. I remember Eleanor telling me shortly before Mark and I got together that he had a 'crush' on me. His behaviour planted the idea in my mind that perhaps I was also interested in him.

Mark and I first got together on a camping trip to the Lake District in the first week of September 2004. A group of around twenty of us went on this trip, which was purely social; although some of us were involved in political and environmental campaigns, others were not. We all stayed in a big camping barn and the core contingent (including me) stayed for a week. Kate and Mark arrived together a few days late. Kate also left a few days early, but Mark stayed until the end of the trip . . . Mark and I were first intimate on the last night of the trip.

'Something's happened. I'm sorry. I don't know what to say.'

Mark was barely coherent. Was he sick? Katja gripped the phone and tried to make sense of what he was saying. Finally, he blurted it out: 'After you left the Lakes, I got off with Lisa.' He sounded like he'd been crying.

She laughed with relief. 'Lisa's great! Was it really that bad?'

He went silent for a moment.

'I thought you'd be upset.' Mark had seemed to embrace the idea that it was OK to love more than one person, but he was clearly still a mess. Perhaps they had more talking to do.

The next time she saw Lisa she brought the subject up. They were sitting on the edge of the stage in the Sumac Centre bar, and Katja leant in so they wouldn't be overheard.

'You don't mind?' Lisa asked.

'I was with Owen when Mark called to tell me! He was still in an absolute state. I sometimes think he needs more affection than I can give him.'

They talked for a while about how to keep it all open and friendly and make sure everyone was able to be honest about what they felt. Lisa was emotionally intelligent and easy to talk to. Katja couldn't think of a better person for Mark to be with.

* * *

Wednesday 15th September

2100

Call from Source.

The landlord had been around to the house complaining . . . The landlord has given them a months notice to get out . . .

2226

Text from Source.

'If all this comes on top can we consider moving to Cornerstone, Speak tomorrow.'

I stared at the sea.

It was just a casual comment in a text message, but it jarred. I thought back to that time and the trouble with the landlord at Wiverton Road: he kept coming round unannounced, and eventually we had to change the locks. He was furious and talked about eviction, but Mark and I drafted a long letter about tenants' rights. Emotionally things were better. We were really close and fired up about keeping our home. Or so I thought.

Behind the scenes, Mark Kennedy was asking his handler if he could move out of our house and go and live with Lisa at the Cornerstone housing co-operative in Leeds, just a few days after they first kissed. Given everything else that had happened, it was stupid to feel hurt by that, but I did.

* * *

It was official: the G8 summit would take place in Scotland. That month's Dissent! meeting was in Edinburgh, so it was a big deal and a hectic weekend. Mark and Katja hired a minibus and ferried people north. They were at meetings all day and slept in a tree-house at the local protest site at night, and there was barely time to think about their relationship. But Mark had clearly been thinking, and when they got home, he surprised her:

'I think I'd like to meet him. Owen.'

Owen turned out to be enthusiastic, so they made a plan. The next time she saw him they would take a trip to Nottingham and the three of them would have a day out. Owen was laid back about it, and she felt sure that it would go OK. As they drove Owen's van towards Nottingham, however, she had a sense of foreboding.

It was late when they arrived. The house was already asleep, so she pulled out the futon in her downstairs room for her and Owen to share. She woke before dawn and lay for a while, listening to his breathing, holding her own breath as she waited for sounds from the rest of the house. Mark was usually an early riser. It was strange that the place was so quiet. Unable to stand it any longer, she went upstairs.

She found Mark lying on his back, his face pale in the grey light. The scaffold bed made him look small.

'It's me. Are you awake?' she asked softly.

He didn't answer, but she saw that his eyes were open, and she realised he was crying. She climbed up next to him and put a hand on his face. His skin was clammy and cold. She watched a tear leak from the corner of his good eye and run down his temple. His whole body was shaking. She put her arms around him and laid her head on his chest.

'What is it, Mark, what's wrong?'

She didn't want to assume that he was in this state just because she had brought her lover home. After all, it had been his idea.

He didn't answer. They lay in silence for what felt like a long while. Gradually he stopped shaking and began to apologise. He talked about his childhood again, how the open relationship brought back those feelings of abandonment and turned him back into the little boy who lost his dad.

'You know, if you don't want to do this, I can just go downstairs and ask him to leave,' she said.

'No, no, I want to,' he insisted. 'It's just hard for me.'

She squeezed his hand.

They spent the day at a protest site in the nearby village of Mansfield Woodhouse. Housing developers wanted to cut down ancient woodland, so activists had built tree-houses from pallets and tarpaulin in the centuries-old trees. These flimsy fortifications, connected by a network of rope walkways, meant that the site couldn't be evicted without specialist access teams. The aim was to send a message to the developers: destroying Sherwood Forest will cost you.

As they approached the gate, Katja saw that new constructions had gone up. Rickety towers poked through the trees, wood and scaffold bars covered with pieces of hardboard and corrugated iron, a shanty town spreading upwards. There were only a couple of people around, but that was OK: the idea was for Mark and Owen to get to know each other. They both put on climbing harnesses and set off for the upper levels to work on the walkways. Katja stayed on the ground, collecting litter.

Despite his emotion at the house, Mark quickly seemed at ease. He and Owen chatted as they worked on the ropes. Katja looked away before they caught her watching.

* * *

Whilst at the site Source replaced two of the ropes that were in a dangerous condition through wear. Source also re-tensioned the cargo net as it was also unsafe.

The day had been all about Mark, Owen and me doing something together for the first time, yet in the handler's logs, Owen isn't named at all. Mark's notes record 'On Tuesday 5th October I went to Mansfield Woodhouse protest site to help with refurbishing some of the walkways and clearing rubbish.'

He goes on to note that 'There were only 3 people on the site,' effectively erasing both Owen and me from his report. I scoured the documents looking for any reference to Owen. There were none for any of the times he, Mark and I were together. In fact, the only one I found was from the following year.

Tuesday 22nd March 2005
1520 Call from Source . . . about taking the marquees to Lanarkshire

for the Festival of Dissent. Apparently the poles are missing. It appears that Owen (Katjas boyfriend) took them to [the squat] after their use in London. I told Source to leave it to [someone else] to sort out as Source has no time.

That is the first time Owen is mentioned. Mark described him as 'Katja's boyfriend'. By then my relationships with both Mark and Owen were over, and I had moved to Barcelona, as Mark and his operational managers knew full well.

Owen's absence from the logs, and the fact that my relationship with him was recorded only *after* Mark and I had split up, was curious. Mark made no effort to cover the fact he and I were together, but he seems to have drawn the line at letting his handler know that his girl was sleeping with another man. I wondered what they would have said about that in the police canteen. Where Mark came from, 'you could get punched for looking at a man's pint'.

The significance of our open relationship was undeniable. 'She had multiple lovers and I didn't consider her a proper girlfriend,' Mark told the tabloids in 2011. In fact, it had just been me and him for the first ten months. Yet reading the files about the open part of our relationship left me more confused than ever. Mark Stone went out of his way to appear needy and insecure, while Mark Kennedy was trying to leave me and move to Leeds. On the face of it, all those long emotional conversations we had were simply unnecessary. I struggled to find a narrative that made sense. Perhaps he was just improvising. Perhaps the concepts of truth, falsehood, love and deceit had ceased to exist for him.

The police certainly didn't hesitate to use our openness against us. In May 2015, the police lawyers had served a defence stating that by entering into a relationship, Naomi, Lisa and I had all 'voluntarily consented to run the risk that the other individual may have misled her about some or all aspects of his identity or personal background . . .' It went on to say that we were 'further put to proof that they did not freely and voluntarily accept the risk of being deceived by a potential partner by engaging in what are pleaded by them as "open relationships".'

The police barristers seemed to think it was normal to lie to the people you slept with, and that simply entering into a relationship with someone meant consenting to be deceived. A horrible view of the world, and one that came very close to saying we were asking for it. They withdrew that defence as well. But the fact that they considered using it at all stayed with me. To the police and their lawyers, our choice to have open relationships made us fair game.

Of course, I had no idea what the Investigatory Powers Tribunal would make of all this. The logs were full of anomalies that I felt sure were significant, but I was reluctant to raise them in court. Although Mark and I spent many hours talking through the personal and political complexities of our open relationship, one thing that never came up was how I might explain it to a judge.

CHAPTER 25

Standing on the grounds of a glassworks that burnt down in 1971, the Bounds Green Campus of Middlesex University was a strange mix: modernist, steel-clad university infrastructure superimposed on industrial decay. Exposed pipework painted in primary colours decorated its mezzanines. An open-plan corridor known as the 'indoor street' called to mind a covered market. In the 1980s and '90s it was filled with hundreds of students studying engineering and design. A vibrant place, right on the cutting edge, it housed the university's mainframe computer, at a time when most people didn't even know what the internet was.

The campus closed in 2003. Little more than a year later, there was no electricity or running water. The rooms were littered with obsolete IT hardware and scattered with broken glass. It was close to Alexandra Palace, where the official European Social Forum would be taking place, and it had been squatted as accommodation for people taking part in the many alternative political and cultural spaces that sprang up around the official event.

Tens of thousands of people were converging on London to share ideas in an enormous festival of international solidarity and global, ecological and social justice; a whirlwind schedule of over a thousand meetings, workshops, seminars, rallies, demonstrations and cultural events, all to be crammed into just three days.

Katja's fears about the lack of transparency in the process had been borne out, and she and her friends had decided to throw their energy into a series of fringe initiatives instead. Mark had been involved since the beginning, going back and forth to London to attend meetings, and acting as the main information point for his activist friends in Nottingham.

Operation Pegasus – Contact Log (2004)
Saturday 5th June
There are plans for an alternative European Social Forum when the official one takes place at Alexandra Palace.

In fact, there were to be a dozen 'Autonomous Spaces' across London, from Whitechapel to Tottenham and from Embankment to King's Cross. The W.O.M.B.L.E.S. 'Beyond ESF' would be the largest of these events.

Sunday 22nd August
Middlesex University will supply the lecture theatres for the conference/workshops. They will squat nearby buildings.

Mark worked flat out in the days before, to make sure the Autonomous Spaces were a success.

Friday 8th October
2346 Text from Source. 'Mission accomplished 1000 plus carpet tiles liberated from a skip. Off to Bounds Green soon to open an empty building . . .'
Date Change
0116 Text from Source. 'Success at Bounds Green. Off to my sleeping bag now, night.'

He was part of the team that cracked the squatted buildings: sweeps of torchlight puncturing the darkness, footsteps echoing on concrete. Katja joined him to help get it ready and start welcoming people and bringing the desolate campus back to life.

There was food, accommodation, workshops and meeting spaces for autonomous social movements from all over Europe, all free entry, run by volunteers and funded by donations. There was live music every night, direct action protests every day, and a campaign aimed at keeping the official ESF accountable, democratic, transparent and free from corporate control.

> Saturday 9th October
> Source says that the Alternative ESF organizers have really got it all together in a short time . . . They are very organized around the whole thing, accommodation, maps, and the event itself . . .
> the translators [are supplied] by Babbles (Bay balls) who are a collective of anarchists who put the call out for translators via E mail. They supply to events such as the European Social Forum and the People's Global Actions.

Katja was working with Babels, a network of mostly professional interpreters who were supporting the main Forum. She was trying to extend their work to Beyond ESF events, and Mark offered to help her with that as well. Conference interpreting equipment was expensive, so they were building alternatives themselves.

* * *

> 1230
> Call from Source.
> Source is going to be tied up . . . this afternoon and needs the materials to build the sound booths . . .
> 2030
> Call from Source who is now travelling to a south London location to collect materials already purchased by this operation to build the AESF sound booths for use by the translators.

I laughed. 'What a bastard.'

'Who?' Ben asked.

'Mark,' I replied. 'No wonder he was able to make himself so useful. He was sending his handler on errands, like buying the materials to make the interpreter booths. He used to complain that other people were disorganised, but *we* didn't have a team of assistants, did we? We couldn't just delegate the tasks we took on.'

* * *

'It is the G8 in Scotland. We are staying in an illegal squat. There are three days of protest left, and the police have given us twenty-four hours to leave. At the moment the police are not stopping people from going in or out of the building. What do we do?'

The scenario was presented as a role-play, in a workshop on resolving problems by consensus in large groups. The walls were covered with posters and charts setting out the principles, pre-requisites and shared assumptions necessary for non-hierarchical decision-making to work.

The participants divided up into groups to discuss the situation, and then nominated 'spokes' who would present their views to the 'spokes council' and then report back. Anyone could listen to the council meetings, and groups could pass messages to their representatives, but only nominated 'spokes' could speak.

Katja had to leave early to prepare the evening session on international networking, so she never found out what the group decided, but she was amazed by the system, which effectively enabled a thousand or more people to feed into a manageable-sized meeting that could make a decision everyone participated in. It was an impressive feat.

* * *

Operation Pegasus – Contact Log (2004)
Friday 18 October
0815
Call from EN59 . . . Discussed the implications of closing the Bounds Green Squat.

███

█████████████

███

███████████

1440 Meet with EN59 for briefing . . .
Consideration of the ground commander to raid the Bounds Green squat.

███

████████████████████████

███

████████████

. . .

1655 Call from Source and the above discussed. Source says it would be dangerous to raid the Bounds Green Squat . . .

It was curious, the way their conversations mirrored our own. I wondered then what it must have been like for Mark, to go straight from a workshop about consensus decision-making to defend our spaces, to a conversation with his commanders about evicting the space he had worked so hard to create. I tried to recall why it might have been dangerous to raid the Bounds Green squat, but I couldn't. In any event, the raid never came.

* * *

Operation Pegasus – Contact Log (2004)
Thursday 14 October
1515

DISCLOSURE

Call from Source
Katja [and one other] have been invited to talk to the ESF on Saturday
and have agreed to do so.

The official ESF was a kaleidoscope of cultures, languages and ideologies. Every corner was alive with groups, workshops and panels, discussing the pressing social, political and environmental issues of the time. Dissent! wasn't part of the official programme, but they sent a delegation to speak about the G8 anyway.

Katja gripped the podium. There were hundreds of people in the room. The seminar was titled 'G8 Global Protest and Poverty' and it was organised by Globalise Resistance, and Make Poverty History. The Dissent! Network had been added at the last minute. There was no seating for them on the panel, and the Socialist Workers Party activist chairing the event made his closing comments before inviting them to speak, as if to make clear that they were an afterthought.

They introduced Dissent!, and Katja explained its links to the international alliances that had emerged in the 1990s to resist the World Trade Organisation and 'free' trade agreements. She stressed the network's commitment to rejecting capitalism, imperialism and feudalism, and explained that they were calling for civil disobedience, setting out the plans for protests at the G8 summit in Scotland, which included a camp that would be both accommodation and a space where people could organise.

'What are you going to do about violence?'

Katja couldn't see who had shouted the question. She peered into the audience, squared her shoulders.

'It depends what you mean by violence,' she began carefully. 'I presume you're talking about protestors breaking windows. It's funny, isn't it? Capitalism kills thousands of people every day. You only need to take a walk around the workshops at this Forum to get a sense of what violence is. I think broken windows are quite irrelevant in that context.'

She went on to talk about the importance of direct action in bringing about political change. Dissent! would not be trying to control how people chose to protest. Looking out at the sea of faces, she couldn't tell how it had been received. The meeting chair stepped in.

'We're not the ones ordering the dropping of bombs on innocent women and children in Fallujah, are we?' he said.

Katja felt grateful. Although there was clearly no love lost between them, he had backed her up.

Police were at the entrance when they got back to Middlesex University. Tactical support group officers in riot gear, and FIT: the 'Forward Intelligence Team'. They were a common sight at demonstrations and outside political meetings, their cameras and notebooks a message to anyone taking part: we know what you are doing, we know who you are. She turned her face away, but she could feel their lenses follow her as she passed.

Inside, there was a buzz of conversation about the Indymedia servers. A week earlier, the FBI, acting on behalf of an 'unnamed foreign government', had seized servers in London, taking around twenty independent media outlets offline at a stroke. The Electronic Frontier Foundation (EFF) had just issued a statement saying they would be taking legal action:

> Secret orders silencing the media should be beyond the realm of possibility in a country that believes in freedom of speech . . . seizing entire servers because of a claim about some pieces of information on them is blatantly illegal and improper. It appears the government forgot this basic rule, and we will need to remind them.

Katja read the statement and sighed. How free were they really? She wondered. The Dissent! Network stood for civil disobedience with maximum respect for life, but already they were being called 'violent'. What room was there to act when the media routinely called protests 'violence' while reporting brutal atrocities as if they were business as usual? She was glad she had said what she did in the seminar, but she also knew that the police were bent on criminalising protest and singling out leaders. Her comments on the podium might have put her in the firing line for both.

Mark wandered over and put his arm around her shoulder. 'Penny for your thoughts?'

Sunday 17 October
2230 Call from Source . . . Source explained that having the 'FIT' teams right in peoples faces with a TSG team behind them was a good tactic that 'freaked' the protestors.

* * *

National Public Order Intelligence Unit - Briefing Paper, Friday 12 November 2004
The purpose of this document is to provide an intelligence overview in relation to the United Kingdom G8 Summit for the period from Saturday 6 November 2004 to Friday 12 November 2004 . . . Further intelligence has been received following the recent European Social Forum (ESF). . . At the London ESF two females referred to as ▮▮▮▮▮ and Katja both from the Dissent network spoke to the audience . . . NPOIU comment: Katja is believed to be Kate WILSON from Nottingham Sumac and ▮▮▮▮▮ is subject to further NPOIU research.

CHAPTER 26

I spoke out at a massive public gathering in the UK about organising a protest and I was afraid of police persecution in response. It turns out I had every reason to be. Mark wasn't even the only undercover officer at the European Social Forum. We know of several others. The Forward Intelligence Team, another of the Met's political policing units, were also there, to 'be in peoples faces', attacking burgeoning movements that were building links around the world to bring about desperately needed change. Protest is a vital part of any healthy society or political system and the police were systematically working to undermine that. They were there to make us feel scared.

When our group of eight women first issued our claim in 2011, a tactical decision was made to focus only on the unlawful sexual relationships. Even in 2017 I had to fight my own legal team to get my right to protest included in my claim. By 2020, though, I was on my own. I could say whatever I liked. I was convinced that the entire secret political policing apparatus must be unlawful. The police defence insisted that all their operations were legitimate and lawful, but they offered no evidence to back that up. I no longer had lawyers to tell me not to pursue it. I just needed to persuade the Investigatory Powers Tribunal to order the police to provide evidence for how the operations were 'justified'.

To do that I was going to need to find my own evidence. I sat in the boat's cockpit, watching frigate birds swooping high on the trade winds. I had no idea how I was going to do it, but I had two months to prepare my request. Lockdown was lifting, and a two-day, in-person hearing had been scheduled for mid-October. It was time to go home.

Back in Spain, I got called up to work almost immediately, in a public clinic, doing Covid-19 testing and walk-in primary care. It had been almost a year since I had done any nursing. I was nervous, going over and over infection-prevention protocols in my head, acutely aware of what I had missed and how much had changed. When I got home in the evenings, I was exhausted. Being a litigant in person was hard. For everyone else in the case, it was their day job. The police would casually miss a Friday-evening deadline and send documents on the Monday instead, as though it made no difference. For me, the weekends were the only free time I had.

In the middle of August, Dónal brought his mathematics research papers and his copious knowledge of undercover policing out to Catalonia, to help me write my submissions. He was one of dozens of people who stepped in to help during the time I was representing myself. Some, like Ben, Eleanor or my mother, were people I was close to who had also been close to Mark; others were people I hadn't known for long, or perhaps hadn't seen in over a decade, but who had themselves been affected by the apparatus of Britain's secret political police and wanted to fight back. There were still others who had no personal connection to the case, but who freely offered their time to support us because they were horrified by our story, by the criminalisation of social movements and by the police's flagrant disregard for our human rights.

That summer, Dónal and I had to keep apart because I was working in healthcare, but we would meet up every evening, outdoors, in masks, to talk.

'I've been doing a bit of reading about regulatory frameworks,' he said one day.

'A bit of reading' turned out to be an understatement. He had fifty-four pages of detailed notes. He had researched the structures and governance of the National Public Order Intelligence Unit and the regulatory framework they ought to have complied with at the time. That included the National Intelligence Model (NIM), which was a set of working practices adopted by the Association of Chief of Police Officers (which oversaw the NPOIU).

It was complicated and packed with impenetrable acronyms, and it turned out to be exactly the nitty-gritty detail we needed.

The NIM included 'minimum standards' for ensuring intelligence gathering was proportionate, necessary and in accordance with the law. The extent to which the NPOIU deviated from or ignored those standards in its day-to-day practice was the key to establishing whether the operations were lawful or not.

Together, Dónal and I wrote a list of the documents we felt the police ought to be able to provide to demonstrate compliance with those minimum standards. The police, in turn, argued that the material wasn't relevant to the case.

In the run-up to the October hearing, I wrote submissions politely explaining that it was not enough for the police to simply assert the deployments were legitimate, proportionate and necessary. There were clear standards to be met, and the evidence I was asking for would demonstrate or refute their claim. It was already apparent to us that the NPOIU's open-ended, self-tasking and randomly targeted intelligence-gathering practices would not meet the police's own minimum standards.

Sending those submissions felt as satisfying as throwing a half brick at New Scotland Yard.

Two weeks before travelling to England, I left work so that I could isolate before attending court. I didn't see another human being for fourteen days. Then I drove through the night from Barcelona to the port at Bilbao.

DISCLOSURE

Just as my ferry was pulling away from the dockside, I received an email from the police legal team. It said that they were 'constantly reviewing the available evidence' and, having considered their position, they had decided 'not to contest the Article 8 claim at paragraph 103'. My right to a private life had been breached, they said, not only by the sexual relationship, but by the rest of Mark Kennedy's operation and by the other officers as well.

I paced up and down the tiny windowless cabin.

What did it mean?

I could feel the boat pitching as it pushed its way out into the Bay of Biscay. I wanted to call Ben, Eleanor, Dónal, but we were already out of signal range. For the next twenty-nine hours I would be at sea.

By the time I arrived in the UK I was in a panic. What was their game? Why had they sent this letter just before the hearing on disclosure? Was this yet another attempt to pull the rug out from under the process by making last-minute admissions? They were still insisting that the operations were lawful, accepting only that the interference in my private life had been disproportionate, in the particular circumstances of my case. All I could think was 'What are they trying to hide?'

Yet when we got to court, Perry, the barrister speaking for the Met, made it clear that the admissions were in no way intended to reduce disclosure. As far as I could tell, there was no hidden agenda. It was very disconcerting indeed. Were we simply winning? Had I just thrown my entire weight, full tilt, at an open door?

'Miss Wilson?'

'Bear with me, my notes have got a bit out of control.'

I shuffled the papers on the narrow court table in front of me, buying time. High above me, the Tribunal chair tapped his pen on the judge's bench. The police's last-minute admissions had thrown me off-balance, but there were still a lot of other matters to be resolved.

'The next issue is neither confirm nor deny,' I declared, finally, having got my thoughts in order.

The police requested permission to 'neither confirm nor deny' on three separate questions. The first was whether they had a policy of providing a fake romantic partner for their undercover officers.

The 'fake partner' was a tactic that had been used by both Rod Richardson and Lynn Watson. They told the people they were infiltrating that they already had a romantic relationship. On occasion this person – probably another cop playing the role – would attend social events. This provided a reason for not getting romantically involved with their targets. By sending Mark in as a single person, it appeared they intended for him to have the option of forming intimate relationships with the people he spied on.

The second question was whether 'Ed' and 'Vinny' had, as we suspected, been police officers; and the third was the question Lisa and I had been asking ourselves ever since Mark was uncovered in 2010: where was Mark Kennedy on Boxing Day, 2004?

CHAPTER 27

After the European Social Forum, Katja decided to step back from organising against the G8. Mark tried to talk her out of it. He said the network needed her, but she was done.

'It doesn't "need" me, Mark. Even if it did, that would be all the more reason for me to go away. I don't want to be a leader.'

She wanted to move back to Europe, at least for a while. In December 2004, she told Mark she was planning to leave the UK.

She tried to soften the blow. She explained that she wouldn't be dropping out completely, and she would be back in time for the G8. He responded by becoming more intense. He surprised her with tickets to see her favourite country band. In the run-up to Christmas he spent a whole week in London with her and her family.

And yet, having made her decision, part of her was already imagining life in a new place.

Tuesday 14th December

██

██████████

1600

To safe location to meet with EN21 and EN59

1610

Meeting convened and both updated about the above problem. The following is a copy of my notes . . .

DCI also made notes. DCI outlined the issues that he wanted to address and those were, Source's Taskings, Where the operation had got to, Close the year and plan next year . . . Katja moving out in February. Implications discussed . . .

Katja leant close to the mirror to apply mascara. She almost never wore make-up, and suspected it made her look a bit wide-eyed, as though someone had just stabbed her with a pin. The dress was good though: skin-tight, knee-length and bright red. She did a little twirl. It was made of a shimmery material that changed colour depending on how it caught the light.

'Come on, we need to get going,' her mum called up the stairs.

She skipped down the first few steps, fastening a red rhinestone necklace around her neck as she went. Mark was at the bottom, and she paused halfway for effect. He looked her up and down.

'You look . . . just wow.'

'You don't look so bad yourself.'

He looked fantastic, in fact, in a black suit and white dress shirt, open at the neck.

They posed together in front of the Christmas tree while her dad took a series of photos, and then it was time to leave. Her mum was taking them to the National Theatre. The play was a spectacular stage adaptation of *His Dark Materials*, in which the daemons and other animals were depicted by masks and puppets that lit up from the inside.

During the interval they got drinks and went out onto a balcony overlooking the South Bank. Everyone was discussing how the play compared to Philip Pullman's trilogy, but Mark hadn't read the books.

'I've never even been to the theatre before,' he said, playing to his laddish lack of culture. 'I'll be honest with you, this is the first time I've worn a suit.'

Her mum laughed and Katja looked at him sharply, but his eyes were shining and he was obviously loving the play, so she softened and linked her arm through his.

'You should wear one more often.'

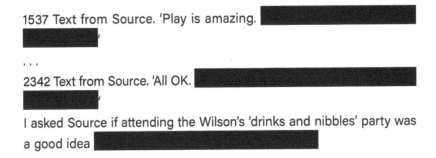

1537 Text from Source. 'Play is amazing. ████████████
████████'

. . .

2342 Text from Source. 'All OK. ██████████████████████
████████'

I asked Source if attending the Wilson's 'drinks and nibbles' party was
a good idea ██████████████████████

Mark shook a collecting tin for hours, charming donations from
commuters as they came out of the station, and everyone sang
until they were frozen. Finally, when no one could feel their
fingers, her mum collected up the song sheets and they all went
back to the flat where her dad was waiting to warm them up with
shepherd's pie and mulled wine.

Thursday 16th December
1700 Source is engaged 'Carol singing' outside Putney rail station with
Katja, family and friends raising funds for Amnesty International.

The table was piled high with snacks and party food that Katja
and Mark had picked up from the supermarket earlier that day,
and there was Christmas music on the stereo. A group set up
around the coffee table to count the donations and announce to
everyone how much money they had raised.

2142 Text from Source. 'Everyone is so posh, I fit right in.'

The party was over and everyone except Mark and Katja had
gone home or gone to bed. They were on the sofa, lit only by the
lights of the Christmas tree. The last few days had been delightful,

and she was beginning to wonder whether moving away was a mistake.

'I wish you would come with us. The cottage in Devon is perfect for Christmas. We could toast chestnuts on the fire. Christmas Day with my family is always lush.'

He said he would be happier in Thailand, soaking up some winter sun. A family Christmas would only make him sad.

CHAPTER 28

'More than 11,000 people are now thought to have been killed in South East Asia, after an undersea earthquake sent enormous waves rolling across the Indian Ocean. The quake measured 8.9 on the Richter Scale, the biggest in the world for forty years. Waves up to 10 metres high engulfed the coasts of many countries . . .'

Katja looked up, then put down her book and moved closer to the TV.

'300 have been killed in southern Thailand, including some tourists, and hundreds of people are missing . . .'

Her dad came in carrying a glass of wine.

'Isn't Mark in Thailand?'

Where had he said he was going? She racked her brain, cursing the casual way they had said goodbye. No, it was worse than that. Less casual. They had been like teenagers, trying too hard, asserting their independence. Their indifference had carried an unspoken message: 'I don't own you. What you do when you are apart from me is your own affair.'

He hadn't told her where he was going. Kickboxing. That was all he said: a kickboxing course in Thailand. She tried to imagine it, students sleeping on embroidered mats, getting up at dawn to fight and train. Wooden huts with open verandas looking out onto a lush tropical landscape. On a hillside, maybe? Higher ground?

'Across six countries in southern Asia, the death toll is now rising, as the terrible picture of damage emerges. Here is the moment where

*the ocean starts to spill onto the street. These pictures are from ama-
teur video by holidaymakers in Thailand, from the popular resort of
Phuket.'*

The TV showed a wobbly shot of water rising over a seawall
and spilling onto the road. There were palm trees, and she felt a
stab of pain. Mark was a sun worshipper. Would he really have
gone all the way to Thailand and stayed away from the beach?

*'It is thought more than 10,000 British tourists could be affected by
the disaster, but at the moment accurate casualty figures for Britons
are unknown . . .'*

She dialled his number. It went straight to voicemail.

'Hey, Mark, I'm watching the news. When you get this, get in
touch. Please. I just want to know you're OK.'

* * *

'In response to my request for further disclosure the police have
also applied to neither confirm nor deny the question of whether
Mark Kennedy went to Thailand in December 2004.'

The judges were getting impatient with me adding yet more
questions to be resolved.

'What relevance is that to your claim? Were you with Mr Kennedy when he went to Thailand?'

I was determined not to be put off by the judges' impatience.

'I wasn't with Mark when he went to Thailand, but I did pick
him up from the airport when he supposedly got back. If you look
at the bundle, on page 280, it is mostly redacted, but at the very
bottom there's a note from Mark's cover officer. He watched me
arriving at Heathrow Airport to collect Mark.'

Operation Pegasus – Contact Log (2005)
Wednesday 5th January
0700

DISCLOSURE

1030

1130

1220

1420

1530

Engaged there.

1600

1935

In fact, the disclosure for that day was almost all redacted, but log entries were made more or less hourly, throughout the day. That seemed odd, if Mark had, as he claimed, been on a plane at the time. Then, just before 8 p.m., we got a glimpse of what was happening:

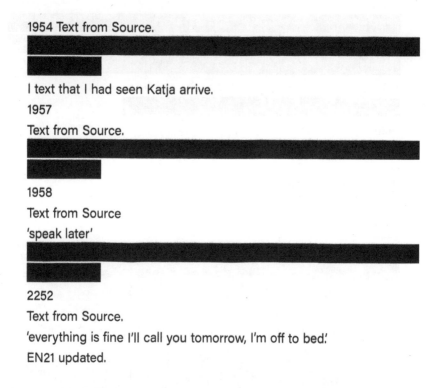

1954 Text from Source.

I text that I had seen Katja arrive.
1957
Text from Source.

1958
Text from Source
'speak later'

2252
Text from Source.
'everything is fine I'll call you tomorrow, I'm off to bed.'
EN21 updated.

It was all wild speculation, but I was left with the distinct impression that Mark may not have been on any flight and that his handler had perhaps driven him to the airport and dropped him off, ready to play the part of my lover arriving home.

* * *

Mark seemed paler and thinner. At first he didn't want to talk about it. When he did, he said he had been far from the coast

206

when it happened, and in no danger, but as soon as he heard, he had rushed to the area to help with the rescue effort. He spoke about digging the body of a dead child out of the sand.

He became fascinated by geography, even signing up to study it on a distance learning course. Katja held his hand at the Natural History Museum, where they went to see the display about tsunamis. From time to time she glanced at his face, watching for signs of distress.

A long tank contained a model of a coastline, with a beach and tiny trees and houses on the right, and the land sloping down to the left to show a cross section of the ocean floor. There was real water in it which provided a tiny simulation, over and over, of how a tsunami builds in size and strength. They learnt that tsunami meant 'harbour wave', and that they were often almost undetectable far from shore, because the energy is spread through the entire depth of the water. However, as that energy reaches shallow water, it is compressed; the wave slows down and its height begins to rise, and can reach up to 100 feet, devastating coastlines for miles inland.

* * *

'The Defendants I think would accept that they had a duty of care to protect Mark Kennedy's emotional welfare and Mark Kennedy's welfare in general.'

I glanced at the judges and then back to my notes, turning the page.

'They note, at page 281 that Mark is in Putney, at my parent's house, when he returns to the UK. EN107 is given a full briefing. EN59 and EN21 are also updated, although there are a lot of redactions and it is not clear what they are updated about. However, there are several comments about us and how worried we were.'

1610 Call from Source. Source and Katja have spent the afternoon at the Natural History Museum . . . People have been calling Source saying that they are glad that Source is safe and well ████████████████ ██ ███████████████████████████

'Now you see, at the end of that section, the Defendants have redacted one line? That line was actually disclosed to me unredacted in 2018.'

I fumbled through my files looking for the page.

'I have it here.'

I read aloud from the disclosure.

'We will have to watch the effect on Source of these people showing that they care when we are lying to them.'

I looked up. The judges did at least seem to be listening.

'My side of that experience was that my boyfriend went to Thailand for Christmas, and I saw the news of what had happened, and I thought he was dead.'

To my surprise, my voice broke. I swallowed, trying to shrink the lump in my throat.

'His managers watched me pick him up from the airport. They claim they don't know we were in a relationship, but I can assure you that when I picked Mark up that day, having feared he might have died, it would have been absolutely evident to anybody watching that we were together.'

I coughed, trying to hide my tears.

'It is all right, I understand,' said the Chair.

I don't think he did understand though. I still have a green satin sarong that Mark gave me that January. It was a gift, supposedly from Thailand. For all I know it was from Camden Market. They were definitely lying, but to this day I can't be sure what the lie was.

The Tribunal upheld the police's application for secrecy on all three points: fake romantic attachments, 'Ed' and 'Vinny', and Boxing Day 2004.

CHAPTER 29

Operation Pegasus – Contact Log (2005)
Thursday 27th January
2244 Text from source. '. . . I will be going to London to see the Flamenco
. . .'
Friday 28th January
Source covered technically whilst at Putney and Sadlers Wells
2305 Text from Source. 'All Ok in Putney'

'That's nineteen.'

'What?'

'I have counted at least nineteen separate occasions between February 2004 and February 2005 where Mark texted his handler to say he was spending the night with you at your parents' place in Putney,' Ben explained.

We were stuck in the UK. I couldn't risk being trapped abroad when the case finally went to court, so I found a room where we could spend the winter, at a housing co-op in the Derwent Valley. There were thirteen of us at Wild Peak, including my old housemate Ronny, who was living there with her new partner. We shared mealtimes and Ronny's vegan cake, and isolated from the outside world as much as possible to keep each other safe. I helped prepare vegetable beds, ready for springtime. We took it in turns to chop wood to feed 'the Beast', a roaring furnace at the centre of a complex heating system that kept all the buildings cosy and warm.

It had been a long while since I had lived in a community. It felt like coming home.

Ben joined me at the beginning of December. Our room was in an outhouse called 'the Barracks'. It contained a desk, a sofa and a camping stove, with a bed above them on a platform up in the rafters.

That tiny space would become our base of operations for the final straight. The walls and floor were soon covered with documents, notes and mind maps. The trial was in just a few months, and we needed to distil all those thousands of pages down to just what we needed: the evidence to prove our case. It was all-consuming. Emerging at communal mealtimes was like coming up for air, and even then, we couldn't stay away from the documents for long.

Saturday 29th January
Source will travel to Oxford from London with Katja to make contact with Corporate Watch members so that when Katja leaves the UK Source can meet up with them in sources own right . . .
1623
Text from Source
'Leaving in about 30'

. . .

2027 Text from Source. 'Remember ██████████'
2034 Text from Source. 'Sorry that is the password to get into the Corporate Watch computer system'

'He got the Corporate Watch computer password and sent it to his handler,' Ben exclaimed. 'That was probably illegal, even back then.'

Under the Computer Misuse Act of 1990, it is an offence to gain unauthorised access to computer material or to supply or obtain anything which could be used in a computer misuse offence. Ironically, the laws protecting our telecommunications are much more stringent than ones protecting our bodies or our homes.

DISCLOSURE

Mark would have needed the secretary of state's permission to tap my telephone. Any ordinary police officer would have needed a warrant to search my garden shed. Yet all the NPOIU needed for the things they did was the signature of a senior police officer.

'His handler was there, you know?' Ben pointed out. 'That weekend, in Oxford, watching you.'

I shivered. 'Let me see.'

Sunday 30th January
1135 Call from Source who had rung off to take another call. Arrangements made to meet in Oxford City . . . In Oxford waiting to meet up with Source.
1423 Text from Source.
'This might be difficult.'
I text back that I was 8 miles away.
1430 Text from Source 'OK I'm with people but am going to the Vaults Garden Café'
I text back for a location . . . Source then covered technically.
1630
Sources vehicle located outside ███████████████████
1800
Source and Katja at vehicle.
1803
Text from Source
'sorry mate you OK'
. . .
1830 Followed sources vehicle . . .
1835 Call from Source who updated me on the location and activity. Source is still involved with discussions at [someone's home] and says that it is important to stay as it is all of interest to us.

It was creepy, thinking about the handler tracking us 'technically' (which I understood to mean he was using GPS in Mark's phone to locate us) and watching us on the street. It was worse than creepy that Mark went for dinner in someone's private home and texted his handler that our dinner-table conversation was all of interest to the police. Corporate Watch was an open and public research organisation. It wasn't a target of Mark's operation, and Thames Valley wasn't even in the area where Mark was supposed to work, yet he engineered that visit to make sure he had a foot in the door. It seemed that the scope of the operation was expanding, although in accordance with what orders was anyone's guess.

'It is so hard to convey just how arbitrary this all was,' I said. 'I think people just assume there must have been *some* serious crime *somewhere*; because otherwise, what were the police doing there?'

It was my turn to cook. There's a meditative quality to cooking, and as I selected a large pumpkin from the store and took it to the kitchen to dissect, I allowed my mind to wander. By then I had seen all the contact logs and notebooks for the time Mark and I were together (apart from the missing bits from 2003). Shortly after that second trip to Oxford, our relationship ended, but there was one important event I was yet to find. I had videos and photos of Mark at my nan's ninetieth birthday party, but I had found no reference to it in the files.

One by one I crushed cloves of garlic against the heavy chopping board, using the flat side of a knife. I thought back to that day: my parent's living room decked out with flowers and helium balloons, and filled with all my cousins, uncles and aunts.

Once the pot was simmering I wiped my hands and called my mum to see if she knew the precise date.

Operation Pegasus – Contact Log (2005)
Saturday 5 February
1046 Text from Source . . . Source is waiting for other people to get themselves up and out to give them a lift to the Earth First gathering.

DISCLOSURE

My mum checked her diary. The party was on 5 February 2005, but from the contact logs it seemed that Mark had been in Brighton that day, for the Earth First! Winter Moot. As I read on, however, I realised that although he drove people to Brighton for the gathering, he didn't stay.

Source has to be at a function in London with Katja by 1200 . . .
1130 Call from Source who has dropped . . . others off at Twynen (ph) Grange for the E/F ████████████████████████
███
███
███
███
███
████████████████████████████████████
Source will be in Putney till about 6 or 7 then travel to Bristol. I will do the same.

In other words, Mark left a political gathering of a group that formed part of his operational tasking in order to attend my family's private event. It was incomprehensible. If anything, it suggested that personal intrusion was not simply incidental, but a police priority in its own right. Could that possibly be true? What was the point of it?

I looked at the photographs. Mark had introduced himself to my nonagenarian grandmother and her entire extended family as my boyfriend. There he was, standing among us balancing a wine glass and a paper plate of food. And there was Nan, together on the sofas with her brother and sisters. I realised with sadness that they were all gone now.

Operation Pegasus – Contact Log (2005)
Thursday 1st December
1825 Call from Source who has had a call from Katja. Her Nan has died

today . . . Source believes that they may invite Source to the funeral. I told Source that from a position of intrusion we should make excuses as to why Source does not attend.

Apparently it was OK to attend her birthday, but her wake a few months later was a step too far. I put the photographs back in their envelope. I wanted to cherish the moment and the memories. In some ways it was a relief that Nan never found out about Mark's deceit.

1635 Text from Source. 'tied up here will not be able to travel to Bristol till tomorrow if that's OK.' 2000 . . . Source covered on technical.
2350 Text from Source. 'Night. All OK'

Mark was supposed to meet his handler in Bristol, but he stood him up. He stayed on after the party, and spent the night with me in Putney instead.

My eyes scanned quickly down the page, looking for the end. I felt itchy and irritable at the gratuitousness of it all.

Monday 7th February
1500 Text from Source. 'Katja is just pulling out of Dover.'

There it was: I left the country at 3 p.m. on 7 February 2005. The night of Nan's ninetieth birthday had been the last night Mark and I spent together.

According to the police logs, the relationship lasted 475 days.

It was exciting when it started, then comfortable and domestic, and over time we grew apart. The irony was our relationship would hardly have made a chapter in a memoir if it had been real. But Mark was a fictional character, contrived by the British state to violate me and undermine the values I hold most dear. And I can recall it all in such detail because EN31 was sitting round the corner the entire time, writing it all down, watching our lives unfold.

PART THREE

PART THREE

CHAPTER 30

Operation Pegasus – Contact Log (2005)
Sunday 6 February
1000 Met with Source. Debrief, diary and future movements . . .
2123 Text from Source. 'all OK at Cornerstone.'
2358 Text from Source. 'Off to bed all OK night.'

Lisa spent six years with Mark, far more than my 475 days. The logs show that Mark went straight from my bed in London, to a debrief with his handler, to her bed in Leeds. The same day. He didn't miss a beat. Almost six years later she lived through the horror of watching her relationship unravel in real time.

We had started this claim together, and yet a decade later, I was the only one to have been given disclosure. It wasn't fair.

For the most part the Tribunal were kind to me as a litigant in person, but they didn't like it when I tried to talk about the other women.

'We are dealing with your claim; we are not dealing with other people's claims,' they said.

The police wanted the Tribunal to consider my relationship with Mark in isolation. It was the only way they could credibly claim that no one knew Mark was having sex, and that he acted alone. After all, to miss one relationship might be regarded as misfortune, but to miss dozens was something else.

Sir Stephen House claimed that the evidence had 'not established that any other officer or member of staff knew or ought to have known that MK was conducting a sexual relationship'. At the time his statement was served, at least six women had been granted core participant status in the public inquiry because of sexual relationships that they had with Mark Kennedy, and four of them had already received compensation and public apologies from the Metropolitan Police. I was personally aware of at least eleven sexual relationships that Mark had had. He was just one of many undercover officers to have deceived women into sex, all fictional characters, seemingly working from the same creepy playbook: mirroring our interests, quick to fall in love, winning us over with their sob stories, charming us with their little-boy-lost routines. Some were known to have gone on to be managers and trainers in the political secret policing units, overseeing new generations of police officers who violated women in the same way. It was completely implausible that an entire police unit could have failed to notice multiple relationships spanning many years.

I needed the Tribunal to see the wider context, so I kept pushing for more information, and finally, I had something to show for it.

From the fourth witness statement of Sir Stephen House, 3 December 2020

I SIR STEPHEN HOUSE of the Metropolitan Police Service . . . WILL SAY as follows . . .

First, it is the Claimant's case that Mark Kennedy conducted a sexual relationship with . . . other women whilst deployed. It is understood that the Claimant's case is that the conduct of such other relationships is relevant to the issue of knowledge or acquiescence on the part of more senior officers as regards MK's conduct in relation to the Claimant, and that it is relevant also to the issue of whether the Respondents have breached Article 14 [the right to freedom from discrimination] . . .

The Claimant has invited the Respondents to review contact logs, MK's undercover report books and any related policy decisions to identify references to [these] other women . . . The references . . . are set out in schedule form at Annex 1.

There was a click on the line as Lisa answered.

'Hi, it's Kate. How are you? Did you get my email?'

There was a long pause, so quiet I could hear birdsong down the line.

'I did. Did you read the bit about my dad?'

Her voice was low. I felt a pit open up inside me. If the police had had an ounce of decency, they would have disclosed these things to her a decade ago. She shouldn't have been finding this out through me.

From the fourth witness statement of Sir Stephen House, Annex 1
Wednesday 29 November (2006)
1357 Text from source. 'I have been asked to attend a funeral. No date yet, Lisa's Dad died last night.' I told source to pass me the details when known. I asked if she was just after a lift. I said I would clear it with the SIO.

Monday 4 December
1025 I called DI Hutcheson and informed him of our movements for the week including attending the funeral of Lisa's Father on Thursday . . . DI Hutcheson agreed sources movements for the week . . .

Thursday 7 December
Source is in Wales for Lisa's Father's funeral. No reporting will follow

'He was in the mourners' car with my family. They approved him doing that.'

I took a deep breath. I could only begin to imagine her anger, and wasn't sure how she would react to my next question. Yet no account of the damage done by Mark and his operation would be complete without Lisa's story, and she had to tell it herself.

'Would you be willing to make a witness statement?'

Another pause.

'I want to tell my story,' she said, 'but it shouldn't be like this. I'm reading about how they spied on me and my family in an appendix to a witness statement, in a case about somebody else. We started this claim together and it's hard, being sidelined like that.'

She asked what making a witness statement involved. I realised I had no idea. Like everything else, we would have to figure it out as we went along.

Eleanor took on the task of coordinating possible witnesses, and she and Lisa began working together, going through the annex to House's statement, which listed references to them both.

In the meantime, Dónal joined Ben and me in Derbyshire. There was so much to do. We compiled profiles of all the officers mentioned in the documents, and wrote reports on what the disclosure could tell us about the various issues. We were at it all hours in our little Barracks headquarters, with barely enough space for the three of us to sit down. Dónal would slip out at night to catch a couple of hours sleep in his van, and Ben and I would climb up to our bed in the rafters, above the strange tableau of pages of notes, lists of ciphers and folders left open at the last page worked on, just visible in the wintry light of dawn.

From my point of view, the most significant file from the period after Mark and I separated was the authorisation document of 26 May 2005.

OPERATION NAME: PEGASUS
RIPA Application
Force requesting authorisation: NPOIU.
[The Officer in the Case is EN107]

. . .

Subjects: Five subjects of the deployment are listed, including Kate Wilson and Eleanor.

DISCLOSURE

[The personal details of these subjects are listed. No additional information is included]

. . .

Intelligence Case

Includes the following:

The National Public Order Intelligence Unit (NPOIU) is currently undertaking an intelligence gathering operation, codenamed PEGASUS, which is focussed against two social centres where various anarchist groups meet known as The SUMAC Centre, Nottingham and the CORNERSTONE Co-operative in Leeds. [MK] has been involved in a prolonged infiltration of these premises and after named subjects since July, 2003. The main organisers and planners involved with these premises are [Eleanor and one other] at the SUMAC and WILSON [and one other] at the CORNERSTONE.

It was nonsense. I never lived in Leeds. At the time it was written, I wasn't even living in the UK. I was never an organiser or planner at Cornerstone. Even the police lawyers accepted that it was absurd, though they offered no explanation for how it came to be recorded in an official authorisation and signed off by a police Commander.

That wasn't the only curious thing. Sir Stephen House's statement included a list of all the authorisations for Mark's operation, and the narrative it presented was strange.

From the first witness statement of Sir Stephen House, Annex 4

18/05/2005 (EN114), Review of the progress of Operation Pegasus notes that 'the criteria for the initial authorisation still remains constant at present.' The Officer in the Case is changed from EN59 to EN107.

25/05/2005 (EN114) Cancellation. Application for authority to cancel the renewal application submitted on 14/02/2005 in which there was an administrative error. Following the appointment of EN107 as Operational Head on the departure of EN59, a review of the authorities to date revealed that 'The previous review and renewal forms were not completed

221

correctly and pages had been omitted! As a result, EN114 was instructed to cancel the previous renewal application and apply for re-authorisation on correct form. Cancellation is granted by Acting Commander Mitchell.

26/05/2005 (EN114) Application. This is the first mention of Kate Wilson in any authorisation document. She is listed as one of the subjects of the deployment and described as one of the main organisers and planners at the Cornerstone co-operative, Leeds . . . Authority is granted by Acting Commander Mitchell.

I put down the folder and paced up and down. Three strides took me from one end of the Barracks to the other.

EN107 took over the operation. When did that happen?

It was decided that the existing authorisation was unacceptable, and a new application was filed. Why?

And why was the only discernible difference between the old and the new applications that Eleanor and I had been added to the list of names?

Eventually, Ben grew irritated.

'What's the matter?'

I stopped.

'I don't know, but something happened in 2005.'

We had a letter from EN59, written in 2019, where he described leaving his job.

In general terms my recollection is that the work load was high and during this period I operated under significant stress levels. When I left the unit, a review of the deployment was carried out . . .
I left because I no longer had confidence in the structure of the NPOIU. I felt I was marginalised.

DISCLOSURE

Despite my best endeavours, I was unable to secure the changes which I perceived necessary to move the unit forward and develop. Professionally I did not want to be associated with work carried out in the manner which I was observing and, due to the ambient situation, had no realistic recourse to seek redress open to me.

Evidently EN59 left under a cloud. That was in March of 2005. The departure seemed to coincide with an internal NPOIU Review of Systems and Structures carried out that same month. The report was scathing. It noted that the NPOIU had failed to gain national accreditation and highlighted a lack of training, and a breakdown of trust and communication within the unit. It singled out senior management referring to deficiencies 'inherited from former managers and exacerbated by promotion within the unit, causing a stagnation of original thinking and a lack of external experience'. It stated that 'whilst appearing critical the situation is easily remedied by the external recruitment of qualified and experienced Senior Investigating Officers (SIOs)'.

It was unclear whether the stagnant and unoriginal manager in question was EN59 or his successor. All we knew was that EN59 was replaced by EN107 in March of 2005.

I got up and made crumpets in the toaster (a recent acquisition that had led to a lot of snacking in the Barracks instead of eating proper food) and settled back on the sofa. Dónal had gone home, but we had him on the phone. The three of us were going back over everything we had, and Ben was reading from the officer profiles.

Our index revealed 119 unique references to EN107 in the disclosure, including one that made it clear she was a woman and

223

several that suggested that she was neither qualified nor experienced as an SIO. The documents reported that 'EN107 was not a trained SIO. EN107 was the deployment manager and in the absence of a SIO had to carry out/assume this role.' The RIPA application of 26 May 2005 records, under Operational Head comments, 'The deployment will be directly managed by myself even though I am not a qualified SIO' and is signed by EN107.

Ben summarised the references made to her in the contact logs.

'She took over control of the operation shortly after the relationship between you and Mark ended. Naming you and Eleanor as targets was one of the first things she did in that role.'

I wished I knew why.

In EN107's correspondence with the police legal team it was recorded that:

> For MK to have people staying or meeting at his flat EN107 needed to know in advance to have the appropriate authorities in place ████████. ██████████████████████████████████ ███████████████████. It was standard practice that MK should seek approval before any activists or associates attend his operational address.

The logs were full of records of overnight stays with no reference to permission or approval. Nevertheless, Sir Stephen House does note, in his first statement that 'There is no evidence of a formal documented policy that MK would have to seek prior permission for such stays, however, it does appear from the cover officer logs dated 10 October 2005 that once EN107 became SIO, a change in policy or practice resulted.'

I had a niggling feeling that she knew about the relationship, and that the renewed authorisation and the change in policy about overnight stays were some kind of clumsy attempt to make it right.

We saw a handful of recorded decisions allowing Mark to have female activists to stay at his home, all signed by EN107. They represented only a tiny fraction of the occasions when people spent the night at his place, and none of the occasions when he slept elsewhere, so if there was a policy or practice, it was one Mark and his handler frequently ignored. Nevertheless, they did contain one important detail:

Operation Pegasus Decision Log
Decision Number 117 - Signed: EN107. Date & time: 30/11/05 1330hrs
DECISION: permission granted for UCO to allow female . . . to reside at UCO's covert premises for two weeks . . .

. . .

- No change to risk assessment.
Cover officer verbally reminded UCO re Health and Safety – intimate relations etc.

I passed the document to Ben.

'Is it just me, or does that basically say, "Cover officer reminded the undercover officer to use a condom"?'

He studied the page.

'Pretty much, yeah. Although who knows? They might have said "keep it in your pants", or given him guidance on how to treat gonorrhoea.'

Whatever the *'Health and Safety – intimate relations'* note meant, it left little room for doubt that it had at least occurred to EN107 that Mark might end up in bed with someone, although she later denied anything of the sort.

She dismissed it as a standard reference to the principles of conduct, but we checked. The principles, known as 'the 1 to 7', consisted of seven instructions to undercover officers. They mentioned acting as an agent provocateur, taking part in a conspiracy, committing criminal offences, respecting people's right to privacy and to a fair trial, and properly corroborating intelligence. Those were all points that Mark Kennedy probably did need reminding about. However, they contained no reference to health and safety, intimate relationships or sex.

CHAPTER 31

After October 2020, new disclosures came thick and fast. The police had run out of arguments to resist handing over the files. Although they'd had years to process the documents, it seemed they never really thought this day would come. Disgruntled at the scale of the workload, they complained that such sensitive documents couldn't leave the secure building where they were housed, making it impossible to social distance in the workplace or for them to work from home. I imagined grey-suited police officers and lawyers, side by side in a windowless bunker, hurriedly trying to gut the pages before sending them off to me.

They were served late, upside down, at crazy angles and in the wrong order, suggesting they had been shuffled before individually photocopying and scanning each page. Some looked like they had been photocopied several times, to reduce the quality of the image before sending them to me. It felt petty, and sorting it out took hours of my time.

On top of that, I had to keep up with correspondence. I was communicating with Sarah Hannett almost every day, checking what we had received and what was still outstanding, managing ever-changing deadlines, and drafting letters of complaint, detailing the police failures to complete disclosure, and ultimately asking her to intervene to make them comply with the orders of the court. Even where I had full disclosure, it was always without context. No explanations were given as to who would have authored or read the documents, or for what purpose they were made, and the pile of things to read just kept growing.

The trial was booked for April 2021 but there was so much material. Even if we managed to read it, I had no idea how we could fit everything into a hearing that was only scheduled to last eight days. When I lay down at night it was with a buzzing head and a twisting feeling in my gut that we were running out of time.

I had promised myself a real break. We planned to join my parents and my brother's family for the permitted 'three-household bubble' on Christmas Day. Then the Government declared London ground zero for a new, fast-spreading Covid-19 variant and brought in 'Tier 4' restrictions across the Southeast. I had never missed Christmas with my family.

In Belper village, Christmas was in full swing. Supermarkets were decked with lights and purchasing limits were being introduced to prevent panic buying. Every time I heard a carol, it made me cry. We set off to visit Ben's family instead, but road closures forced us off the motorway, and we found ourselves driving down unlit lanes through torrential rain and rising floodwaters. At one point I felt the wheels lose contact with the road. Ben leapt out to push the car to dry land through water that came well above his knees.

Each time we changed our travel plans I checked my email. We were still waiting for one of the biggest instalments of disclosure to date, and with characteristic sensitivity, the police solicitors had said they would be sending it to Ben's sister's address on Christmas Eve.

The package still hadn't arrived by Christmas Day, and 'Tier 4' restrictions were going into force in Cambridge at midnight. We fled back to Derbyshire and prepared for quarantine.

I eventually managed to track the parcel down to a local post office on New Year's Eve. I drove to pick it up, but I didn't want to end the year looking at police files, so I left it unopened, and we saw in 2021 at Wild Peak, with socially distanced dancing on the frosty grass at midnight. The next morning, the whole household trooped down to the river and stripped off to swim in the icy waters of the

Derwent. The river was deep, and as we crossed to the opposite side and back it took all my strength not to get pushed down stream. I felt exhilarated as I scrambled up the bank: beating the current, after so many weeks struggling to keep my head above water.

Glowing from our swim, I decided to face the new disclosure. I sat in front of the pile of paper in disbelief.

'There's more than a thousand pages here.'

'Happy New Year,' Ben toasted the parcel with his glass of gin and tonic.

I had been asking to see the intelligence reports generated by Mark's operation for years. The Tribunal had only recently given serious consideration to my request, but when it rains, it pours. I could see, at a glance, that I had material spanning more than a decade of undercover operations, with reports attributed to Mark Kennedy, some attributed to other undercover officers I had known, such as Lynn Watson and Marco Jacobs, some from the Special Demonstration Squad, the political spycops unit that preceded the NPOIU, and even some from after Mark had been uncovered, where the provenance was unclear.

The police had fought bitterly over every word of disclosure for years. They hadn't even given me my own 'NPOIU subject profile', instead providing only a garbled gist of what it contained. Yet here they had sent a deluge of details relating to events I was not involved in and knew nothing about.

I was given full copies of the personal 'subject profiles' for a number of other people (although, absurdly, still not my own). There was even a big chunk of material covering Marco Jacobs' activities in Cardiff, a city I had never visited.

It was disorientating and overwhelming. Now that we were running out of time, it seemed the police no longer cared what they were sending, they were just dumping it on us. I wondered whether they had simply grown exasperated and run out of resources to sift and redact the information, or whether the tactic had actually shifted from resisting disclosure to weaponising the process. I was a litigant in person; they may have thought I wouldn't be able to process it in time and so they were sending me piles and piles of paper in the hope that it might drown me.

It might even have worked, but we were thrown a lifeline.

As it happened, Charlotte had never quite given up on my case. Ever since she let it go, she had been searching for a firm of solicitors who might be able to take it on for free, and at the end of December 2020 she contacted me with news: she had found one.

My days as a litigant in person were almost over. Everything was about to change.

One by one, little videos popped up, until they completely filled my screen. There were two junior barristers, plus half a dozen solicitors from the 'pro bono' department of Freshfields Bruckhaus Deringer, a major City law firm.

Charlotte's was the only familiar face, so we began with introductions. In my nervousness I almost immediately forgot who everybody was, but I would soon come to know them well. Matthew seemed to be in charge. He would step in with his smooth, persuasive manner whenever a controversial issue needed to be resolved. Ricky worked alongside Matthew, and although I dealt less with him directly, I learnt from his co-workers that he was highly respected, with an almost supernatural capacity to handle multiple complex issues at the same time.

Holly was next. She said she would be in charge of drafting witness statements, and her calm demeanour betrayed nothing of the scale of the task that awaited us there.

Finally, there was Charlotte B and Paddy, young, enthusiastic associate solicitors who had started their careers at Freshfields in the field of commercial law, but who now, between them, had the unenviable job of dealing directly with me.

They suggested that we set up a weekly phone call, which quickly ramped up to us speaking several times a week. I didn't know it then but the people on that call were just the team leaders. There were dozens of others, including paralegals and in-house graphic designers, most of whom I never got to meet, who swung into action that day and began work on my case.

Freshfields were coming to it all from scratch. Harriet's law firm, Birnberg Peirce, had given them a briefing, but they still had a decade of catching up to do. Even Charlotte needed updating about everything that had happened over the past twelve months.

'So, Kate, could you talk us through where things are at right now?'

'Well, yeah, I mean, the case is complicated. They have made a lot of admissions over the years. They have since withdrawn some of them, as well.'

I could see Charlotte shaking her head, recalling the dramatic changes in the police defence.

We discussed the history of the claim and the ongoing disputes about disclosure, and I listed the police's repeated failures to comply with directions. When I had finished there was an incredulous pause. I think if Charlotte had not been in the meeting, the other lawyers might not have believed me when I told them how various teams of police lawyers had consistently failed to meet almost every deadline set by the Tribunal, causing years of delays in the case. Freshfields were appalled. Eventually Ricky suggested that they move the meeting on.

'I think we need some more time to think about this. Honestly, I have never come across *incompetence* as a litigation strategy. I'm not really sure how we should respond.'

Freshfields called the case 'Project Hale'. Email lists and software platforms were set up, and Paddy and Charlotte B introduced me to their 'Secure File Transfer system', asking me to send them everything – all the disclosure, correspondence, submissions, transcripts, directions and rulings – from the last twelve months.

The lawyers were concerned that with only three and a half months to the actual, final hearing, there wasn't enough time to prepare. They wanted to request a delay. I was dismayed. I knew they were right, but I hadn't realised until that moment how much I was counting on it all being over. I didn't think I could cope if the trial date were moved again, and I said as much to Matthew, expecting to be reasoned with and persuaded to request an extension. To my surprise, he said that he understood, and that we would aim to go ahead for April as planned.

It wasn't until the trial was over, and we were unwinding together in a bar, that I discovered exactly what that meant for them. They resolved that they would just have to do whatever it took to meet the April deadline, and I don't think anyone got any sleep for the next ten weeks.

Ben and I were already working all hours, but it didn't escape my notice that we were soon exchanging dozens of emails a day with Freshfields. If I messaged Charlotte B or Paddy at one or two in the morning it rarely took them more than ten minutes to respond.

It was agreed that they wouldn't take over the case until after the next hearing, because it was unrealistic to get the new team up to speed that fast. I would go to the hearing in London on 22 January to represent myself, and then cheerfully break the news to everyone in person that I had found legal representation for the remainder of the case.

Unfortunately, that plan began to fall apart almost as soon as it was made. Covid-19 rates in London were rising, and I received an email from the Tribunal cancelling the hearing.

I was still officially a litigant in person, so I continued corresponding with Sarah Hannett, trying to figure out what should happen next. With no court date, the existing directions became meaningless. There were no longer any deadlines or any plans for resolving outstanding issues. Freshfields observed my clumsy attempts to deal with the resulting disorder, and eventually they politely asked me not to send the Tribunal any more emails. Charlotte Kilroy QC and Freshfields Bruckhaus Deringer stepped into the melee with a sternly worded letter on 21 January 2021, trying to get the process back on track.

That same day, the River Derwent began to flood.

Ben and I were tripping over each other in the tiny Barracks, collecting the piles of paper into boxes and moving them onto the high bed to keep them safe from the water. Once that was done, we joined the others in the main house, piling stuff on the dining table and moving whatever furniture we could upstairs. We drove all the vehicles onto the hillside, and then went over emergency evacuation protocols together – first priority: make sure the children are safe.

We were up all night, watching the river as it advanced across the fields. By morning the whole garden was underwater. We were lucky. It had not yet come into the buildings, and the level was starting to recede, but the Barracks looked like a houseboat, and the fields had been replaced by a boundless expanse of water, dotted with lonely trees. The shimmering surface was a reminder of what was at stake. Floods like that on the River Derwent used to be a once-in-a-decade occurrence. Now they happen almost every year. Yet the NPOIU described Mark's work against climate change campaigners as 'the priority area for domestic extremism'. They worked hard to undermine movements in Britain that were fighting to get the climate crisis taken seriously. They took the side of capitalism and fossil fuels. People will die because of what they did.

'History's going to judge them, whatever the IPT says,' I muttered, as we moved the files back down to the ground floor and got back to work.

CHAPTER 32

As I went through the files we had accumulated over the previous twelve months, preparing to upload them to Project Hale, I felt a strange misgiving. I realised I was a bit reluctant to give up control after a year of speaking for myself. Charlotte and I had had our disagreements in the past. Now I was instructing a vast team of lawyers from a monolithic corporate firm. Would they understand the political issues that mattered so much to me? Was I making a bad choice?

My worries spiked during our next call.

'So, Kate, I have been reading the files, and I think we are going to need to address the issue of serious criminality here. The Tribunal are obviously going to be concerned by things like "aquatic attacks on ships". Talk us through that.'

Aquatic attacks? I had no idea what they were talking about, but it sounded like they had seen something in the files that they considered serious crime.

When the call was over, Ben and I turned to the documents. We eventually found what they meant. The phrase appeared in intelligence reports about a protest in 2003 against Defence & Security Equipment International (DSEi), an arms fair in London.

NPOIU Intelligence Report (2003)
Date: 20/08/03
Force: NPOIU
Source Reference: [MK]

KATE WILSON

Handler/Officer Reporting: [EN31]
This information was gathered during the Earth First Summer Gathering ... DSEI Workshop. This had the greatest attendance of all the
workshops ... There will be an aquatic attack on ships possibly on the
6th September.

And later,

[MK]
01/09/2003
... On Tuesday 02/09/2003 there is a meeting to finalise the plans for
an aquatic assault on the ships.

Ben started to chuckle.

'I remember that action,' he said. 'I filmed it, actually. Check
this out.'

He typed something into YouTube and pressed play.

From: Kate Wilson
Date: Tue, 2 Feb 2021 22:25:30
To: Project Hale
Subject: A bit of light relief . . .
Hello all,

I have been asked to consider some of the allegations
of more serious criminality mentioned in the intelligence
reports, such as 'aquatic attacks'. It does sound a bit
serious, so I looked up the specific 'aquatic attack' in
question, which took place in 2003. I found this:

I sent them a link to the three-and-a-half-minute video Ben shot
in 2003. It showed a dozen or so people riding inflatable dragons,
which he recalled had been on sale at Toys 'R' Us.

They launched themselves into Albert Dock in East London in

an attempt to stop a military vessel from docking at the arms fair. An evil-looking police RIB chased them around the harbour. Most of the activists didn't even have paddles, they just used their hands.

'Apparently people were briefly arrested under a by-law banning swimming in Docklands,' my email continued, 'but later released without charge. Four people did spend a day in jail following other actions against the same arms fair, after refusing to pay fines. The judge said that the Defendants were "genuine, highly principled and motivated" and acknowledged that the actions they took part in were important to a democratic society. I suspect that will set the tone for most of what passes for serious crime in the reports.'

At the next Teams meeting, I asked if they had found time to watch the video. I was politely informed that they had. I thought I heard a suppressed giggle. 'The *Mission Impossible* soundtrack was a nice touch,' someone remarked.

* * *

From the second witness statement of Eleanor to the Investigatory Powers Tribunal
The Sumac Centre was an open community centre with a café, a bar and regular public meetings and events. It also had a basement which was primarily used by a vegan catering collective. It was used by hundreds of local people, and was run by volunteers, many of whom were active in a variety of different campaigns – campaigning around environmental issues, animal rights, anti-war, trades unions etc. I was part of the collective that ran the bar there and Kate also volunteered occasionally . . . I recall that I first met [Mark Stone] at the Sumac Centre in Nottingham where I believe I was one of the first people he met in our community . . .

The Serious Organised Crime Authority (SOCA's) report into Mark's operation also spoke about the Sumac Centre. It said: 'At the initial application stage, a detailed intelligence case was submitted that clearly articulated the extremist nature of the identified groups and the associated criminality . . . on a geographic basis as well as targeting extremist elements of specific groups. Nottinghamshire, and in particular the SUMAC centre . . .'

One of Mark Kennedy's RIPA applications, targeting the Sumac Centre, used variations of the word extremism (extreme, extremist, etc.) no fewer than twenty times in four pages.

We tried to explain to the lawyers that while the centre had indeed been a space where activists organised, it wasn't actually an underground bunker housing a military training facility and a factory for making bombs. For many people, it appeared, the actions of the police have an air of legitimacy simply because they are the police. SOCA seemed to take the targeting of the centre seriously, and we could tell it would take more than our word to convince the legal team.

One day, I found a seventeen-minute video shot in February 2004, just as the Metropolitan Police were signing off on Mark Kennedy's continued infiltration of our community. In it, Eleanor and Loukas introduce the Sumac Centre, and escort the viewer around the café, garden projects, catering collective and bar.

It showed the place to be exactly how we remembered it, and as we watched the video with the lawyers, I felt, for the first time, that they were beginning to understand why we felt so strongly that the operations had been an unlawful interference with our rights. A community café where people gathered to discuss politics was deemed a legitimate target for police interference. Was that what democracy looked like?

In early February 2021, the Tribunal indicated that they too thought the question of the legitimacy of the operations was one that needed an answer:

'We consider that the issue . . . is not merely one of proportionality, as conceded by the respondents, but whether or not the interference was in accordance with the law.'

I was crouching on the floor of the Barracks, marker pen in hand. Ben was on the sofa with his laptop balanced on one knee. It was late, but we were both feeling inspired. At last, we not only had a legal team willing to state our case, but also a Tribunal that was prepared to listen. It was time to think seriously.

I wrote 'Justification?' in the middle of a sheet of paper and drew a bubble round it.

'Come on, let's brainstorm. How did they justify it?'

It proved surprisingly difficult to pin down, and we soon realised we were not the only ones to have struggled.

We had a folder full of official reviews and reports about the NPOIU and Mark Kennedy's operation, written by an alphabet soup of organisations. In 2008, the National Coordinator for Domestic Extremism (NCDE) reviewed Mark's operation and noted that there were no recorded 'terms of reference'. They complained that aims and objectives simply evolved as 'roll-on opportunities' presented themselves. Mark's operation was not conducted to 'evidential standards', and there was no apparent corroboration of the intelligence gained.

'Managers spoken to were unable to produce recorded or formal evidence of the value of the investigation,' the report continued. 'The cover officer had difficulty in articulating what "offences" were under investigation, tending to confirm that the focus and style of the infiltration concentrated on ongoing intelligence, rather than crime prevention.'

SOCA complained, in 2011, that 'the NPOIU lacked any form of operational impact or outcome assessment to quantify the success of an operation.' They concluded that the 'lack of any real measure of success or otherwise of the operation makes proportionality in its widest sense difficult to justify to the public'. In fact, both the

NCDE and SOCA reports were secret and internal, never intended to be published. It is likely that it never even occurred to Mark's commanders that they might one day be asked to justify what they were doing to the public at large.

Her Majesty's Inspectorate of Constabulary (HMIC) reported in 2012. It was the only report on my list that had been written for public consumption. Like the other investigations, it noted that 'the lack of specific outcomes makes an objective assessment of success extremely difficult'. Nevertheless, it did make some effort to justify Mark's operation, and it gave a few retrospective examples of its 'success'. Those included the policing of three climate actions: the Kingsnorth Camp for Climate Action, in 2008; an action to stop a coal train at Drax power station in 2009; and a planned action at Ratcliffe-on-Soar power station, also in 2009, which led to the pre-emptive arrests of 114 people (including Mark Stone).

But history had not been kind to the conclusions of the HMIC report. Protestors, including two eleven-year-old twins, brought a legal challenge against the policing of the 2008 Kingsnorth Camp. The operation was criticised by internal policing reviews that specifically identified problems with the handling of intelligence from inside the camp. Police had to pay compensation for unlawful searches of people entering and leaving the area, and there was an overhaul of public order policing in order to avoid repeating the mistakes of Kingsnorth. It was not their finest hour.

The policing of the Drax and Ratcliffe actions had fared no better. Both were well known, and not as successes. The mishandling by the police and the Crown Prosecution Service of Mark Kennedy's involvement in those actions led to miscarriages of justice, with forty-nine convictions overturned and the collapse of the trial of six more.

'Wasn't Mark one of the main people planning both those actions anyway?' I wondered aloud.

'Yes, that's partly why the convictions were overturned,' Ben replied. 'But look here. The NCDE actually raised that issue back in 2008. They say "The profile and role of the UCO in UK-based activities is high . . . He is often the first of a small, trusted group of core conspirators, sometimes no more than two or three persons to discuss and plan future criminality."'

The HMIC report described the direct-action protests against the Ratcliffe-on-Soar and Drax power stations as 'serious crimes', and compared them to racist violence and nail bomb attacks by fascist groups like Combat 18. My first reaction was shock that those non-violent protests against climate change could ever be considered 'serious criminality'. Then it struck me: if they were, it posed a dilemma for the police. Either Mark played a central role in organising serious crime, or they were targeting political protest involving only minor offences – in which case, why was he there at all? They couldn't have it both ways.

I chewed on the end of my marker and looked at what I had written down. With no clear justification for the spying, the other two branches of my spider diagram, 'necessity' and 'proportion-ality', were difficult to assess. Both were relative concepts. The intrusion had to be proportionate to the aims of the operation, and necessity was assessed by looking at whether those aims could be achieved by any other means. Without clear aims to work with, it was all a bit of a blur. Nevertheless, I was increasingly sure that we could demonstrate that the spying had not been necessary in a democratic society.

We collated examples of the seemingly limitless scope of the operations. Reporting about obviously lawful political activity (such as people's attendance at open political meetings and participation in lawful protest) far outweighed reporting of anything resembling crime. Both were overshadowed by the extensive reporting of trivial, or deeply personal details, about people's private lives. Participation in lawful protest was routinely characterised as 'extremism' by the police, without any clear definition of what that meant. Operation Pegasus described 'Source' as living with 'several people known to be involved in extremism'.

That was me, Eleanor, Ronny and Loukas. The police were clearly satisfied that we were exactly the kind of people they should be spying on, yet intelligence and reporting on Mark's housemates indicated that Ronny worked for a vegan catering collective. Loukas was the organiser of a campaign against local Post Office closures and wanted to create a local social forum. Eleanor was made a named target of the operation, but in response to repeated requests, the police lawyers eventually informed us that no intelligence case for that decision was ever made.

Targets of the operation were variously described as 'holding an anarchist perspective' or 'furthering extremist ideology' (which apparently included veganism and wanting post offices to keep serving their communities). One authorisation from 2008 stated that it was very rare for 'collateral intrusion' to occur, because the officer spent the majority of his time with 'like-minded people'. That left little room for doubt that we were targeted for what we believed.

I added 'thought crime' to our brainstorm, followed by 'collateral intrusion'. That was what the police called undercover officers intruding into the lives of innocent bystanders. It sounded like 'collateral damage', as if they thought they were at war.

Several of the authorisations for Mark Kennedy, Lynn Watson and Marco Jacobs claimed that collateral intrusion would be 'minimal', because 'the secretive nature of the subject group is such that any person present during the deployment is within the membership of that group'. Thus anyone who came into contact with the undercover operation was, by definition, a legitimate target. I thought about the reports on my parents, on our family trip to IKEA. I thought about the reports on the death of my nan.

Ben and I presented our ideas to the legal team. They were concerned that we had too many arguments. If we approached the case from so many different perspectives, we risked losing focus. So, Ben suggested we come at it another way.

'Let's start at the beginning. The initial target of Mark's deployment, the Sumac Centre, and the justification for that.'

He turned to the very first RIPA authority for Mark's operation. 'It says here that the Sumac is "a centre used by persons involved in extremism". This is the "detailed intelligence case" that SOCA talked about, but it's really not detailed at all. Unless all they meant was that it contained a lot of words.'

He began highlighting specific bits of the intelligence case.

'It lists groups that meet (or in some cases used to meet) at the Sumac Centre and talks about criminal acts. But it doesn't establish any actual connection between the acts and the groups. It just says "some groups use the Sumac Centre, demonstrations happen in Nottingham, and some people, somewhere, are extremists", as though saying those things in the same sentence somehow establishes a link.'

He traced his finger along a line on the screen, and read a section aloud, 'Northamptonshire Police have experienced difficulties between persons involved in hunting and hunt saboteurs. These difficulties have involved several serious assaults which have been classified as grievous bodily harm.'

I wasn't sure where he was going. GBH actually sounded quite bad. 'They are deliberately vague about who was assaulted,' he clarified, 'The GBH was committed against hunt saboteurs, but that's who they are proposing to spy on.'

I was shocked. Whatever you think about their political beliefs, spying on people for being the victims of crime ought to be a no-go, even for the police.

'They targeted the anti-fascists instead of the racists as well,' Ben said, pointing to where the intelligence case described 'people who oppose extreme right-wing politics'.

'Since when does opposing extreme right-wing politics make you an extremist?'

'Yeah, even the police acknowledge that! Well, kind of. They say, "Anti-fascism is a very sensitive area . . . where people from across the spectrum of the population have protested."'

'Right,' I said. 'World War Two springs to mind.'

'The Peace Movement were extremists too, apparently,' he replied.

I laughed.

'Seriously, look, it is described as "a traditionally extreme left-wing movement". They use the example of that big demonstration in London.'

I nodded, remembering that day in February 2003, when millions of us marched through London in protest against the illegal invasion of Iraq. 'They say peaceful demonstrations took place in Nottingham around the same time. And that's it. Satisfied they have demonstrated the "extremist" nature of something, they go on to say that those entirely peaceful demonstrations "have been supported on occasions by persons known to frequent the Sumac Centre".'

Ben was on a roll. He was reading out extracts from the intelligence case in a voice dripping with sarcasm.

'They talk about an action called Foil the Base. Have you heard of it? Apparently, activists were trying to incapacitate a military base? Although it does say here that a large police presence foiled the protestors' plans.'

He winked, obviously pleased with his dreadful pun. I rolled my eyes.

'Seriously? I was on that demo as well. I think it was organised by CND. We took silver balloons and tinfoil to decorate the fences. It was all very symbolic. We wore tin foil hats!'

It was Ben's turn to roll his eyes.

'Thankfully, the intelligence case leaves that embarrassing detail to the imagination.'

He wrote up his thoughts about that first RIPA authority for the legal team, explaining how the whole justification hinged on the fact that lots of groups and individuals 'used' the Sumac Centre, without mentioning that it was an open community space with a café and bar, where 'using the centre' might simply mean eating a fried breakfast or drinking a beer.

All Mark's future authorisations leant heavily on that initial intelligence case. They used phrases like 'the case remains the same' and cut-and-pasted entire sections from one document to the next. The initial justification was key, because any retrospective outcome of a fishing expedition could not be considered evidence of the need for it in the first place. The decisions would have to have been lawful and justified at the time they were made.

'An open-ended operation like that would almost inevitably encounter some kind of crime eventually, even if it were only by accident,' Ben added. 'If that were a lawful way to conduct undercover operations they would have undercover police officers in every pub.'

'In our community, I think they probably did.' I laughed. Ben reached for his beer.

CHAPTER 33

In February, Holly began work on the witness statements. She asked for a list of women who might be willing to speak out. I put her in touch with Lisa and Eleanor, and said there were others as well.

Like me, Lisa believed in open relationships, provided they were built on honesty and trust. I recalled how, in the twelve months after my relationship with Mark ended, he 'reluctantly' continued to expand his horizons. He and I would meet up for long, friendly dinners in Barcelona or Berlin, and he would tell me about his complicated love life. Despite claiming to be unsure about open relationships, he always seemed to have several women on the go at any one time. Fifteen years later, I was finding their traces in the operational files.

Operation Pegasus – Contact Log (2005)
Monday 21 March
2250 Text from Source. 'Sarah is coming to Belfast as well? Don't know her.'

From the witness statement of Sarah to the Investigatory Powers Tribunal, 9 March 2021
I have been involved in environmental campaigning since 1999 . . . I first recall meeting Mark on the eve of travelling from England to Ireland [in the spring of 2005]; Mark had not initially planned to attend . . . but he offered to be

the driver for the trip . . . Mark flirted with me frequently during this trip . . . we were hugging as we hiked around the hills. It was obvious we were both interested in starting a relationship.

Friday 1 April

Sarah the American girl travelling with Source . . . intends to stay in Clare until next week when she will link up again with Source . . .

From the witness statement of Sarah to the Investigatory Powers Tribunal, 9 March 2021

Soon afterwards I went to visit Mark in Nottingham . . . we began a sexual relationship. I then returned home to Spain . . . Mark communicated with me by telephone and email when we were not together. Despite his primary relationship with 'Lisa', he fostered the relationship with me, and encouraged me to believe that . . . our relationship could be a serious emotional relationship . . .

Friday 6 May

1725 Source received a call from Sarah in Spain. Discussed the visit to Spain in June. Sarah was happy that Source could come over . . . Sarah will travel back with Source . . .

Wednesday 25 May

1700 Me engaged telephone calls re travel to Spain to [EN21] and Sarah . . .

From the witness statement of Sarah to the Investigatory Powers Tribunal, 9 March 2021

Not long after my trip to Nottingham, Mark visited me in Spain. It was a 28-hour bus ride each way, and I knew that Mark was very busy. I remember being swept off my feet, knowing that Mark had made all that effort . . . we had a very intense and sexual week.

Mark Kennedy handwritten police notebook
Saturday 4th to Sunday 5th June engaged re travel to Barcelona. In Barcelona I was picked up by American Food Not Bombs activist Sarah . . . I remained in bed for most of Monday . . . On Friday 10th June 2005, having spent some days in Reus, [others], Sarah and I travelled to L'Ampolla to work clearing the site for the land project. We camped . . . On Monday 13th June to Tuesday 14th June I was engaged in travelling from BCN to the UK with Sarah . . .

Operation Pegasus – Contact Log (2005)
Tuesday 21 June
1720 Call from Source who has received a text from American Sarah inviting Source to stay with her [and others] in Edinburgh. Source is happy with this situation.
1722 [EN107] updated.

From the witness statement of Sarah to the Investigatory Powers Tribunal, 9 March 2021
Mark and I both attended the G8 in July . . . We arrived ahead of other activists and helped build a convergence camp in Stirling.

* * *

Holly worked closely with each of us in turn to draft the statements. She emailed me written questions about my own statement and explained, section by section, what I needed to cover. Section A was the introduction. It set out basic facts about my own background, and the details of my relationship with Mark. It took the deep and turbulent emotions and memories I had navigated since receiving those first disclosure documents, and charted them in simple, matter-of-fact terms: how I got involved in political action, how I met Mark, and what our relationship was like.

'What about after the sexual relationship ended?' Holly asked.

'I didn't see Mark again until the G8 summit in July 2005,' I said. 'Things got a bit weird after that.'

* * *

Katja hummed an ironic 'Happy Birthday' to herself as she unpacked her belongings from the evidence bag: Property of Edinburgh Police. Looking up, she saw Mark, about fifty metres away, walking down a path between the tents.

She had been in Scotland for about four days. Most of her friends had been there longer, working to set up a vast tent-city, known as the 'Eco-village' or the 'Hori-Zone'. Everything was already up and running when she arrived and she felt like an outsider.

Mark was a key part of the organisation, coordinating mini-buses that took protestors to and from actions and events. She had seen him briefly, but the break-up still felt raw and he was busy, so she didn't get a chance to talk to him on his own.

Many of her old friends had become 'their' friends while they were together, and since she left it felt like they had become 'his' friends. It was clear that he had been talking about her. A few people mentioned how hurt he was, and she had an uncomfortable feeling he was playing on the idea that she was a heartbreaker. That seemed unfair: he was at the camp with Lisa and she was there alone.

She found herself keeping away. The camp had many moving parts, so it wasn't hard to avoid him.

The medics' meeting was off-site, in a flat in Edinburgh. When Katja arrived, it had already begun. She gestured a silent apology and sat down. The only face she didn't recognise was introduced as Lynn from Leeds, a thin woman with straight dark hair. The main item was to organise shifts for the medical marquee at the Eco-village, plus roving teams of first aiders to tend to any injured protesters. Katja put her hand up for a street medic crew. They would cover a demonstration in Edinburgh the following day.

That was where she was arrested.

They picked up her whole team, allegedly for 'coordinating riots from a first-aid van'. When the demonstration was over, they released them all without charge. Her co-detainees had been presented with intimidating folders of information about themselves, but the police were surprisingly paternalistic with her.

Some friends drove her back to the camp that evening. She finished unpacking her belongings and folded up the evidence bag, stuffing it into her tent. Then she began putting the laces back into her shoes. As she pushed them through the eyelets, she tried to think it through. It was as if they had no background information about her at all. They seemed to think she was refusing to answer their questions because she was being threatened. It was very odd. They even asked who in the first-aid group had 'got to her'. She felt quite offended at that. If she hadn't resolved not to talk at all, she might have given them a piece of her mind.

* * *

Gisted RIPA Review – June 2005
Operation ▉▉▉▉▉▉▉▉
Operational Head Comments
I directly manage this operation. As previously detailed within the review for [operation name]. ['Lynn Watson'] has worked extremely hard in this review period to build upon their existing legend and infiltrate both CIRCA [the 'Clandestine Insurgent Rebel Clown Army'] and the Action Medic Network. ['Watson'] has been invited by the Action Medics to

provide coverage during the forthcoming summit which offers us an excellent opportunity to obtain details of their [indecipherable] communication and numbers involved [indecipherable] all of which are priority issues for the [operation name] intelligence cell . . . [Signed by EN107, dated 27 June 2005]

There was nothing in the disclosure to throw any real light on what happened at the G8. All I knew was that despite avoiding Mark, I still ended up spending time with an undercover cop. The arrest in Edinburgh made very little sense. Lynn had definitely been at the meeting the day before. She knew we weren't coordinating anything, we were just there to offer first aid. So why did the police arrest the medics? Indeed, what were the police doing infiltrating a first-aid group at all?

Soon after the Edinburgh demonstration, there was an outbreak of diarrhoea at the Eco-village. It began after the police closed access to the camp on 7 July, under the Prevention of Terrorism Act. Five thousand people were trapped on the campsite, and they wouldn't let anyone in or out, including the pump-trucks that emptied the toilets. When people started to get sick, it spread fast.

Had Lynn been in the meetings where the medics team gave out instructions about handwashing, and what people should do if they felt unwell? Did she help us set up treatment marquees and sort out saline drips, or tally the numbers of people falling ill as a result of the police blockade? Was she reporting our health and safety concerns to her superiors? Was she gloating to them about how the sickness was breaking our morale?

Possibly not. She may have been off by then, painting her face and priming her squirty flower, preparing to move in on her other official target group.

Mark Kennedy, meanwhile, was sleeping with two different women at the camp. He was openly together with Lisa, but he also took time to encourage and nurture his relationship with Sarah.

There were at least five other undercover officers at the Stirling Eco-village, from both of the principal spycops units, the SDS and the NPOIU. Several of them were working closely with Mark in the transport team. He can't have believed that his behaviour would go unnoticed. If he really had thought (as his superiors claimed) that he might be disciplined for what he was doing, he was sailing very close to the wind.

'Well,' Holly said carefully, when I had finished my account of the G8 summit, 'that could all be really useful. But we need to set it out as evidence, and let the Tribunal draw their own conclusions.'

CHAPTER 34

'Evidence' meant setting aside our emotions and opinions and sticking to the facts. The way we were reading the files was changing, as we stopped focusing on specific events and memories and began looking past them, in search of patterns and themes. We began to notice meta information in the contact logs, such as the way certain sections were highlighted, or notes were added for the attention of the SIO, suggesting that the logs must have been passed up the chain of command. There was also a surprising amount of financial information littered among the calls and texts from Source.

Wednesday 14 July
'£20 food kitty and £1.80 toll. Let me know a time to meet tomorrow. All well here, speak tomorrow.'

Friday 23 July
1311hrs Text 'Non receipted cash. £12 on 22nd lunch and legend, £6 on 23rd launderette and lunch £5. All OK just hanging out ▮▮▮▮▮▮▮▮

Saturday 24 July
2032 hrs. Text. '£14 cash no receipt for evening meal.'

Wednesday 28 July
1350 Call . . . £8 unreceipted Kitchen fund.

Monday 23 August
0952 Text from Source. '£7.26 bread and milk etc.'

Reading these little notes, I had a sudden flashback to Mark slipping receipts into his glove compartment for his 'tax return'.

In one of his *Daily Mail* interviews in 2011, he claimed that his operation cost £200,000 a year in expenses alone. He described how handlers drove around in expensive cars. 'They had seven . . . If we all had a meeting it looked like the CIA had turned up or something – seven identical flash cars in the car park of a pub.'

What he didn't mention was how his handlers were bean counting, right down to the last tin of Heinz. The logs were filled with references to expenses and operational finances. I had a sudden vision of EN31 as a balding man in a grubby shirt, who worried about his blood pressure and spent his days making spreadsheets of overtime and expenses, on a laptop, in a Holiday Inn.

It dawned on me that secrecy created an aura of glamour and mystery around the unit that probably wasn't deserved. It was unlikely that slick bad guys in sharp suits ran surveillance from expensive cars with blacked out windows. Let's face it, this was Britain, and the Metropolitan Police.

Then we hit on something interesting.

Operation Pegasus - Contact Log (2006)
Wednesday 26 April
Time now GMT +1 hour
1530 . . . met Source from the ferry . . . Then to Amsterdam.
. . .
2010 Whilst with Source, Source received a text message from [a woman] saying that she was at Central Station and could they meet to find some accommodation together. Source then left us to meet with [her].
2235 Call from Source who has booked into a hostel at 69 Singel

DISCLOSURE

Amsterdam . . .
2346 Text from Source. 'All OK. Still out will call tomorrow'

Thursday 27 April
0915 Call from Source. Caught up on news. Very interesting. 40 euros
last night out with [the woman].

It took a bit of searching, but I managed to track the woman
down, and she also made a witness statement. She told me about
the sexual relationship she had with Mark, from late 2005 until
the spring of 2006. They would meet up at activist events around
Europe.

'The hotel stay was Mark's idea. I would not have been able to
afford a hotel at the time.'

We already knew that Mark spent public funds on developing
his sexual relationships: he had given me a mobile phone and a
bicycle. However, the fact that his handler recorded him spending
public money on a shared hotel room and a night out with a
woman, without question or comment, seemed like a new level.

It was evident that the camp against the 2005 G8 summit in
Scotland had not been an exception. During key moments, such as
overseas deployments and action camps, which were closely moni-
tored by his cover officers and where senior managers were taking a
special interest, Mark Kennedy was often sleeping with more than
one woman, and maybe charging it to his police expenses account.

From the witness statement of Sarah to the Investigatory Powers Tribunal

Mark often expressed his love and stressed how important
I was to him . . . Open relationships were not uncommon
in the environmental movement in the UK at this time, and
there was no attempt to keep our relationship secret . . . Lisa
also knew about our relationship.

In the spring of 2006, Mark again came to visit me, accompanied by Lisa and a few others who all stayed at my house. I had helped Mark to organise a speaking tour in relation to the Saving Iceland group . . . we went together to a couple of the events I had helped him to set up locally.

It was clear that Mark could be quite nasty about the women he deceived:

Saturday 8 April
1045 Call from Source . . . Sarah is such a control freak. She had told them to stay in the room she said they could stay in and not wander about the building . . . Source told her that Source did not realise it was a fascist squat.

I also noticed that, after we separated in 2005, his tone changed when he talked about me from admiration to irritation:

Sunday 12 June (2005)
1145 Call from Source. Katja has called Source and is unhappy because Source has been to Spain and not looked her up. Source explained that Source had been busy and had not had time . . . I told Source that I would be keen for Source to meet with Katja as she had been a good contact for us in the past and she still had excellent contacts throughout Europe.

Monday 13 June (2005)
0013
Text from Source
'. . . Have sorted Katja's life out for her again . . .'
I asked if Katja was staying with Source and what was the situation with Sarah . . .
1017 Call from Source . . . Source bought Katja dinner last night whilst

she discussed her problems and life situations.

Monday 10th October (2005)
1050 Call from Source ... Had beers and pizza with the depressed Katja last night ... Katja may go off to Australia herself. Source comment 'depends which way the wind is blowing at the time'. Source will be able to replace Katja as contact in Berlin with [another woman] who respects sources abilities ... The Iceland talk has fallen through because Katja was too laid back and lazy to put it on the agenda.

Tuesday 11 October (2005)
1230 Call from source ... Source said that Katja has become a nightmare, she ... has no energy for anything.

The trip to Barcelona in the spring of 2006 was no exception:

Friday 7 April (2006)
Source had a call from Katja who asked for sources eta in Barcelona. She said she was ever so busy and could only fit them in between 4 and 7. Source said this was typical Katja where everything has to revolve around her. Source told her that they were also busy and that if they could not meet then so be it.

I felt wrong-footed and taken aback. I contacted John and Eleanor and asked about what happened after I left the UK. They said Mark had obviously been upset by me leaving, but that he had also told my friends I was unstable and that he was worried about my mental health. That surprised me, but it made some sense. By manipulating the way our mutual friends saw me, and making me feel guilty for breaking his heart, he left me isolated. I was living far away so I didn't always notice, but I had definitely felt it in July 2005, at the G8 protest camp.

A few months after the awkwardness at the G8, Mark reached

out, presumably because his operation required it. He came to visit me in Berlin and he made a point of staying in touch after that. It was clear from the contact logs that he didn't like me very much. Nevertheless, he went out of his way to make himself my principal link with the UK.

I went back and read his emails from that trip. They were affectionate and emotional, with no trace of his obvious disdain:

From: Mark Stone
Date: Thu, 02 Mar 2006 10:01:12 +0000 (GMT)
To: Katja
Subject: wow!
Wow! you know how to make a boys heart jump. Well you got yourself a date, I'll be in Madrid from about the 22nd March and am driving home from BCN on about the 10th April . . .

Life is good, been doing some cool stuff, with the campaign, but we can chat about that when i see you . . . Looking forward to being back in Spain, Lisa hopes to be coming as well . . . Looking forward to seeing you beautiful girl,

Love Love Love,

MarkXXXXXXXXXXXXXXX

The contact logs also revealed that despite his irritable comments to his handler, Mark did meet me that evening in Barcelona, and mindful of how busy I was, he made a point of showing up on time.

Saturday 8 April
1640 Text from Source. 'Tonight talk at Casi Casa, near the Guinardo metro station. All ok talking to Katja.'

DISCLOSURE

I listened as he told me about his relationship problems, with Lisa and Sarah both on the tour. I affectionately told him that he was making a bit of a mess of things, and that people were going to get hurt if he wasn't careful. To me, it was a lovely evening, spent with my friend and ex-lover. I thought I had it all figured out.

On 11 April we left Barcelona for the UK: me, Mark, Lisa and another friend. The atmosphere was light; perhaps they found it a relief to be leaving the tensions of the previous days behind. We had fun on the drive to Bilbao. On the long overnight ferry ride, I remember sitting together in the bar, watching for whales and dolphins in the Bay of Biscay.

Mark didn't see Sarah after that. She later told me that she found out he had been telling her friends she was needy, mentally unstable and difficult. She broke up with him, and never spoke to him again.

I wondered what I would have done if I had known then that he was saying similar things about me.

My neck ached. I realised I had been clenching my fists and holding my breath. 'I need to clear my head.'

Ben barely looked up from the files. I slipped out of the Barracks and made my way across the garden and into the field. The landscape was dusky. Behind the clouds, the sun was already low: I had missed the day again.

Long strides and the rhythmic crunch of frozen grass steadied my inner turmoil a little. I was angry at what I was reading, but also at myself. My failure to notice things at the time meant he had gone on and done it to other women. It must have got easier every time.

The thin tape of an electric fence was barely visible in the low evening light. Gingerly I stepped over, watched by a dozen sheep of different shapes and sizes. I walked more slowly. A few scattered as I approached but others came ambling over, to see if I had brought them anything.

As always, Badger was the first. By far the boldest of the bunch, his face, with its black, brown and white stripes, was instantly recognisable. The others kept their distance, but he nuzzled my hip and let me bury my hands in the oily wool of his back. I breathed in his musty smell of lanolin and grass and sighed, sitting down on a hillock.

'I just thought Mark couldn't disappoint me any more, you know?'

That was the truth of it: I was dismayed to find that I still had illusions about my ex-lover. I probably couldn't have admitted it to anyone except the sheep.

After Mark was outed, there had been a series of shocks: the day I found out he was a cop, of course, but also later on, when I learnt he was married; when I read the press interviews he gave in early 2011 and realised that I didn't know the man who had the face of my old friend. Those were all pivotal moments, but they were a long time ago. I thought I had come to terms with what he was. Yet reading the logs and the other women's statements turned my stomach. Despite everything, I found myself unprepared.

Badger thrust his proud Roman nose into my shoulder. I gave him a final scratch and stood up, stretching the cold out of my limbs and causing a minor stampede.

I bowed slightly to the flock.

'Thank you for listening.'

It was fully dark when I picked my way back across the field, towards the rectangles of yellow light spilling from the house.

CHAPTER 35

From the first witness statement of 'Lisa' to the Investigatory Powers Tribunal

My relationship with Mark started off quite casually. Then in early 2005, Kate moved abroad, and Mark began spending more time with me . . . Mark told me he was in Thailand in late December 2004 . . . When he returned he told me of his harrowing and gruesome experiences there (such as helping with the relief effort and discovering the dead body of a child), and we became closer in the aftermath with him opening up to me about this and me providing him with emotional support.

From the second witness statement of Eleanor to the Investigatory Powers Tribunal

I lived with Mark when he and 'Lisa' first got together, and I recall talking to him about their relationship . . . I remember Mark telling me that he fancied 'Lisa', and I know that they got together on a camping trip in the Lake District in September 2004 . . . They started off fairly casually . . . by the time of the Festival of Dissent in April 2005, they were very much in love . . . They were very obviously a couple from then on. I clearly remember talking to 'Lisa' about her relationship with Mark and knowing how serious it was. Mark also told me of his dedication to her and absolute love for her.

They remained very happily a couple for many years. Everyone knew they were together. They went on a number of holidays together . . . I would have described 'Lisa' and Mark as life partners, and I expected them to be together for a very long time.

From the first witness statement of 'Lisa' to the Investigatory Powers Tribunal
From around April / May 2005 to October 2010 Mark and I spoke almost every day, either on the phone or by email.

'Lisa' Exhibit 1: email from Mark to Lisa 2 October 2005
hey beautiful girl, just wanted to email you to tell you how much I love you. Which is lots and lots and lots. In fact I could not even imagine quantifying it, that would just be wrong, it's just a wonderful lovely thing that grows and grows . . .

From the first witness statement of 'Lisa' to the Investigatory Powers Tribunal
When we met up we would do all the normal things that couples do . . . My friends reacted well to our relationship. Mark was charming and became well-liked . . . He became friends with everyone I was friends with . . . Our relationship quickly became very close . . .

I had wondered how Lisa would be able to capture all those years of shared life and intimacy in a witness statement. The answer was immediately obvious: you can't.

Most of the text had clearly been taken from the original statement she made in 2011, written by our lawyers in the aftermath of the discovery, just when her life was falling apart. It had been reduced even further, by necessity, to fit the task at hand; and yet, as a ship in a bottle evokes the vastness of the ocean, little details in her statement somehow conveyed the immensity of what she had been through.

As a witness, rather than a claimant, Lisa was not granted the same kind of evidence in disclosure that I was. She was not given the full contact logs and notes for the years she and Mark were together, only disjointed extracts, where she was specifically mentioned by name. It also appeared, from the disclosure we had, that the police became more careful about how things got written down shortly after my relationship with Mark ended. We could tell we were not seeing everything that was there. Nevertheless, the logs showed similar evidence of a close and romantic relationship with 'Lisa' as they had with me.

Sunday 23rd July 2006
2050
Call from Source who is at [Lisa's] where she is cooking using her new pots ████████████████████████████████ ████████████████ Source may be going to the pictures with [Lisa] . . .

'Mark bought me those pots when I moved into my new flat in 2006,' she told me. 'They were expensive, Le Creuset. I still use them.'

It was the kind of gift we knew the operation used to gain favour, to 'increase the bond'. No policy decision to buy cookware for Lisa was ever disclosed, but Mark mentions the pots to his handler, and the police considered it necessary to redact part of what he said about the gift, seemingly because it was tradecraft – a 'sensitive technique'.

The logs also showed how Mark spent time with Lisa's family, and how they travelled together in the summer of 2006.

Tuesday 22 August
Source is going with 'Lisa' [and one other] to the Earth First gathering in Wales via Worcester and Kidderminster to collect tents.

Wednesday 23 August
1510 Call from Source . . . This evening Source is going to Lisa's brothers house 15 miles NE of the camp and will stay there overnight . . .

The following week was the Camp for Climate Action, which would be targeting the Drax coal-fired power station – a single point in Yorkshire that on its own emitted more carbon that year than many countries.

The 31 August 2006 was a day of action. Mark, Lisa, Lynn Watson and I were all part of a group that planned to get into the complex, and maybe get up on the coal buckets. The plan was to shut the place down, if only for one day. We wanted to inspire people to think big, stop talking about the politicians and start physically disrupting the root causes of climate change.

Operation Pegasus – Contact Log (2006)
Wednesday 30 August
2138 Text from Source. 'We leave at 9 then split off when possible my part is to distract the security guards . . .' I text Source to confirm that Source would not be involved in getting onto the bucket itself.
2211 Text from Source. 'Yes minor role'
2220 Text from Source. 'Ok, there are a number of groups determined to get in . . . get onto the bucket and not damage it.'

Thursday 31 August
0809 Text from Source. 'Morning, all ok, 7 people already inside'
EN21 sent a text asking if spirits in the camp were high.
0818 Text from Source. 'Very'

Just over two hours later his tone had changed:

1041 Text from Source 'Beaten up very bad and nicked . . . Broken fingers, lots of blood on head. Nicked for assault.'

I text Source saying 'Keep me updated, be as calm as possible, don't give them any excuses.'

1046 Text from Source. 'Going to local nick then I want a hospital'

I text Source saying that custody would have to send them to hospital and that I would arrange what I could from my end.

1120 From DI Hutcheson. Source has been arrested for criminal damage and assault.

1140 From DI Hutcheson the allegation is that Source punched a PC and cut his lip. May be charged for court tomorrow.

Friday 1 September

1024 Text from Source 'Morning the boot marks on my back are showing now'

1038 Text from Source 'Leaving today staying in Leeds overnight' . . .

Lisa will be leaving the site with Source tonight

1205 DI Hutcheson updated.

From the first witness statement of 'Lisa' to the Investigatory Powers Tribunal

At the Climate Camp at Drax Power Station, which we attended together in August 2006, Mark was badly injured by the police and was taken to hospital in police custody. I have been shown Mark's own notes on his injuries following this event, which reflect my recollection. I was very worried about him and, as soon as he was released from police custody and hospital, I took him back to my flat . . . he stayed with me for the night, and I took care of him. He left the next day. I remember protesting that he was going back to work too soon when he clearly needed looking after . . .

Friday 1 September
1904 Text from Source 'The bath water was red after I washed my hair'
. . .
Saturday 2 September
1300 Met with Source at a safe location near Leeds.

Mark Kennedy was arrested twice at the 2006 Camp for Climate Action, once on Tuesday 29 August, after locking himself to the gates of a nuclear power plant in Hartlepool; and again, two days later, outside the fence at Drax, for criminal damage and assault.

His managers must have been watching when he left that Camp with Lisa, still covered in his own blood. It's hard to imagine how they were able to leave their fallen officer alone and injured, with only his surveillance target for company – unless, of course, they knew full well that she was harmless, and that he would be safe.

Wednesday 13 September
1750
Meeting with O-50, O-97, O-28 & O-23

[The redacted text concerns discussions about the need to remove MK from deployment immediately]

I explained ███████████████████ Source was returning to number 5 and that Source had Katja staying there.
. . .
1904 Call from Source. Long discussion re the above situation and instructions. Reason for leaving suddenly discussed.
. . .
2022 Call from Source who was obviously in a bad way as far as the

way in which the whole incident had been managed, resulting in the situation that we had now placed Source.

. . .

2337 Text from Source. 'Explanation that my mother is seriously ill has gone down ok, but everyone is concerned and Katja wanted to come to Portugal with me.'

For ten days, we – Mark's girlfriend and his ex-girlfriend – looked after him. Then he and his handler concocted a lie about his mother being taken ill abroad and pulled him out.

On 22 September 2006 it is recorded that Commander Gormley granted Mark conditional authority to recommence communication with subjects of the operation by phone or email. In fact, he never lost touch.

'Lisa' Exhibit 1: email from Mark to Lisa: 18/09/2006 10:30
Hi lovely girl . . . Mum is ok to travel they are still not sure but it looks like she has had a bit of a relapse again. I think the panic thing hit her which made it appear a lot worse. Still it is all a bit worrying as I know you understand. She is booked in with her own hospital when we get back to Ireland. I'll be out there for a bit to sort everything out. I'll get an Irish phone number so you can chat to me then . . . Miss you so much sweetheart,
Love and hugs,
Mark Xxxx

From the first witness statement of 'Lisa' to the Investigatory Powers Tribunal
I had a six-year relationship with a man who I believed was open and honest with me; I believed him to be my primary partner, my best friend, my future. I believed he was a like-minded person with whom I had a lot in common. I loved

him so deeply, in a way I am not confident I will experience again. However, my partner turned out to be leading a double life, and was not in fact the person I believed him to be at all, but the opposite in many ways, and he was placed in my life to deceive me by an employer who would inevitably one day pull him out.

On 18 October 2006, EN31 filed an update to the use and conduct authority for Mark Kennedy to resume 'full physical contact with the subjects', after over a month of absence. In the following weeks they kept a close eye on him.

From the first witness statement of 'Lisa' to the Investigatory Powers Tribunal

It was known by many others in our political and social community that we were in a relationship; we would kiss and hold hands in public, and stay in the same tent at festivals and protest camps. When I was staying in Nottingham, it was well known that I stayed with him in his house, and others from within our community would come over for dinner whilst I was there. When Mark stayed with me at Cornerstone, it was obvious to those living in the house (about 14 people) and to anyone popping over that Mark was staying in my room. When I moved out of Cornerstone, it was widely known that Mark stayed with me at my flat . . . whenever he was in Leeds.

Operation Pegasus – Contact Log (2006)
Thursday 23 November
I again reiterated to Source DI Hutcheson's instructions to spend less time in Leeds and that I had been instructed to contact DI Hutcheson every time there seemed to be a need for Source to go to Leeds.

After Drax it appeared that Mark's commanding officers may have made a half-hearted attempt to stop his relationships. The prohibition was being 'reiterated' so it was evidently not the first time it had come up. We have not seen the original instruction, and DI Hutcheson's reasons for the prohibition were not revealed, but the implications are clear.

From the first witness statement of 'Lisa' to the Investigatory Powers Tribunal

Mark met my family . . . They were devastated to learn of Mark's true identity. Most notably, Mark supported me through my father's illness and death in 2006 . . . Mark met my extended family at my father's funeral . . . he intruded on my family's private grief . . . I asked him to attend the scattering of my father's ashes, but he said he couldn't get the time off work . . . I had wanted him to be there with me.

Operation Pegasus – Contact Log (2007)

Tuesday 8 May

1535 Call from Source who has been invited by [Lisa] to assist her to take some of her elderly relatives up to the mountains of Wales to spread the ashes of her recently deceased father on the 26th May. I advised Source that the term collateral intrusion immediately came to mind. The spreading of her father's ashes with her close relatives is a highly personal and private matter and that although Source was considered to be a close friend by [Lisa] that it was an intrusion into their private lives that should be avoided at all costs. Source said that they had left the door open but had intimated that they would be away at the time and may not be able to change it. Source will not attend.

Both the prohibition on spending time in Leeds and the entry about the scattering of ashes were highlighted in red in the contact logs, for the attention of Mark's superior officers. He was subjected to an increased use of 'technical' (GPS tracking) to determine his location during that period, suggesting that his managers might sometimes have doubted him.

Lisa and Mark went on a number of holidays together, some of which are recorded in the logs as 'Rest Days', meaning that Mark was officially off-duty, but he was still pretending to be Mark Stone. His managers knew about that as well.

SOCA (Serious Organised Crime Agency) Review of Undercover Deployment in support of HMIC review of the National Domestic Extremism Unit, 2011

KENNEDY also spent significant amounts of time in recreational activities with subjects of his infiltration and other activists. This included holidays, walking and climbing excursions, entertaining, attending social functions and co-habiting for both short term and extended periods. There is also evidence that on occasion KENNEDY spent rest days with activists.

One such holiday was a cycling trip Mark and Lisa took across Denmark, on the way to the 2007 G8 summit in Germany:

Operation Pegasus - Contact Log (2007)

Wednesday 30 May

1540 Text from Source. 'Cycling is the way forward. Customs called me sir and waved me through at the front of the queue wishing me a happy holiday.'

1737 Text from Source. 'On board'

Thursday 31 May

1158 Text from Source. 'Calm seas and lovely sun good book and ok coffee. All ok here.'

. . .

1326 Text from Source. 'At Esbjerg'

. . .

1609 Text from Source. 'All going well, last train journey then cycling to coast to camp somewhere'
1611 I text Source. 'Excellent thanks for that let me know eta into Rostock when you can'
2123 Text from Source. 'All ok 80 k ride. Pitching up tent. About the same tomorrow to Gedser.'
2128 I text Source. 'Amazing!'

These entries are remarkable because they imply that Mark was travelling alone, although Lisa was there, and his handler obviously knew:

Sunday 3 June
1032 I text Source 'Thanks matey. Keep in touch when safe to do so'
1117 Text from Source. 'Leaving for Reddlich in 10 minutes.'
1119 I text Source. 'Good thanks mate. Is that with others or just Lisa'
1120 Text from Source. 'Just L. But others are making their own way.'

The cagey and inaccurate reporting of who Mark was with implied there was an awareness among his handlers that what he was doing could blow up in their faces. Perhaps there was an operational decision to cover up the relationship. Or perhaps Mark was effectively out of control, and they just hoped that he would calm down of his own accord.

Shortly after that trip in 2008, Operation Pegasus was externally reviewed by SO15, Counter Terrorism Command. Their report appeared to raise concerns about the quality of Mark's evidence, pointing to the 'length of time the operation has been running with no investigative/evidence gathering strategy'. It referred to authorities being granted according to 'a locally adopted system . . . in contravention of the UCO standards manual' (no copy of this obviously important document was ever provided). The review noted that Mark's intelligence could not possibly be used as evidence, and highlighted that it was 'imperative to undertake work to corroborate and test the veracity of the information' he was providing. It also noted that Mark had a '"blanket" authoriza- tion for participation in crime' and noted that this raised 'concern regarding the ongoing management of this policy as the UCO is often in the company of others when conducting activities that may be problematic when numerous arrests are made for minor crime.' (This was a prophetic comment, as Mark was arrested just a few months later, alongside 113 people while planning an occupation of Ratcliffe-on-Soar power station, leading to the police and the Crown Prosecution Service effectively colluding to conceal his role from the Criminal Court and the Defence). Despite all this, the conclusion of Mark's managers was to extend his deployment beyond its natural end:

Association of Chief of Police Officers of England, Wales and Northern Ireland
Council Committee on Terrorism and Allied Matters
National Coordinator Domestic Extremism - Minute Sheet
11 August 2008

The original Operation Pegasus commenced in April 2003 and is an infiltration of extreme left wing groups which (to date) now includes:

... The UCO is an experienced police officer with 23 years service, married with children. He/She is trained as a climbing expert inclu- sive of Policed rope access training, a qualified driver with 5 years

DISCLOSURE

Tactical Support Group driving experience, ███████████████
███████████████████████████████ In addition he has training
in ███
███

. . .

In legend, the UCO is engaged in a 'lifestyle' method of infiltration regarding these groups, and lives an open life within the community and anarchist networks . . . Operation Pegasus should have reached conclusion in 2008 as this would have represented a 5 year deployments period. The operation and deployment has been extended until 2010 with MPS support and review of health and safety of the UCO.

Everything that happened after that date is firmly on the heads of those senior officers who decided to keep him in.

CHAPTER 36

From the second witness statement of Eleanor to the Investigatory Powers Tribunal

In late 2008, I was single, and I recall that Mark began flirting with me. He took me out to a punk gig and we got very drunk, and afterwards we slept together. I knew that we would not get into an involved relationship, as he was so intensely involved with 'Lisa' at the time. I was also disappointed that our long and close friendship did not seem to translate into a strong intimate connection. However, we continued to sleep together in an occasional manner for around nine months. We were never 'in a relationship' but were friends who had sex and (I thought) cared for each other.

My friends in Nottingham knew about our sexual relationship. We made no attempt to hide it, and I recall us kissing in the public bar at the Sumac Centre. As I explained above, our political community was very close and often gossiped, so I expect that many in our community in Nottingham would have known . . . Indeed, that is why somebody called me to tell me that Mark was an undercover police officer on the morning after he was exposed. 'Lisa' also knew about it and I think it likely that her and my mutual friends in Leeds would also have known about it. My sexual relationship with Mark ended when I got together with someone else in the summer of 2009.

DISCLOSURE

* * *

Eleanor and I didn't see much of each other that year, but I did run into Mark in January 2009, at a meeting in Strasbourg. He didn't mention that he had been seeing her. Instead, he told me he had always held a candle for me. If I wanted to, he said, we could rekindle the spark. He also spoke urgently about how he had been in secret meetings learning to make incendiary devices. He invited me to join him.

I declined both offers. I recall, even then, feeling quite worried about my friend. He was behaving erratically and showing signs of paranoia.

When I first met the other women in our court case, Helen, Alison and Rosa all described how the men they had been with – John Dines, Mark Jenner and Jim Boyling – appeared to suffer intense mental breakdowns in the final months of their deployment. Mark was no different. From mid-2009, his mental health appeared to deteriorate.

It seems that feigning mental illness was a key part of their 'exit strategy'; and there was a twisted logic to that. It allowed them to leave the relationships and disappear without raising questions about who they really were. But there was a shiver of something cold and inhuman in it too. Sent to live a lie for years at a time, chipping away their moral compass and their sense of self, these men were then ordered to fake a breakdown, at a time when cracking up might be the only performance they had the resources left to give.

Whatever the truth of that, the distress it caused their partners was very real, and lasted long after they disappeared.

* * *

From the first witness statement of 'Lisa' to the Investigatory Powers Tribunal
In around April 2009, Mark was involved in the planning of an action to occupy Ratcliffe-on-Soar power station. A meeting he attended was raided by the police and subsequently Mark's home was searched . . . After, Mark started to become very agitated and stressed and I spent time caring for his mental and physical well being. Over the following months, Mark appeared to have some form of mental breakdown. He became very paranoid and was always looking over his shoulder. I was extremely worried about him.

From the second witness statement of Eleanor to the Investigatory Powers Tribunal
Throughout their relationship, 'Lisa' would visit Nottingham regularly, and I would see her then. She moved to Nottingham in 2009 to spend more time with Mark . . . I saw 'Lisa' look after Mark in 2009 as he seemed to have a breakdown, and I saw how worried she was about him.

From the first witness statement of Sir Stephen House, Annex 4
[Mark Kennedy's] withdrawal strategy commenced after April 2009 and his arrest at Ratcliff-on-Soar Power Station.

26/10/2009 Application for authority to renew Operation Pegasus [for one week] for the minimum activity necessary to extricate Kennedy from the deployment safely. Authority to participate in criminal activity is removed as Kennedy will not physically deploy . . . 'MK told the activists that they were leaving the UK for the USA to join family relatives as he was annoyed and frustrated that activists had implicated him in the Ratcliffe-on-Soar operation.'

From the first witness statement of 'Lisa' to the Investigatory Powers Tribunal

In October 2009, Mark told me that he was going to visit his brother in America, but did not give any idea as to when he would be back. He sold his car, packed up his house and was in an agitated state. I was extremely worried; I didn't know if he was ever going to come back and I was very concerned that he might deliberately cause harm to himself. We stayed in regular contact by Skype calls whilst Mark was away and he visited me once, at the end of November 2009, saying that he'd had to come back from the US for something work related. He asked me not to tell anyone he was in the country. In January 2010, Mark returned and announced that he had bought a narrow boat.

From the first witness statement of Sir Stephen House, Annex 4

Request for cancellation of authority to deploy Kennedy as part of Operation Pegasus is granted by ACC Ackerley on 10/02/2010. A summary of the intelligence case and his withdrawal strategy is set out and notes, in particular, that Kennedy has provided an 'immense amount of pre emptive intelligence over the last 7 years to many police forces. The intelligence has formed the basis of numerous policing operations.' His withdrawal strategy commenced after April 2009 . . . Before his return to his police force, he will be fully de-briefed and a final risk assessment completed.

From the first witness statement of 'Lisa' to the Investigatory Powers Tribunal

I had moved onto my own narrow boat the previous January. Together, we brought his boat to Nottingham from Lincoln, where he had bought it. Initially Mark did not want to be seen in public, or let anyone know where he lived but, by the end of February 2010, he was beginning to be more comfortable and seemed less on edge about being seen . . . During this period Mark appeared to be depressed and confused about his career options. He was behaving erratically, for example he had dramatic mood swings and often changed his plans at the last minute. He also started a relationship with another woman . . . but he wasn't honest with me about that relationship in the way that I had come to expect . . . I believed in open relationships provided they were built on honesty and trust; they do not work when there is no trust, and Mark's [other] relationship was confusing and destabilising . . .

NPOIU Intelligence Report (2010)
5x5x5 Information Intelligence Report Form A - 04/08/2010
ORGANISATION AND OFFICER [O-148]
EARTH FIRST GATHERING 31/07/2010 - ATTENDEE 'MARK'
At the Earth First Gathering beginning on 31/07/2010 at Ashbourne, Derbyshire there were several people that helped set the camp up. Mark a white male, 5'8"-10" tall, mid to late 30's, of thin build. He had earrings, multiple tattoos, long brown hair worn in a ponytail and a goatee beard . . . He is married to another one of the organisers . . .
NPOIU Comment: Mark piw Mark STONE DOB 07/07/1969

That was new. Reporting about people's relationships (one-night stands, partners, break-ups, even childcare arrangements) was very common in the police reporting. When Mark gave evidence to the Home Affairs Select Committee, in 2013, he claimed, 'I was not the only person deployed . . . [there were] other undercover officers. There are also many informants within the environment that I was working in . . . So where Mark Stone lived, who his girlfriend might have been, what car he drove, was all intelligence that I am sure was coming into various different police departments around the UK.'

DISCLOSURE

Yet 'Mark Stone' began his first relationship in 2003, and the first intelligence we saw mentioning a partner was filed in July 2010.

It was inaccurate. Mark wasn't married to the activist. Nevertheless, they *were* in a relationship. It was frankly remarkable to find any reference to Mark Stone's romantic attachments at all.

The reason for the change in reporting seemed to be that, in March 2010, Mark Kennedy became a civilian.

From the first witness statement of Sir Stephen House
MK was a former Metropolitan Police Service officer who in April 2003 and thereafter at all material times until his resignation on 16 March 2010, was seconded to the National Public Order Intelligence Unit ("NPOIU") under the pseudonym of "Mark Stone".

Mark Kennedy resigned from the police in March. So why was Mark Stone still hanging out with us in July?

* * *

The *Guardian*, Thursday 13 January 2011
Mark Kennedy: secret policeman's sideline as corporate spy
The undercover police officer whose unmasking led to the collapse of a trial of six environmental protesters on Monday apparently also worked as a corporate spy, according to documents seen by the *Guardian*.
Details of how Mark Kennedy went from police officer to businessman reveal the extent to which shadowy corporate firms appear to have developed links with the police . . .
From 2003 until around March last year, Kennedy lived in the midst of the protest movement with the fake identity Mark Stone. Remarkably, he appears to have used that same undercover identity . . . to venture into private practice . . .
. . . [A] friend of Kennedy said the implication he went on

to work for private security firms 'fits perfectly' with his behaviour. Kennedy was becoming agitated and, unusually for someone who earned the nickname 'Flash' for his impressive wealth, he started running out of money around the time he resigned.

. . . But if Kennedy was seeking to use the fake identity provided by police to continue his life as a spy, there was one crucial obstacle: he would almost certainly have had to hand in his fake driving licence and passport, meaning he would need to travel abroad under his real name . . .

From the first witness statement of 'Lisa' to the Investigatory Powers Tribunal
In July 2010, Mark and I went on holiday together to Italy, where we attended an animal rights gathering to give a climbing workshop. One day, whilst we were up in the mountains together, and Mark was on a bike ride, I found . . . a passport which had expired in 2008, which was in the name of Mark Kennedy. The passport referred to Mark Kennedy having a dependent. I also found a mobile phone, on which there were messages from what appeared to be two children referring to Mark as 'Dad'. I was in a state of extreme shock, and did not know what to think . . . I was scared to approach Mark for fear of what I might uncover, particularly whilst I was alone with him in a remote location . . . I desperately wanted to believe in the person that I thought I knew.

* * *

From: Flash
Date: Thu, 12 Aug 2010 15:32:53
To: Katja
Subject: Re: Hi

DISCLOSURE

Well Hey,

firstly great to hear from you and good luck with the medicine im sure you will be awesome. Congrats to your brother and his wife as well and i hope your Mum and Dad are fine and dandy and enjoying themselves. So I now live on a boat and am currently having a chill out after a bit of hectic time. Had a superb trip to Italy climbing and came back to EF set up, so I'm having a few days, then working hopefully before doing the set up for another gathering with Activist Tat Collective which is about the 24th. So let me know where you will be between 18th - 24th. The gathering is in Northampton and although i will be there to sort out marquees etc. I'm happy to come and find you. I was hoping to get over to Wales to see Lisa's brother with her which is next week sometime about the 19th, but would be so nice to see you so i am determined to try and sort it out before you go back.

    Love Mark xx

It was mid-afternoon when Katja pulled into Burton-on-Trent. She parked her car in a deserted residential street near the river and was locking the doors when a voice startled her.

She spun round, gripping the key in her fist, only to see Mark walking down the road. She relaxed slightly. He was smiling, although he seemed to be looking past her.

'This your new wheels?'

'Jesus, Mark, you scared the life out of me. How did you even know I was here?'

'I saw you park up.'

He reached out to hug her.

'Well, it's good you're here,' she conceded. 'It saves me harassing the other boats to find out where you're moored. Lead the way!'

'I thought I'd take you for dinner first.'

After dinner they walked by the river. It looked beautiful in the summer evening light. She reached out and took Mark's hand, and thought, not for the first time, about the strangeness of friendships between ex-lovers. She was no longer attracted to him, but felt totally comfortable touching him. She supposed the physical intimacy would never be altogether lost. He would always be more than a friend. She looked up at his face. He looked troubled.

'What's up?'

He told her that he had started another relationship, and it was causing difficulties with Lisa. Not for the first time, she wondered aloud whether it was necessary for him to have so many lovers. It always caused him stress, and this time it seemed messier than ever.

She thought back. He had been on edge in Strasbourg, and although she hadn't seen him since then, she knew from talking to mutual friends that he had been in a bad way. People said he had been depressed at his fortieth birthday party. Was that what all this was?

She stopped walking and pulled at his hand, making him turn to face her.

'I don't know anything about this new relationship, but I do know you have a really good thing with Lisa. My advice? Don't do anything hasty because you're anxious about your life. Take a breath. Take it slow, and, you know, don't fuck it up.'

'I can rely on you not to mince your words.'

She thought she had upset him, but then his shoulders slumped.

'You're right, I know. I just need to be more careful.'

She wasn't totally sure what he meant, but with that, he changed the subject, turning and striding back towards the moorings.

'Come on, let me show you my boat.'

Just as Katja was about to head back to London, Lisa arrived, having driven from her brother's in Wales. It was dark already, but it was such a long time since Katja had seen her, she decided to stay a while longer. The three of them sat drinking tea in the boat's little saloon.

Katja and Lisa caught up. Mark mostly listened. Katja thought her friend seemed happy enough, a little tired from the drive, perhaps. In reality, Lisa was already living with uncertainty. She had found the passport in the name of Mark Kennedy and text messages from his children, and she had begun the research into his background that would bring it all crashing down.

* * *

From the first witness statement of 'Lisa' to the Investigatory Powers Tribunal

I believed that I had found a deep, long-term connection with Mark, and that we would share a long-term future together. It was with him that I talked about really important life decisions, like my decision to enter the healthcare profession, and it was with him that I discussed moving onto a narrow boat to live. The boat was very much a joint project of ours . . . Mark moored his boat next to mine for a large part of [2010] . . . [He] appeared to be depressed and confused about his career options . . .

NPOIU Intelligence Reports (2009)
DATE/TIME OF REPORT - 25/08/2009 1740 hrs
INTEL SOURCE or INTEL REF Nº. [Mark Kennedy]
Whilst at the Earth First Summer Gathering at Seathwaite Cumbria on the 22/08/2009 activists discussed their belief that 2 'activists', that they had known for some time, could have been Undercover Police Officers . . .

The two activists under suspicion were Lynn Watson from Leeds and a white male with short blond hair from Nottingham called Rod.

As far as Watson was concerned the main gist of the conversation revolved around the fact that . . . Watson has not maintained any sort of contact via Facebook, Email or phone . . . They discussed how they still knew people from years ago who still occasionally keep in touch and that was going back to a long time before the internet, today it is so much easier to keep in touch.

[Someone] then associated this behaviour with Rod saying that people always knew he was a UC and he suddenly disappeared abroad.

Character traits were also spoken of, including the fact that no family members had ever been seen, and neither of them were ever around at Christmas . . .

Watson seemed to always be un-contactable for a couple of days each week . . .

From the first witness statement of 'Lisa' to the Investigatory Powers Tribunal

Over the course of summer 2010, various inconsistencies started to appear in Mark's account and further clues about the possibilities of undercover policing activities started to appear. For example . . . doubts in people's minds about who Lynn [Watson] really was . . .

In October 2010, Mark said that he had to go to the US again to see his brother. Whilst he was away, I told a friend about the discovery of the passport and the phone. We decided to investigate it further using online ancestry websites.

We made some searches under the name 'Mark Kennedy' and also under the names of the children from the text messages. We did some further research, and found a marriage certificate from 1994 . . . with the occupation for Mark as a police officer. I also found birth certificates in the names of the two children, which again gave the father's occupation as 'police officer'. We identified an address in Ireland and a telephone number. I still clung to the belief that somehow it would not be true, or that Mark would have an explanation. I was also very scared for my safety at that time . . . One of my friends called the number we had found, and Mark answered. I then called Mark on his mobile, and told him that I knew where he was and that he had to come back to explain himself. He asked me to tell him what I thought I knew, but I refused to be drawn over the phone.

Mark came back that night, 20 October 2010. He arrived in Nottingham in the middle of the night and turned up at an address where four friends and I were waiting for him. Mark eventually admitted the truth that he had been an undercover police officer . . . Finding this out has broken my heart, devastated my life and shattered my trust in people . . . the fact that this disregard for my mental health was sanctioned by the state is a fact that I may never fully be able to process. It has impacted on my core beliefs and values . . . The shock and trauma from that initial discovery still impacts on my mental health today . . . It is devastating to think how much influence this person, with the oversight and direction of the police, has had on my life.

* * *

At 16:57 hours on 21 October 2010 activists published a short statement on the Indymedia.org.uk website, along with photographs of Mark Stone:

Mark Kennedy/Stone exposed as undercover police officer
This is a statement from a group of people who have considered Mark 'Stone' a friend for the last decade.

Mark 'Stone' has been an undercover police officer from 2000 to at least the end of 2009. We are unsure whether he is still a serving police officer or not. His real name is Mark Kennedy. Investigations into this identity revealed evidence that he has been a police officer, and a face-to-face confession has confirmed this. Mark claims that he left the police force in late 2009, and that before becoming an undercover officer he was a Metropolitan Police constable.

Please pass this information on to anyone who may have been in contact with Mark in the last decade, both in the UK and abroad.

CHAPTER 37

The other statements were nearly done, but mine still had a long way to go. Once the part about Mark was finished, I had to write the rest. There were intelligence files mentioning me in the disclosure, starting in the late 1990s and going right up until 2014. The later documents, created after we started the court case, were from the 'Metropolitan Police Counter Terrorism Command', and they were apparently sent to the Spanish police.

The first noted that 'the two known addresses provided by WILSON have been co-operative type communal addresses', as though that alone could somehow explain why the anti-terrorist police would be sending personal information about me to a foreign police force. They went on to explain I was known to the National Domestic Extremism and Disorder Intelligence Unit (NDEU) for attending the Earth First! Summer Gathering in 2007, and that I had been arrested at the 2006 Climate Camp and the 2005 G8 (although 'No Further Action' was taken).

Six months after their first report, on 22 September 2014, Counter Terrorism Command had produced a second one:

███

██████████ update in relation to the activities of Kate WILSON, a known UK activist with XLW (Extreme Left Wing) sympathies. WILSON continues to reside in the city of Barcelona ████████. WILSON is undertaking a leading role in anarchist / ecologist protest groups centred in Barcelona ████████. WILSON is driving an Opel Astra, Spanish VRM – 3981GMP ████████

Not long after that report was written, I found the GPS tracker hidden under my car.

It is curious that Counter Terrorism Command seemingly neglected to mention, in their list of my 'known activities', that my principal activity at that time was, in fact, an ongoing legal action against the Metropolitan Police for violations of my human rights.

I laughed nervously.

'Just because you're paranoid . . .'

I wanted to make light of it. I had always believed that the spying didn't begin or end with my relationship with Mark, but it was still deeply unnerving to see hard evidence that I was right. If I had dwelt on the emotional impact of it all, my statement could have run to thousands of pages. However, with Holly's guidance I somehow pared it down, and soon, the only section left to write was the part about my contact with other undercover officers. The disclosure about them had finally arrived.

I opened the email, which contained extracts from the police note-books kept by Rod Richardson, Lynn Watson and Marco Jacobs. They had taken a long time to come because the extracts had to be typed. I was not permitted to see samples of their handwriting. Nevertheless, the first thing that struck me when I read their notes were the differences in style.

From the police notebooks of Marco Jacobs, 2004
29th July 2004. I was deployed in Northampton for legend building purposes. After spending the morning from about 9:30am in the town centre, I was busking from 12:15pm to 1:00pm in Abington Street near the junction with Fish Street. During this period £3.26 was placed by passers by into my rucksack which was on the floor in front of me as I played. After this, I spent time in The Bear Public House, Northampton,

from 2:15pm to 3:00pm, then the Wine Vaults public house, Northampton from 3:10pm to 3:45pm. Whilst in these premises I spent my time talking to staff and customers.

After building his 'legend' on the streets of Northampton, Marco Jacobs went on to make contact with his target groups at the Earth First! gathering in August 2004. From then on, his was an active operation. Yet the notes I was given contained very little political information. Meetings were described as 'general in nature' and mostly recorded only names and little details about the people he met.

For the three-month period from the beginning of February to the end of April 2005, we had notes relating to his activity on forty-two separate days. Twenty-eight describe it only as 'social in nature'. Of the remainder, twelve involved him being in a pub. Only four days in that period recorded activities that unequivocally took place outside a drinking establishment. Those were collecting leaflets from someone's house, staffing a street stall about the G8, picking someone up from London to give them a lift, and looking at empty buildings for possible squats.

Lynn Watson was more interested in personal interactions: her reports were filled with deeply confidential details about people's family lives, including relationship break-ups, house purchases and even fostering children. These mostly seem to have been picked up while dining as a guest in their private homes.

By contrast, Rod's notes were clipped and procedural. Nevertheless, they contained a surprise. Apparently he and I had met in London while I was still a student.

From the police notebooks of Rod Richardson, 1999
Notes recommenced at 21:30hrs/27.3.99. At 11:00hrs . . . The meeting covered various topics all relating to the organisation of the June 18th day of action . . . A white female called Kate from Oxford took my mobile

number and asked if I could help with sending off mail which I said I would . . . Notes finished at 22:30hrs (Signature: Rod)

Notes recommenced at 16.00hrs on 13 April 1999 . . . Kate seemed to appear to be a very active organiser and was very keen for me to attend future meetings. She made several phone calls to unknown groups and was obviously someone who had their finger on the pulse. I left shortly afterwards.
Notes completed at 16.25hrs. (signature: Rod).

Notes recommenced 12.15pm 28/4/99. At 10.05 I received a message on my mobile . . . from a female I know as Kate . . . I phoned back at 11.45 approx and I left a message on her mobile number saying for her to call me back and arrange a time to meet . . .

Notes recommenced at 23.30hrs on the 30th April 99. At about 15.00hr (30/4) I received a phone call from a person who I know as Kate. She asked me if I could come to [an address] in Putney from 18.30hrs onwards to help with posting leaflets to various organisations . . . [I] was met at the door by the girl I know as Kate. She invited me into the house . . . Nothing of any relevance was said through-out the evening and I left at about 22.00hrs. I established that the house belonged to Kate's parents who weren't there.
Notes concluded at 23.55hrs (Signature: Rod).

'He was inside my parents' house.'

Ben looked up from the report he was reading.

'What?'

'Rod Richardson. He came to my parents' home. In 1999.'

I felt hollow. How on earth was I going to tell my parents that Mark hadn't even been the first undercover police officer I brought into their home?

'It says here we spoke on the phone every couple of weeks

that spring. I don't remember it, but he describes me as "obviously someone who had their finger on the pulse". He was spying in Nottingham just before Mark. There's nothing here about the time he was in Nottingham, but he was there, he lived with John and he helped set up the Sumac Centre, right at the start. He must have briefed Mark about us all.'

I always thought that I had made the first move with Mark, but maybe even that bit of my story was a lie. I thought about all the things that had attracted me to him, from the moment he first sat next to me in that NASA meeting. He told me he grew up in South London, near where I did. He said he liked country music and caravans. He seemed to like everything I did. Had I been chosen in advance, studied, carefully reeled in?

I remembered hanging out with Rod in Nottingham in the early 2000s, yet nothing was disclosed from his later reporting, after he moved to Nottingham. Had he not mentioned any of those encounters? Or were those files destroyed?

There was a scattering of other documents from other officers, from the years before 2003, but not as many as I expected. I have photos of a demonstration in London on 1 May 1999. Jim Boyling is pictured in a crowd moving through an Underground station, and he is clearly talking to me. Yet there was nothing in the disclosure about that demonstration, or my involvement in that group. I was told that there was nothing about me on 'IMOS', the database where Special Branch kept their political files. As with all the gaps in the disclosure, there was no indication of what that meant. Had my file never existed? Had it been destroyed? Had I simply asked the wrong question, thereby enabling them to insist there was nothing there? It was frustrating, but we only had weeks before the trial, and I had to work with what we had.

I began with the notebooks for Lynn Watson and Marco Jacobs.

The first important fact I discovered was that Lynn had been at the Dissent! Meeting in Manchester in April 2004, when Mark and

I arrived together late and arguing, just before we went to Dublin. She reported that 'Catia from Nottingham' would be preparing the agenda for the next meeting. Because of the misspelling I missed the reference at first. She also noted that 'Catia' was going to the May Day demonstrations in Dublin where she would 'host a G8 workshop to publicise Dissent!'

She made no mention of Mark Stone, but of course she knew who Mark was. They were serving officers in the same unit. In her undercover role, Lynn joined the Dissent! Finance Working Group, alongside Mark and me. It is hard to imagine, as a police officer trained in intelligence gathering, that she would have failed to notice the tensions between us that weekend, or the way that we arrived, spent the night together, and left together the next day.

From the limited disclosure I received, it seems that Lynn Watson never once recorded my relationship with Mark in writing, even though a one-night stand I had with someone else, which she heard about on the grapevine, made it into her intelligence reports. It seems she didn't record Mark's relationship with Lisa either, even though Lisa and Lynn were friends, part of a tight-knit social and political scene in Leeds. However bad Lynn might have been at reading people, she knew about Mark and Lisa.

From the first witness statement of 'Lisa' to the Investigatory Powers Tribunal

[I] remember discussing my relationship with Mark with Lynn. For example, after my father died, she expressed her sympathy and asked how I was doing, and I remember telling her that Mark had been very supportive and that he had attended my father's funeral. I also recall being at a meeting at her house in around 2008, when Lynn asked me how things were going in my relationship with Mark and told me how sweet we seemed together. I told her things were going well . . .

DISCLOSURE

Marco Jacobs also attended Dissent! meetings. On 16 September 2004 he writes:

> I attended the Sumac Centre and met [name redacted] who I had met at the Earth First Gathering. This was in preparation for travel to Edinburgh for a Dissent! G8 gathering. I travelled up on the Friday morning in a minibus having stayed at [Ned's housing coop] the previous night . . . I travelled back to Nottingham and stayed at [Ned's housing coop] on the Sunday night (19th September).

He then lists the people he met that weekend. Neither Mark nor I am on the list, but I realised we must have been there, and Mark's notebooks agreed:

> On Friday I drove to Scotland, Edinburgh in a minibus with the following people, Katja, Marco, [and five others]. We drove to Edinburgh for the dissent gathering. Whilst there we stayed at the protest site in Bilsten Glenn. During the weekend I was present at a number of meetings for the Dissent network. These included Funding, ESF Day of Dissent, Actions, Convergence Centres etc. The minutes of which have been documented.

Lynn was also in Edinburgh that weekend, though she didn't travel up with our group. She doesn't mention me, Mark or indeed any of those present by name in her notes, but she writes:

> At 1000hrs of Saturday 18th September 2004 I attended the DISSENT! Meeting at the Church Hall above the Forest Café. At the meeting and throughout the weekend there were between 50-60 people present.

I felt a flush of anger. The police case was that there had been at most 'limited contact' between me and other undercover officers. In fact, at one point I had been put to proof over whether I had ever met them at all, yet they must have known that Lynn and Marco had been in a lot of the same places as Mark and me, and that Rod had been in my parents' home.

Their constant changes of position, their 'non-admissions', and their combative, secretive and inconsistent approach to my case meant that years later, I was still having to dig through haphazard and piecemeal disclosure to find snippets of information that disproved their denials.

I was frustrated at myself as well. I had missed the reference to 'Marco' when I first read Mark's notes from September 2004, skimming over it as I remembered other, more personal events from that summer, such as Mark kissing Lisa in the Lake District, and the landlord threatening to kick in the door at Wiverton Road. I had forgotten that Mark and I organised and drove the minibus to Scotland.

So, Marco Jacobs was with us in the minibus and throughout the weekend. He couldn't possibly have failed to notice that Mark and I were together.

I felt a tug at the back of my mind. I was missing something. But when I tried to chase the feeling, it was already gone.

CHAPTER 38

For a moment I had no idea where I was. I became aware of the sloping roof of the Barracks, just a metre above my head, the patterns made by frost on the skylight, and Ben breathing gently by my side. 3.17 a.m. I wondered what had woken me.

I could feel that nagging from my hindbrain again. Something about Marco Jacobs. He spent that weekend with us, in a group of just eight people. He must have known that Mark and I were a couple.

Moving slowly so as not to wake Ben, I made my way to the steps at the foot of the bed and down to the ground. The night air was cold, but the concrete floor still held some warmth from the underfloor heating, so I pulled a cushion off the sofa and sat in my dressing gown, going through the files.

There was a letter written from Marco answering questions from the police solicitors in 2018. Marco was asked if he recalled meeting me between 2003 and 2005. He replied:

I did see her at a few other G8 planning events, for example a G8 planning meeting in Glasgow in early 2006. She was usually in Kennedy's company, but I saw them more as a pair of organisers not a couple. I saw no behaviour which indicated a relationship (holding hands, etc). I did not know they were in a relationship. I don't think I ever actually spoke to her.

I realised he must have meant the Edinburgh trip. By changing both the date and the city he had concealed a mistruth. If pressed

293

it could pass for a simple slip of memory. At the same time, those errors subtly put him in the clear, because in early 2006 Mark and I were no longer a couple.

I had witnessed a similar process in Mark's media interviews: fictitious narratives made up of little bits of truth. I wondered if it was part of undercover officer training, or if it just came naturally to men who had told so many lies.

There it was again: the feeling that I was missing something. Where had I read these words before?

I found the passage paraphrased in Sir Stephen House's first statement. He described Jacobs saying he spent time with Mark and me, but he made it even more vague, editing out the 'G8 planning meeting in Glasgow', and referring only to 'a meeting in early 2006'. That explained why I didn't think of the 2004 Scotland trip. By 2006 Mark and I were no longer together and I spent the first half of that year in South America, so Marco Jacobs couldn't have seen me at a meeting then. I'd assumed that he had confused me with one of Mark's other girlfriends. But no, that wasn't what he'd done.

I was getting closer.

From the first witness statement of Sir Stephen House
In response to the question, 'To your knowledge, was there a policy or practice of permitting or encouraging UCOs to engage in sexual relationships with those being reported on in order to better integrate and/or elicit intelligence', 'Marco Jacobs' responded: 'I am not aware of any policy relating to this. I did not make use of a such a provision in any case, hence no knowledge of a policy' . . . There is no evidence therefore that "Marco Jacobs" knew or ought to have known of the intimate sexual relationship.

House appeared to think there was no reason to doubt Jacobs' word. With that the tangle came loose. Jacobs *did* have sexual relationships while he was undercover. I knew that. And House would have known, when his statement was signed, that the Met paid compensation to two women because of it (though they refused to make any formal admissions at the time). Jacobs served alongside Kennedy, in the same unit, and they would both have seen each other with women. They were all covering for each other.

'What are you doing?' Ben murmured, peering down through a crack in the planks. 'Come back to bed.'

I climbed back up to join him, but I was too wired to sleep. I needed to speak to the women from Cardiff who had been in relationships with Marco. Their stories were the proof we needed that Mark was not just a rogue officer, and that the practice of undercover officers having relationships was not limited to the 'historic abuses' of the defunct and discredited Special Demonstration Squad.

From the witness statement of 'ARB' to the Investigatory Powers Tribunal

My name is 'ARB' in these proceedings and my identity is protected by an anonymity order . . . In 2001 I moved to Cardiff . . . I first met Marco Jacobs in around May 2005 at a Cardiff Anarchist Network meeting. Marco came across as amiable and chatty and, after the meeting, we watched a folk band in the pub together. During the gig Marco flirted with me and offered to walk me home several times, but I declined, feeling that he was trying to initiate a sexual dynamic which I did not want at the time.

I subsequently saw him . . . in September 2005 . . . [and] at a Defend Council Housing Rally in London in early 2006. We went for a drink together after the rally and met up with my sister and one of her friends. When we parted company Marco said to me: 'I'll see you next time and we can talk about us.' I remember those words clearly because I found them both surprising and flattering. I remember checking with my sister to make sure I had not misheard him.

Application for RIPA Authority for Marco Jacobs, 24 June 2006
Intelligence Case, includes the following:
In January 2006, the SIO added the objective of physically moving location to the Cardiff area to enable infiltration of the Cardiff Anarchist Network (CAN) in order to gather intelligence on their non-legitimate protest activity and to renew contact with [named subjects of the operation]. This objective was completed in April 2006, with [Jacobs] now settled into covert premises in the Cardiff area and contact established with [named subjects] and other members of CAN, especially 'ARB'.

From the witness statement of 'ARB' to the Investigatory Powers Tribunal

Marco and I formed a close friendship . . . he told me that he was a truck driver from Northampton and that he was separated from his former partner, who used to physically abuse him . . . he took an interest in me personally and shared my political views. He would assist me with DIY tasks in my house and met my work colleagues on several occasions . . .

I placed a lot of trust in Marco at a time when I was very vulnerable because my father was severely ill with cancer . . . he died in 2008. Marco provided support to me, including meeting my parents . . . He also attended my father's funeral. Marco told me that he understood what I was going through as his mother had died of cancer when he was young and his father had died in 2005.

In the summer of 2008, shortly after my father's death . . . Marco sought to begin a sexual relationship with me. I recall being in the pub with Marco and him telling me that he didn't want to go home. I invited him back to my flat. I recall him saying that he thought I was amazing and that he did not think I should be going out with [my boyfriend at that time] (he said that finding out that I was . . . had been like a 'knife in his heart', or words to that effect). He also told me how struck he had been by me when he first saw me.

Marco told me he wanted to cuddle, so I agreed to share a bed with him. I recall getting ready for bed and putting on pyjamas. However, Marco wanted to have sex and was very assertive. In the end, I was persuaded . . . The following morning, Marco told me that he loved me.

I ended my relationship . . . in late August 2008 in the belief that Marco and I would begin a relationship. However, when I told Marco that . . . he seemed shocked. Although we slept together on two further occasions. Marco then sent me text message saying that we should just be friends and that his feelings had changed. I was surprised and extremely hurt and upset, and believed that Marco had deliberately misled me about his feelings so as to persuade me to sleep with him . . .

NPOIU Intelligence Report attributed to Marco Jacobs, 18 October 2008
['ARB' and her boyfriend] are no longer involved in a relationship but continue to associate through activism.

From the witness statement of 'ARB' to the Investigatory Powers Tribunal
From October 2008 I remained in contact with Marco, but our interactions became less frequent . . .

I know that Marco also had another relationship with [a woman] in the summer of 2007. [She] was another female member of CAN . . . Marco attended the G8 in Germany with her in 2007 and, although I did not attend . . . I recall hearing from my friends that they shared a tent and were holding hands around the campsite . . . I recall her being very upset when Marco broke up with her . . . I remember asking Marco why he had broken up with her . . . he had previously told me that he liked her so much . . . he said that he no longer felt comfortable with the age gap between them – he was in his mid-forties and [she] was in her mid-twenties. It appeared to me that [they] had shared an intense relationship . . . and that he had been very important to her.

Marco's involvement with CAN became less frequent in late 2008 and he left the Cardiff area in August 2009. He told me that he had been offered a job as a gardener in Corfu . . . he remained in contact with me by postcards and text messages until approximately November 2009, when all contact ceased . . . [I] became very concerned that something might have happened to him. I searched for him . . . and even posted on a missing person's website.

Looking back . . . I feel that I was exploited at a particularly vulnerable time of my life . . . I did not socialise a lot or have a lot of close friends and came to depend upon Marco to a considerable extent for emotional support. I still do not know whether Marco was lying about the death of his mother and I regard the support he gave me during this time as a gross intrusion into my grieving . . .

I and others whose lives were affected by Marco's actions brought claims against The Commissioner of Police for the Metropolis, The Association of Chief Police Officers, and the Chief Constable of South Wales Police on 8 March 2012 . . . The claim was settled out of court . . . no admissions were made . . .

CHAPTER 39

Each woman's story was unique, yet read together they were hauntingly similar. And with each new account, the police denials sounded more and more hollow. In all we presented seven witness statements; six first-hand accounts of abusive and deceitful relationships conducted by serving police officers, and a final statement that would bring them all together and look at the wider picture.

By 2021, Harriet Wistrich had represented a total of seventeen women deceived by undercover officers into relationships, and her witness statement described patterns that were repeated over and over again.

From the witness statement of Harriet Wistrich to the Investigatory Powers Tribunal
In 2011, I was instructed by eight women who had been deceived into entering into long-term intimate relationships with serving male undercover officers during the period 1987 to 2009 ... All eight of the women who instructed me in 2011 had been involved or associated through their friendship networks with political groupings organised around issues of environmentalism and/or social justice campaigns at the time ... All eight of these women were deceived by undercover officers into entering into long-term and intimate sexual relationships ... They experienced undercover officers using common methods when grooming them ... Those common methods included mirroring the

women's personal background and interests (for example, by mirroring their music tastes as Mark Kennedy did), being unusually attentive and committed (for example, by moving into a shared house very early into the relationship as Bob Lambert did with Belinda, and Jim Boyling did with 'Rosa') and appearing to be an ideal lover and or soul mate (for example, by writing letters, emails and poetry professing their love at an early stage in the relationship). Many of the undercover officers created false narratives about difficult childhood experiences and other traumas in order to appear vulnerable, drawing on the women's empathy and in order to build trust. For example, John Dines told Helen Steel that he had lost both of his parents, which brought them closer together, and Mark Jenner told 'Alison' that his father was killed by a drunk driver when he was eight years old . . .

There were also striking similarities between the disruptive way in which the undercover officers exited the women's lives and relationships. For example, all of John Dines, Jim Boyling, Mark Jenner and Mark Kennedy appeared to be having mental breakdowns and then claimed that they were moving abroad. They manufactured false narratives that sought to explain why they suddenly needed to disappear from the relationships despite having intensely professed their love. In doing so, they pulled on the heartstrings of these women and caused them to become extremely concerned and anxious about their well being when they disappeared . . .

All of these women were in their twenties and thirties at the time when the undercover officers entered into relationships with them . . . Some of my clients have told me that the timing of these relationships during their optimum child-bearing years, and the impact of these relationships on their subsequent ability to trust, meant they lost the option to have biological children or had children later than they otherwise would have . . .

A total of 27 women, including all eight of the women who instructed me in 2011, have been granted 'Core Partic- ipant' status in the UCPI because they were deceived into sexual relationships by male undercover officers employed by the SDS and NPOIU . . .

In my view, it is likely that many other women may have been affected by such conduct by many other male officers but have not come forward, either because they do not want to re-live painful memories, or because they are still unaware of the deception . . .

The sheer number of officers who engaged in relation- ships while deployed undercover, the length of time over which these relationships took place, and the persistence of the practice without correction until Lisa discovered that Mark Kennedy was an undercover officer and exposed him to her circle of friends must, in my view, undermine any assertion that these were the independent actions of a few rogue officers. I believe that this was a systemic problem in the SDS and the NPOIU, characterised by (and the result of) scant regard for the personal dignity and integrity of the women involved.

CHAPTER 40

The legal team sent my statement back again. Eighty-five pages, filled with new highlights and questions in the margins. Each and every thing I said was cross-referenced and meticulously fact-checked against more than three hundred pages of exhibited evidence. It had been going on for days, and it was driving me mad.

'You'll be grateful for this when you're cross-examined,' Paddy said.

'Oh. Will we all be cross-examined?' I asked. 'Do the other witnesses know?'

I had written so many statements and submissions over the years. I had been to court two or three times a year since 2012, but those were all just pre-trial hearings. Actually going to trial would be a different matter.

In my whole life I had only ever appeared in the witness box once. Twenty years earlier I had testified in defence of a close friend who stopped a deportation flight. I had, and have, no doubt that my friend did the right thing, and I was keen to tell the court why. Nevertheless, cross-examination may have been the worst thirty minutes of my life. By the end, I couldn't have told you my own name, and was convinced that I was going to jail myself.

I thought of our vulnerability in this case. I tried to imagine being grilled like that, by lawyers bent on discrediting us. I felt intensely protective of my witnesses.

Then again . . . It was hard to see how a police barrister bullying victims of sexual misconduct by serving officers could ever be a good look. I was, I admit, a little curious to see how this would play out.

Ben and I sat on one of the large, stone benches in front of the Royal Courts of Justice. I had rarely seen people sitting there, and as I shifted my position, trying to get comfortable, it became obvious why. It took serious design to make a seat that awkward.

I was just wondering why, if they wanted to discourage loitering, they had bothered to put benches there at all, when we were interrupted by the arrival of Matthew and the rest of the Freshfields team. They all wore sharp suits and matching black satin Covid-19 facemasks. It was a far cry from our video calls: they looked absolutely formidable. As we made our way up the marble staircase to the courtroom, I realised with awe that, although my friends and I brought the side down a bit, we were the best-dressed team in the room.

It was fun to be out of lockdown, taking our places in court, doing something real. The hearing started with a litany of safety announcements about social distancing, handling documents and wearing masks. Then Charlotte Kilroy began.

'Sir, there are three matters for determination, as I understand it, today. The first is the cross-examination of Sir Stephen House. The second is the cross-examination of the Claimant's witnesses and the third is the timetable for the hearing.'

I smiled, realising how much I had missed Charlotte's cool delivery.

'The Defendants have chosen not to advance any evidence from those in their current or former employment who could address the factual issues from first-hand knowledge. Instead, they have produced Sir Stephen House's witness statement. They candidly admit he has no first-hand experience with any of the factual matters.'

The Tribunal chair interrupted Charlotte to ask whether the

Tribunal had in fact asked for House's statement.

'What the Tribunal said,' she replied, 'is that they wanted the respondents to comply with the duty of candour and cooperation with the court. Now, that does not mean a statement from someone who knows nothing about what is going on . . . we are in a peculiar position where this is simply a summary of material with Sir Stephen House lending it, apparently, some legitimacy or extra weight because he is a senior police officer . . . In their submissions for this hearing, the Respondents say things like, "He has nothing useful to add, nothing further to add," and is "unable to shed light on a disputed factual issue". Well, we would agree with that, but if that is the position, then no weight should be attached to his inferences or opinions at all.'

When Charlotte had finished, the Tribunal turned to the police barrister.

'Could we just clarify that a little, Mr Perry? There can be no doubt that it must be for the Tribunal to reach conclusions itself, but in doing so, it is conceivable that we might be influenced by an officer of the standing and experience of your witness. So, there is a difference between saying that it is our ultimate responsibility, which we all know it is, and saying that we pay no regard whatever and give no weight whatsoever to the views he has expressed.'

'Very well,' Perry sighed. 'I am not relying on his expressions of opinion and I ask you to disregard them.'

I felt a mix of elation and rage. House's infuriating opinions were officially unfounded and irrelevant. That had been our view all along, so it was good news, but the flip side was that we would not get the opportunity to question a single police officer about what had happened. I wanted to see them all on the stand: Mark's handler, the senior officers who ran the deployment, even Mark Kennedy himself.

The police were not presenting statements from those officers, so they could not be called as witnesses. The only officer we would ever have been able to question was Deputy Commissioner Sir Stephen House. The police's original intention had been that we would receive no disclosure at all apart from Sir Stephen House's statements. We would have been able to cross-examine him, granted, but we would have been going in blind.

Now, of course, the tables had turned. We had seen a lot of the same evidence that House had. We were in a position to ask detailed questions about his reasons for interpreting them in the ways he did. I wanted to see him sweat over his answers, under the stares of the Tribunal judges, and the affected women, who would have packed into the public gallery to watch him squirm. It wasn't to be. For the police, losing his evidence altogether was apparently preferable to having House take the stand.

The second question before the Tribunal was the status of our witness statements. Again, Charlotte explained the position.

'The Claimant has advanced witnesses of fact, witnesses with first-hand knowledge of what occurred. All of the Claimant's witnesses are advancing accounts of events that happened to them . . .'

The police legal team may have shared my sense of how putting us on the stand would play out. A few days before the hearing, they informed the Tribunal that they did not intend to cross-examine any of us. It almost felt like they were proposing a deal: 'We won't cross-examine your witnesses but you don't get to cross-examine ours.' My legal team explained that this was not the school playground and that wasn't how it worked.

'Now, the respondents have said that they do not seek to cross-examine but, they say, that does not mean they accept the evidence of these witnesses in its entirety. Well, again, clarity is required because if the respondents do not accept the assertions of primary fact that are made in those witness statements, they must put that to the witnesses. It is not, in my respectful submission, open to the respondents, having passed up the opportunity to cross-examine, to then make submissions that those assertions or that evidence of primary fact is wrong or that people are not telling the truth, that they are incorrect, and so on.'

Again, Perry, on behalf of the police, opted for what must have seemed the lesser evil.

'In relation to the Claimant's evidence, may I just again make it clear we do not dispute any issue of primary fact.'

Unlike House, we were willing to be subjected to cross-examination if necessary. Still, it was a relief to hear that we wouldn't be. Not only did that decision mean we would not face questioning, it also meant that the police were not disputing the facts in our statements. It amounted, for example, to an official admission that Marco Jacobs had sexual relationships while under-cover.

All that was left was to set the timetable for the eight-day trial.

It seemed that the balance of power had shifted.

CHAPTER 41

My phone rang on our way to the Tube. It was a journalist, asking for comment, but when I started to tell her about the day's hearing and the decision about Sir Stephen House, she responded with blank surprise.

'I'm sorry, I had no idea you were in court today, I was looking for your views on Saturday's events.'

The *Telegraph* Newspaper, 15 March 2021
Sarah Everard vigil: How the police turned on women paying tribute to murdered woman
The vigil for Sarah Everard was supposed to be a sombre, peaceful affair – a chance to remember a young woman who was taken from a busy road as she was just trying to walk home . . .

They were met with the full force of the Metropolitan Police, who seemed determined to shut down the gathering . . . As night fell, just half an hour after a minute's silence was held for Sarah, the scene had disintegrated into chaos, with women being pulled off the bandstand . . .

Cries of 'arrest your own' rang out, as scenes of women being detained by largely male officers angered everyone.

I wasn't on Clapham Common that night. Ben and I were still on our way to London. We watched it later on the news, the police wading in, attacking and arresting the assembled women. Even so, talking to journalists that week about sexism in the police, I could tell that something had changed.

The hashtag #MeToo went viral in 2017, just as the IPT case was beginning to get moving. This was different. On 9 March 2021, PC Wayne Couzens, a serving firearms officer in the Metropolitan Police, was arrested for Sarah Everard's kidnapping, rape and murder. I always thought sexism would be one of the harder points for us to get across, but now the headlines were full of misogyny in the police, and Police Commissioner Cressida Dick was nonsensically telling women that if they felt threatened by a police officer they should 'wave down a bus'.

Everyone was asking who actually did police the police. (Bus drivers were quick to point out it wasn't them.) A deep-seated culture of sexism in the Met was coming to light.

My claim alone could not prove a pattern of sexist discrimination, nor would multiple relationships by just one officer be enough. But the crux of our case would not be the attitudes of individual officers. It was a systemic disregard for women's dignity that made it possible for the abusive relationships to take place.

* * *

Operation Pegasus – Contact Log (2005)
Thursday 6 October
2030. Met with Source in the *Reeperbahn* area of Hamburg. Katja now arriving tomorrow not Saturday. She has no money and Source asked for authority to give her 50 euros if necessary. Authorised.
Various discussions then about the need to use this trip to make and develop contacts which will be further developed over the next 2 years leading up to the 2007 G8 in Germany.
2300 Meeting concluded.

DISCLOSURE

The Reeperbahn area of Hamburg seemed a strange place for an operational meeting, particularly at that time of night. It is Europe's largest red-light district. Locals call it *die sündigste Meile* (the most sinful mile). The record of what was discussed in the meeting also seemed remarkably sparse. Could that really have filled two and a half hours?

Ten minutes after the meeting ended, EN31 received a phone call from Mark:

2310 Call from Source who had been 'dipped' by a group of prostitutes and had his passport stolen ████████████████████████████████
██
██
██
██████████████████████████████████

2320 Source met with the prostitute
2328 Call from Source who was walking away from the prostitute. No luck, prostitute denied she or any of the others took the passport.
I then followed Source back to the squat for safety.
2330 I advised Source to report the theft to the authorities tomorrow in the normal manner and that we would take care of the rest.

Was it likely Mark left that 'meeting', encountered the women, had his passport stolen, realised his predicament and made the call, all in the space of ten minutes? Or did Mark and his handler actually visit sex workers that night?

The handler, EN31, was interviewed in 2016. He told investigators that 'the stress of the actual deployments was significant. Part of the debrief process after the deployment was aimed at allowing him to de-compress and chill out.'

Was this what he meant? I had a feeling that we were glimpsing the dirty underbelly of the operation. Details of that evening's expenses were not disclosed.

CHAPTER 42

The barristers were preparing their skeleton arguments, and there was nothing left for us to do except wait. Ben and I escaped to a tiny 1970s holiday cottage on the East Devon coast to look at the ocean and count the days.

The beach sloped down to the water in a series of steep shelves. We walked together along the last edge, feeling the spray on our faces, watching the stones dislodged by our footsteps cascade down into the sucking waves. The grey water looked forbidding, and it was strange to think this was the same ocean we had swum in this time last year, during lockdown in Martinique. My eyes combed the beach, looking for driftwood or interesting pebbles. Our work was done, but our minds were still whirring.

The outcome of the March hearing had significant implications for the upcoming trial. There would be no live evidence and no cross-examination. The final showdown would not be anything like your traditional courtroom drama. Everything would hang on the paper evidence that I had spent so many years fighting for. The barristers would go through those thousands of pages of original police files and present their arguments, and then the judges would decide.

The facts of Mark's operation and our relationship were set out in the logs for anyone to see, and it was clear that the deployment had explicitly used me for operational ends.

DISCLOSURE

Operation Pegasus RIPA Authority Renewal 24 May 2006

Wilson was identified by MK as an influential person in the world of activism almost at the beginning of this operation. As such the operation has utilised her reputation, knowledge, energy and contacts (both national and international) to progress and promote MK's own standing. Her trust of MK has allowed her to 'reference' MK into many leading individuals and organisations.

Operation Pegasus – Contact Log (2005)

Monday 31 October

Katja has . . . asked Source if she could borrow £150 . . .

SIO to consider this request . . .

Handler Comment

The positive effect Katja has had on this operation over the past 2 years, and the people that she has introduced Source to and referenced Source into European and UK organisations is well worth this expenditure.

The real heart of the case would be the question of how far responsibility for the abuse extended. The police evidently obtained an operational advantage by using sexual relationships, which amounted to a big incentive for senior officers to allow them to go ahead. Nevertheless, there were no explicit references to such relationships in the documents. By March of 2021, Ben and I knew those documents inside out, and we knew that there was no smoking gun. However, there were a number of officers who must have been aware of the relationship.

House's statement singled some of them out. Mark's principal handler, EN31, was unquestionably the officer closest to events. Even the police accepted that he 'ought to have known' about the relationships.

EN59, Mark's deployment manager, received regular updates and signed off on decisions like the one to buy me a bicycle. EN107 claimed to have had no contact with Mark until after my relationship with him ended, but the logs showed she was quite closely involved at times in 2004, and her comments about 'Health & Safety – intimate relationships' were difficult to ignore.

House also considered two other officers, EN30 and EN21. I was thinking about them as we walked. House described them both as 'occasional cover officers', but it didn't ring true.

'I think we need to try and figure out what EN30 and EN21's actual jobs were.'

Ben and Dónal had made profiles of all the officers who appeared in the files, and Ben now summarised what we knew.

'The police really downplay EN21,' he said. 'He actually seems to have been more senior than EN31, in some kind of management role.'

EN21 appeared regularly in the disclosure, approving budgets, submitting authorisation applications and even organising Mark's appointments with the psychologist. He played a similar role for Marco Jacobs, suggesting he was far more active in the undercover unit than the term 'occasional cover officer' would imply.

'If I had to guess,' said Ben 'I would say EN21 was probably one of the Detective Inspectors who oversaw the deployment, but it's hard to know. EN30 definitely had more than just occasional involvement as well.'

He reeled off the facts about EN30, who appeared on more than fifty separate dates in our index between May 2004 and April 2006. The evidence pointed to him being part of a close team with EN31. He was drawn in to assist on various occasions in Mark's deployment, particularly outside of Nottingham and abroad. EN30 was involved in the trip to Dublin, in 2004. He was also clearly physically present in Spain, covering Mark in the spring of 2006.

'EN30 is the one who claimed never to have met Mark in person,' I added, 'although the contact logs make it clear that he did.'

'I think he was Lynn Watson's principal cover officer, at least after January 2005,' Ben concluded.

I thought about that.

'We don't actually know if EN30 was a he or a she, do we?'

In the absence of any real information about the ciphered officers, I found myself imagining them. I guessed that EN30 was a man, but there was no solid evidence. I imagined EN59 as a blustering character with sideburns. EN31 was 'Uncle Phil', because of Mark's mythical 'Uncle' from Bristol. The EN21 of my imagination was tall and skinny: I thought he was probably an accountant-type with a nervous disposition. I still have no idea who these people were in real life.

We reached the end of the beach, where the pebbles gave way to red-and-green clay bedrock, and we turned round.

'It bothers me,' I said, 'the way Stephen House has framed the question of who might have known about the relationship, and limited it to just those five individuals.'

We reached the steep steps up the cliff and lapsed into silence. It was impossible to hear each other over the blustery March wind on the cliff top, so we walked on, deep in our own thoughts. It was starting to rain when we reached the point where the cliff path joined the road, so we hurried home to warm ourselves by the electric fire.

When I checked my email, I found yet another witness statement from Stephen House.

From the fifth statement of Sir Stephen House to the Investigatory Powers Tribunal

. . . EN21 was the officer responsible for applying for authorisation of MK as a UCO and carried out a number of reviews under the relevant legislation between February and April 2006 and EN30 between January 2007 and October 2008. The preparation of the applications and reviews required EN30 and EN21 to complete sections outlining the intelligence obtained from the deployment since the last authorisation/review, carry out risk assessment, and comment on matters including the likelihood of collateral intrusion and access to confidential material. They would have been required, as a result, to have a familiarity with MK's deployment over and above what may be expected of an occasional cover officer.

That left us more convinced than ever that we were on the right track.

'There's actually around seventy officers mentioned in the disclosure,' Ben offered. 'I think quite a few of them must have known who Mark was.'

Seventy? I wished, not for the first time, that we knew more about how the unit operated. Taking into account the new information, that EN21 and EN30 were responsible for applications, I realised the same must also apply to other officers as well. EN114 was a Detective Inspector who was 'Authorities Officer' for Operation Pegasus in 2004 and 2005. He would have carried out the same role as EN21 and EN30 during the period Mark and I were in a relationship, yet he didn't even get a mention in the police account.

Meanwhile, Ben went through our research, looking for examples of officers who met Mark face-to-face. In addition to EN30 we also found O-90, who attended an in-person debrief with Mark at 1 p.m. on 24 April 2006, somewhere near Nottingham. 'Representatives of the 5 forces' attended an Operation Penguin meeting on Tuesday 2 December 2003, at Leicester Police HQ, which 'Source attended so that Source could see them and they had an opportunity to see and question Source.' However distant these officers may have been from the day-to-day running of Mark Kennedy's deployment, they knew that he was an undercover officer, deployed as Mark Stone.

The police defence was predicated on the idea that there was a 'sterile corridor', so only the officers closest to the operation could have known that he was a cop. But there was ample evidence that that was not entirely true, particularly as time went on.

DISCLOSURE

Officer O-18 was a case in point. A Nottingham Special Branch officer who appeared more than 118 times in the files, O-18 was the applicant on all the early RIPA forms, starting with Rod Richardson in May 2002, and continuing into Mark's deployment in 2003. After that, control passed to London, but Mark and I continued to live in Nottingham and O-18 continued to appear in the logs and intelligence reports, maintaining two-way contact with EN31. It is likely that O-18 oversaw other intelligence coming in to Nottingham Special Branch about Mark Stone the activist and his known associates. The people providing that intelligence may not have known Mark was an undercover police officer, but O-18 certainly did.

Another example was O-71, who worked on the 'Environment Intelligence' desk at the NPOIU. We know that O-71 communicated with Mark Kennedy via EN31, and met him in person, in London, in 2004, for a debrief about Dublin. He or she would also have been well aware of the identity of Mark Stone. Yet the fourth witness statement of Sir Stephen House said this:

'I understand that the dissemination of sensitive intelligence within the NPOIU was strictly controlled to ensure that a sterile corridor was in place . . . [the Environment Intelligence Desk] would have been unaware that Mark Stone was a UCO.'

As we tried to trace which officers would have seen what in the contact logs and intelligence reports, I realised the 'O-number' officer ciphers were significant in themselves. Officers in the public inquiry were being ciphered using 'EN-numbers' like EN107 or EN31, but in the disclosure I was seeing other ciphers were some-times used. This had been done with absolutely key officers, such as EN59, who was referred to as 'O-24' in all but a few places. The only reason I could see for them to do that was to make it harder for me to cross-reference information and understand what those officers did and what other roles they may have held.

'Do you ever get the feeling they're just gaslighting us?'

That night I dreamt of an office building. The air smelt of bad coffee and, strangely, of cigarettes. I was in a corridor made of partition walls, with a middle section made of glass, looking into offices furnished with gun-metal grey filing cabinets and shabby desks.

Cursors blinked on bulky computer monitors, and men (they were all men) passed from room to room, carrying faded cardboard folders. I couldn't hear their conversations or make out their faces and it felt like none of them could see me, although they stepped round me in the corridor as they passed.

I woke to darkness. The radiators were off and the room was cold. I could still feel the outline of the dream, and the dated scent of cigarette smoke indoors. I nestled close to Ben for warmth and tried to tell him about my dream.

'What?' Ben said, his voice groggy with sleep.

'Just remind me in the morning about glass walls,' I said. 'They don't really separate things at all.'

The next morning, over breakfast, Ben remembered. 'What were you on about last night, about glass walls?'

I thought back. The dream had been incredibly vivid, even down to the smells, and I had woken convinced that the 'sterile corridors' that Sir Stephen House talked about weren't real. In the light of day, it wasn't quite as obvious as it had been in my dream, but I tried the idea out anyway.

'What if everyone knew?' I said 'What if, instead of trying to guess which officers might have been in on the dirty secret, we assume a kind of low-level common understanding? People work in the same building, they know what goes on.'

'A policy maybe,' Ben suggested. 'Not "neither confirm nor deny". More like don't ask, don't tell.'

On reflection, it wasn't crazy at all. In fact, it was the only feasible explanation for how so much evidence of intimacy was unashamedly recorded, and passed from cover officers to DIs and DCIs, seemingly without surprise, comment or concern. It was unbelievable that no one had asked why Mark was spending so much time with Katja's parents, or attending Lisa's father's funeral; unless they already knew.

Even the strange lie that I was an organiser at Cornerstone made a bit more sense, because Mark's new girlfriend, Lisa, was living at Cornerstone at that time.

'Have you noticed the intelligence reports often seem to mix up the women Mark was sleeping with?'

We found a number of instances, from about 2005 onwards, where I appear to have been mistaken for Lisa. Later, Lisa appears to be mistaken for other women. In 2008, a man who was reported as living on a narrowboat with his girlfriend was (mistakenly) assumed by the Environment Desk to be Mark Stone, presumably because Lisa lived on a narrowboat at the time.

The only explanation for those errors was that the people 'adding value' to those reports knew at least something about the sex life of Mark Stone.

'It would also explain how no references at all to any of Mark's relationships made it into the intelligence between 2003 and 2010. Informants and FIT team officers must have reported on who Mark Stone was with, so someone must have been removing those references from the reports.'

'Until he resigned from the police in 2010,' I said. 'Then suddenly we see reports about who Mark Stone was seeing. Do you think the absence of something in the reporting can be considered evidence if it's sustained over a long enough period of time?'

'That is the elephant,' Ben replied.

I laughed. A few years earlier, we had travelled to Zimbabwe to support a conference of small farmers fighting for food sovereignty. A guide had warned us about encountering elephants on the road after dark. 'You won't see an elephant,' he explained. 'You must look for the absence of light. Even at night, there are lights everywhere. But where you see no stars, no streetlights, only darkness? That is the elephant.'

CHAPTER 43

Smiles and hugs, photographers and banners – 'police have crossed the line', 'paid to lie', 'give us our files'. Everything blurred as I passed through supporters into security checks at the Royal Courts of Justice. Then we had to wait outside the allotted room with the police legal team. We avoided each other's eyes, occasionally clearing our throats.

Once we were in the room, I was all business, making sure I had the bundles, swapping numbers with my lawyers so we could text each other questions. When I glanced over at Lisa, she was crying.

'Nine years and six months since we sent that first letter,' she whispered, 'and we're actually going to court.'

She pulled me into a hug, and I wanted to reply, but my voice caught on the lump that had appeared in my throat.

Covid-19 regulations were still in force, so only a small group of us were allowed into the public gallery, in carefully distanced seats.

Charlotte went first. She outlined our evidence, and it was deeply moving to hear all the memories that had turned our lives upside down, all the work we had done on the files over the past three years, meticulously and forensically laid out.

The court heard how Mark's handlers logged endless references to our life together; how it was widely known that we were a couple, and Mark made no effort to hide it, even when he knew we would be spied on by other police. Evidence of the quality and quantity of the time Mark and I spent together just kept coming, and the sheer intensity and volume of the contact could not be interpreted in any other way. They knew what kind of relationship it was. They always knew. They would have been negligent and incompetent if they didn't.

Charlotte also explained what was missing, including all but one of the phones used by Mark Kennedy while he was deployed. The police claimed to have only one phone, seized from Mark Stone during his arrest at Ratcliffe in 2009.

'A report into the contents of that phone,' Charlotte explained, 'describes deeply intimate photographs.'

I heard Lisa shift position on the seat behind me. The photographs in question were private pictures she had sent to her boyfriend. 'What a way to find out the police have a picture of my vagina on file,' she whispered in my ear.

For a moment I was overwhelmed. When I tuned back in, Charlotte had moved on to points of law: where did the burden of proof lie in a human rights case? What inferences could the Tribunal draw from the absence of all that key evidence?

Reporting the trial was difficult, because so much of the police defence revolved around their claims that it was 'unnecessary' for the Tribunal to consider parts of our case, which meant that a lot of the narrative became mired in case law. The police were saying that allegations of institutional sexism weren't important enough to investigate. That naturally felt like something of an insult, but it was a risky strategy for them: if we won the legal point, they had offered little further defence.

The judges asked a lot of questions and seemed well disposed to Charlotte's case. The first sign of discord came at the end of the second day. It was around the thorny question of whether political policing was 'necessary in a democratic society'. Charlotte showed how the initial authorisations failed to demonstrate any serious criminality or 'pressing social need', and how, from those inauspicious beginnings, the operations became broader, rather than more focused, as time went on.

I was utterly engrossed, hanging on her every gesture. Over the years the political nature of the spying had been the biggest cause of friction between me and Charlotte, yet when the time came, she presented the arguments with impressive zeal. Mark spied on me because I was involved in political protest and campaign groups, and it was indisputable that the undercover operations interfered with my rights to freedom of expression and assembly. The entire goal of the undercover operations was to spy on people for expressing our political views.

The judges took issue, however. They interrupted Charlotte to ask whether we were suggesting that spying on people for being involved in political protest violated their human rights. That was exactly what we were saying, she said. The judges made it clear that we had gone too far. I couldn't see Charlotte's face. Sitting behind her, I studied her posture, but it gave nothing away. After court, we filed back to her Chambers for a crisis meeting, around twenty of us in a conference room. I was furious, and also more than a little put out: however obvious the injustice was to me, it was far from self-evident to the judges. We only had one more day to bring them round.

We discussed the pivotal role that Mark had played in organising actions and events. Ben's most recent research was collating Mark 'Stone's' writings. In addition to the Dublin Black Bloc statement, there were other articles for websites like Indymedia, his participation in email lists and online discussions, interviews he gave on the radio, and even a chapter he wrote for a book.

'He was instrumental in the Trapeze G8 Roadshow and the Saving Iceland Tour,' Dónal added. 'Both were about popular education. He was basically travelling around, teaching people about the politics and encouraging them to join political campaigns.'

We weren't just talking about surveillance. They took part, created content and shaped ideas and decisions; they affected outcomes within our movements; and they gathered and stored information about hundreds of people's political opinions and activity for more than four decades. That information was shared with the security services, private companies and foreign police forces.

The manipulation of my thinking and behaviour by someone who was, by turns, a sexual partner, ex-boyfriend, active comrade and trusted, long-standing friend, was far more insidious and all-encompassing than a few discrete examples could ever express; and the implications went far beyond Mark's personal manipulation of me. It didn't even end when his true identity became known.

My withdrawal from political action had been gradual. Meetings and gatherings made me anxious, but I kept going because not to do so would have felt like letting them win. Over time, however, my discomfort demobilised me. It turned out this had a legal name: *the chilling effect*. When the threat, news or experience of state repression puts people off participating in meetings or demonstrations, it is considered an interference with our political rights.

'It didn't just affect Kate. It hit all of us,' Dónal said. 'A lot of the campaign groups we were involved in collapsed in the aftermath of the spycops scandal. Even if we wanted to get back involved, many of those groups just don't exist anymore.'

I thought about the Sumac Centre. It was still there, but when Ben and I had visited looking for witnesses, the place had seemed sad. 'All the old centre users stopped coming in here after that cop was exposed,' the young woman who showed us around explained.

It was hard to know how to pitch it. If I had been presenting the arguments myself, I would have aimed too high. Charlotte had a better sense of how to tread the line. But she had been on her feet talking all day, and was exhausted. She had to take everything we had said and figure out how to present it in court the following day. We decided to call it a night.

On the way home, I was in despair, thinking that this fundamental part of our case might be lost. Ben seemed less worried.

'Haven't you noticed?' he said, 'The judges get grumpy around four o'clock. It's happened at every single hearing, and it doesn't matter who's talking or what's being said. I think they just reach saturation point and want to go home. Don't stress it. Tomorrow is another day.'

The lawyers turned our crisis meeting into a five-page note for the Tribunal overnight, and it seemed that Ben had been right about the mood of the judges. One of them wondered aloud whether Mark Kennedy's operation could even be considered political when all the intelligence he gathered was so trivial.

'You might say,' another interjected, 'that the state has no business spying on the legitimate political activities of its opponents?'

You might, I thought. *You might say that.*

Our case closed shortly after, and we celebrated with a picnic lunch outside. The whole team sat in a wide circle, eating sandwiches and soaking up the sun on a carefully manicured lawn in Temple. We were determined to enjoy it. After lunch we would hear the case from the other side.

CHAPTER 44

David Perry QC got to his feet and my stomach contracted. Yet it soon became obvious that, having effectively discarded the witness statements of Sir Stephen House, he had very little else to rely on. He even asked the Tribunal to consider some of Mark Kennedy's own words to the Home Affairs Select Committee, though he made it clear that he knew other parts of that interview were lies. My stomach began to relax.

Perry described the codes of conduct and training that all officers received, and the ethical and moral standards expected from them at all times. Kennedy's career was outlined: before joining the NPOIU, he had been an experienced police officer of ten years. His record was exemplary. How could his supervisors have known what he was about to do? It was a source of 'profound regret' to the police that no one had asked why Mark was passing quite so much intimate information about so many people to his handlers. They were hanging Kennedy out to dry. A small price, maybe, to protect those higher up the chain.

More than once, Perry made arguments that seemed to support our case, not theirs. 'Rightly or wrongly,' he told the court, 'there was operational benefit to Mark Kennedy developing the relationship with the Claimant, and officers receiving evidence of a developing relationship would have seen it in that context.'

A murmur spread through the public gallery as the irony landed.

He referred to evidence that Mark Kennedy had continued to have relationships as Mark Stone after he resigned in 2010, proclaiming that this showed there was no culture or practice of cultivating sexual partners for operational ends, because the relationships he had in that period could not possibly be linked to the police.

One of the judges intervened. 'The fact that Mark Kennedy may, and probably did, want to have sexual relationships for personal gratification really does not have a bearing on whether it was used as a tactic by the police. There is a confluence of interests there.'

Those politely phrased words contained a harrowing truth. The most likely answer to the question about the purpose of our relationships was that the interests of a corrupt police unit were aligned with the sexual urges of men given power over women. It wasn't a part of the job or a perk of the job: it was both.

In general, the judges showed themselves to be shrewder than I expected. They pushed the police hard for answers about the missing evidence and asked probing questions about how the unit operated.

'I shall want to know who authored the reports, who saw the reports. I do want to understand the process involved,' one of them said.

The court adjourned shortly after that to hold one of their secret hearings behind closed doors, swiftly followed by the weekend. For three days I was on tenterhooks.

On the Monday, the police served more disclosure. The judges were not appeased.

'We have questions no one in court can answer. What was done with the contact logs? You present a witness who by your own declaration has no knowledge of the events at all and has not spoken to the officers involved. That is a very odd witness statement indeed.'

'The difficulty with intelligence flow,' Perry explained, 'is that it appears to have evolved over the lifetime of the deployment, with a new system implemented in August 2006. We cannot really know what happened before that.'

Of course they could know. They just needed to ask the officers who were there. It seemed no one was willing to do that.

Instead, Perry presented a series of internal policy documents from 2006 describing the same 'sterile corridors' and 'firewalls' that appeared in House's statements.

'Our position is that the documents are available and they are the primary evidence,' he said. 'The absence of witness statements should not be taken against the Defendants.'

He explained that in the public inquiry there had been an undertaking that witnesses giving evidence to the Inquiry would not be prosecuted for anything they said. The police's unwillingness to give evidence in the IPT was simply because no such undertaking existed there, and 'not for any sinister reason'.

The officers were unwilling to give evidence because they feared they might be prosecuted for what they did? Nothing sinister about that.

On the question of whether the operations were 'necessary in a democratic society', it seemed that the judges had been ruminating since we made our submissions.

'Would you say that these operations did meet a pressing social need?' one of them asked.

Perry's only answer was to say that the definition of a 'pressing social need' in the context of undercover policing was imprecise. Maybe, he suggested, we needed to ask not whether the operation was necessary, but whether the officers at the time might have believed it was necessary.

'Maybe this whole undercover operation was just misconceived, inappropriate and disproportionate,' the judge suggested.

Were they getting it at last?

There were some troubling moments. In response to our arguments about sexism, Perry ventured that we were making stereotypical assumptions about male and female sexuality, and missing a more fundamental point about 'consensual sexual relationships'.

I tasted bile. In case anything secret accidentally got said, there was a rule that nothing could be reported outside the room until ten minutes had gone by. I closed my eyes and took several deep breaths, counting the minutes before I could vent on Twitter.

12:05 PM · 26 Apr 2021
Kate Wilson (@fruitbatmania) Just in case you missed the point, in among Perry's legal arguments, let's say it loud again: WE DID NOT CONSENT #SpyCops

Another worrying argument came in the form of a warning Perry issued to the judges: it could be 'problematic', he said, if they decided to rule on Articles 10 and 11 (the rights to freedom of expression and association). They should consider what impact their judgment might have on future police practice, as it could mean that authorisations would have to comply not only with Article 8 (the right to privacy), but also with Article 10.

I was astounded. I had assumed that all policing was supposed to comply with the entire Human Rights Act. Apparently not.

Overall, though, the arguments presented on behalf of the police seemed underwhelming.

'I offer no defence for the unlawful behaviour that took place. All of the submissions we have made are to circumstantial inferences to be made based on the materials. The Tribunal can draw the inference it wishes to make,' Perry said. With that, the police closed their case.

It felt like a strange way for it to end. I had spent ten gruelling years fighting their obstruction and obfuscation. They had seemed such an imposing adversary. It was disconcerting to face them in court at last and find they had so little to say.

The final day saw our closing statement, and Charlotte was on fabulous form, hammering home what we had all witnessed: the police had made no evidential case at all about what any of the other officers ought to have known. Perry couldn't answer a single question about how the NPOIU operated in practice, she pointed out. Then she produced a document that dealt a body blow to the idea they had created of 'sterile corridors'.

We had found the email nestled among the organigrams and descriptions of how the NPOIU operated, the same documents the police had relied on as evidence of how their intelligence flow was managed. It was part of a long document, and the police had originally redacted that page. Even when I was a litigant in person, Sarah Hannett always made clear that she could not advise or represent me in any way. The one exception to that rule was that, in her role as Counsel to the Tribunal, she would look behind the redactions the police applied to the documents they sent me. Right up to the last minute we would occasionally receive new versions of documents where Sarah had told the police there were redactions they ought to remove; and there it was:

From: [O-137]
Date: 11th May 2007, 14:04
Subject: RE: Intel flow for views
Dear All,

We have looked at the Intel Flows [diagrams] and our observations are as follows:

1) The flow charts are somewhat 'dishonest'. By this I mean that they do not show us having interaction with the covert side of the house, yet we clearly do. This is in the form of briefings by them to us and taskings by us to them, especially post event with tactics and photos. This is also somewhat the same for the desks . . .

What we all do in the background is what makes the office work especially during events, and usually very successfully. Are we saying that we should not really be doing this and so are trying to hide it or should we be honest with ourselves and openly celebrate the unique things that make the NPOIU successful. In other words, we do what we do to make the job work. If the rules prevent this they are clearly wrong and need changing or amending . . .

I hope this makes sense but we would be willing to discuss further if need be.

[O-137], POPS (Public Order Policing services)

At a stroke, it blew their claims away. Not only did it confirm Ben's and my vision of a working environment in which everyone knew what was going on, it also betrayed a culture that was willing to bend or change the rules to get the job done.

Charlotte then turned to the question of whether the operations were lawful. This turned out to be a complex matter, involving a number of different tests, but once she had walked us through them all she knocked down the entire house of cards with a flourish: there was no basis on which any of the authorisations could be said to be necessary in the first place, because the police accepted that they contained lies.

After that, we thought it was over. In the public gallery we started to pack our things away. Out on the floor, however, they were still talking. Something was clearly up. Legal points were being thrown around, with increasing agitation, and then someone said something about further submissions, even another hearing. We exchanged looks.

The problem, it seemed, was that Perry had said that Mark Kennedy's evidence to the Home Affairs Select Committee contained 'lies'. Charlotte's coup at the end of her closing statement had been to ask whether that might not put him, and by extension, the Tribunal, in contempt of Parliament. It turned out that a fundamental aspect of the British constitution is that the courts cannot question something said in Parliament. Violating the Bill of Rights was apparently a big deal. The Tribunal politely suggested that the police could simply withdraw their reliance on Mark Kennedy's evidence. The police (somewhat less politely, I thought) replied that, having already accepted that they could not rely on the inferences of Sir Stephen House, they would probably have no case left if they lost Mark's statements as well. The decision was, incredibly, deferred to a later date.

I was confused. Did that mean it wasn't over? Something was ending, because the Chair of the Tribunal, Lord Boyd, was saying goodbye and thanking the barristers. Suddenly he was thanking me as well, telling the room how I had filed the claim ten years ago and that I had spent some of that time representing myself.

The immensity of it all suddenly overcame me. I started to cry and the room dissolved. Someone led me by the arm. Someone else collected my things. I wish I could remember who.

CHAPTER 45

Spain lifted its pandemic border restrictions, and Ben and I made our way home. We arrived to find that my house had been broken into and turned upside down. Clearing up the mess and replacing the broken windows felt symbolic. It was time to rebuild our lives. Yet June came and went, and we had no idea when the final ruling would arrive.

The police sent submissions saying that the Tribunal could resolve any possible conflict with the scope of Parliamentary Privilege because much of what Mark said in Parliament had already been said to the newspapers. They sent a table listing things Mark had said to the press, back when Max Clifford was managing his celebrity profile. I was reminded of how distraught I had been reading those interviews. We had come a long way since then. It seemed laughable that, after ten long years, the best the police could do was suggest that the Tribunal look for answers in old issues of the *Daily Mail*.

Hurricane season was heating up. Ben had walked away from his boat more than six months ago, leaving it at anchor while he helped me prepare for the trial. Once my house was sorted, we decided to fly out to Martinique together and make sure his home was shipshape as well.

July turned into August, and we settled into boat life. For the first time in years there were no deadlines, no pressure, just a deep sense of anxiety about the impending ruling. Evenings rolled by like waves. I would sit on deck and watch the sun set behind

Diamond Rock, another day with no news, and nothing to do but wait.

When the IPT finally uploaded its ruling on 30 September 2021, it was already mid-morning in the UK, but it was 5 a.m. for me. I had set an alarm and was out of bed, shuffling around the tiny galley putting the kettle on and making toast. I texted Lisa, Eleanor and the others.

We won.

A grey streak had only just begun to appear on the eastern horizon, and I had slept for less than three hours. I was definitely going to need caffeine before I could manage a comment that stretched to more than two words, but Sky News were already on the phone; I tried to arrange the Zoom camera so that it kept the palm trees and dawn sky out of shot. Somehow it didn't seem to set the right tone.

At the end of the interview, she asked me about trusting the police force.

'It's the big question today, particularly for women. What would you have to say about that?'

My case had continued to run in parallel with the prosecution of Sarah Everard's killer, and in a final twist, the IPT had published its ruling on the same day that the police officer who murdered her was given a whole-life sentence for his crimes.

I tried to sum up my feelings for the Sky reporter, of how my own sense of victory was muted by growing evidence of the ugly cultures still festering within the police.

'We already had a finding that the police were institutionally racist. The Daniel Morgan inquiry recently found the Metropolitan Police to be institutionally corrupt. The IPT today has found that undercover operations were guilty of sexist discrimination. I feel that the Metropolitan Police is an organisation beyond redemption . . . I don't see that they have made any great progress . . . I don't have any confidence that they are going to target the culture of misogyny that exists.'

Watching that interview I am surprised at how calm and articulate I seem. Inside I was reeling. It had just hit me how much had been riding on the decision of that three-judge Tribunal. It gave me vertigo to think what I had given up; how much of myself I had put into the witness statements and submissions; how many years we had dedicated to fighting the case; and how easily it could have all been for nothing. My elation at winning was tempered by the sudden, dizzying realisation that I had made decision after decision to keep going, for eleven years, without any real inkling of what I was taking on, and without ever stopping to consider what it might mean if we were to lose.

'We didn't lose,' Eleanor pointed out. 'We won far more than we ever thought we could win. I am totally overwhelmed. The fact they said the infiltrations were unlawful in our democratic society. It's totally huge.'

It was Eleanor and Lisa who cut through my need to treat it all as one more thing on the to-do list – interview at 6 a.m., send the ruling to our supporters, write newspaper opinion piece, congratulate the lawyers, call Mum and Dad.

'This is really huge, Kate,' Lisa messaged. 'Finally, a court has heard what we've been trying to say for over a decade. You gave it your everything and you made them listen. I'm proud and a bit tearful right now. And angry with them, of course. Basically the full spectrum of emotions.'

I began to appreciate the sheer scale of what we had won. The Tribunal identified what they called a 'formidable list' of breaches of fundamental human rights by the Metropolitan Police. 'This is not just a case about a renegade police officer who took advantage of his undercover deployment to indulge his sexual proclivities . . . Our findings that the authorisations under RIPA were fatally flawed and the undercover operation could not be justified as "necessary in a democratic society" . . . reveal disturbing and lamentable failings at the most fundamental levels.' They called the operation a 'fishing expedition'. It was unlawful, it violated the right to protest and it met no pressing social need.

The police had tried to claim that engaging in a sexual relationship while deployed would be a breach of professional conduct, but the Tribunal considered that argument to be 'materially undermined by the sheer frequency with which Mark Kennedy did conduct sexual relationships without either questions being asked or action being taken by senior officers'. The police failed to put in place systems, safeguards or protections; training of undercover officers in relation to sexual relationships was grossly inadequate; there was a widespread failure of supervision and a disturbing lack of concern on the part of the police about the impact on women. They concluded that the National Public Order Intelligence Unit's approach to its officers having sex while undercover was one of 'don't ask, don't tell'.

It made me smile to see how the words that Ben had used as we walked along the seafront, puzzling over the inner workings of the NPOIU, had passed into jurisprudence. For one tiny moment I even found myself wondering where Mark might be and what he thought of it all.

'I felt awful for years,' Eleanor wrote to me later that night, 'about what I said, that first time you and Mark kissed. I told him you were dangerous! I warned him not to get involved. I hated to think of him smirking to himself, smug in the knowledge of the power imbalance between you. So, I think my secret favourite thing about all of this is that it turns out I was right. He was no match for you in the end.'

Epilogue

**From the opening statement of Category H Core Partici-
pants to the Undercover Policing Inquiry, 25 April 2022**
[T]he evidence that has emerged . . . assessed against the
applicable legal framework, including the unappealed conclusions in the recent case of Kate Wilson v Commissioner
of the Metropolis and National Police Chiefs Council
(NPCC) [2021] UKIPTrib IPT 11 167 H, demonstrates that
the operations of the SDS failed to comply with numerous
basic requirements . . . involved multiple unjustified torts,
including trespass to land and goods, and breached numerous fundamental rights of a wide range of individuals. They
significantly exceeded long-standing parameters set for
the use of police powers, and broke the public trust . . .
As explained below, that indisputable unlawfulness has
implications . . .

The ruling we won in the Investigatory Powers Tribunal didn't
just move the goalposts, it changed the whole game. 'Kate Wilson
v The Commissioner' is now case law. It has been used in the
Undercover Policing Inquiry, in ongoing claims in the High Court,
in new cases before the IPT, in undergraduate law courses, and
even in cases abroad.

However, life, like memory, doesn't happen in ways that can
easily be pinned down in court papers (or indeed books). Even if it
did, in October 2010, everything I thought I knew about my own

life was blown apart. I was a bit part in somebody else's spy story, and the narrative of my life was no longer my own. That is why I fought so hard for disclosure. The police were eventually forced to disclose several thousand pages of secret documents. They are the primary sources for the history of Mark Kennedy's deployment, but also for my own life.

'They don't own our memories. They don't own our lives or the things that we did.'

That is what Eleanor told me when we first started reading the files. However, it wasn't entirely true. Memories are made of sights, sounds, and sensations. They are shaped over the years, reinforced by photographs and the sharing of stories, or blurred and faded with the passage of time. For the most part, our memories weren't written down, and they certainly weren't time-stamped. It was deeply unnerving to discover someone else had been sitting round the corner for years, keeping logs.

The files didn't arrive in the order they are presented here. The process of disclosure was painful, protracted, chaotic and disorganised, and it was not until the very end that I received the files from 2003. Throughout the court process, the police maintained that those documents were 'missing'. We assumed that they had been destroyed. However, on the very day our proceedings in the Investigatory Powers Tribunal finally ended, Mark's handler (long since retired) delivered his own copy of those documents to the Undercover Policing Inquiry.

There was a flurry of correspondence. The Directorate of Legal services of the Metropolitan Police wrote to the Tribunal to make clear that the police had not been aware that the log was still in existence:

Although its absence was regarded as significant and highly unfortunate, it was considered inconceivable that it would be in EN31's personal possession . . . This is particularly so in view of the need for sensitive materials concerning undercover operations to remain within the workplace . . . it was not considered that there was any prospect whatsoever that EN31 would be in possession of the log, having not provided it in the course of more than a decade of inquiries and investigations . . . [EN31 was] a mature police officer of many years' experience, who knew full well what was in issue and who could reasonably have been expected to volunteer any relevant material should it be in his possession . . . To say the least, what has occurred since was unforeseeable and unfortunate. There was no attempt to conceal the existence of any material, nor is it accepted that there has been any failure on the part of the MPS.

By then, protestations that the Metropolitan Police had not failed in any way were background noise. What mattered was that, for whatever reason, EN31 kept his own backup copy of the contact logs. On 1 July 2022, the contact logs covering the weeks when Mark and I first met, were finally disclosed to me.

As soon as the case was over, I turned back to the documents. Freed from the endless rounds of submissions deadlines and hearings, I was finally able to read them as I had always wanted, and weave them together with the shattered pieces of our memories.

It took years to make sense of the files and turn what we found into an historic victory in the courts. Through that process, I became more than a bit part. Yet the findings of the Investigatory Powers Tribunal in my case were not only about me. They reflected human rights violations committed against thousands of people over decades. What was done to us lays bare the lie of democracy, in a country where protest is considered a democratic right.

'I am weeping for you and for all of us,' a close friend wrote when she read the judgment, 'and for the world we might have built if this hadn't been going on.'

DISCLOSURE

Despite a few arrests at demonstrations over twenty years of political activism, I have no criminal convictions. That didn't matter: I, and hundreds of others, were branded 'extremist' and made a target for Britain's secret political police.

The police have been forced to apologise over and over again for their biased and discriminatory policing, yet their powers keep expanding. We are holding on to an ever-shrinking space for defiance of authority, and while we worked to expose a small part of the state's war on progress, they were regrouping and creating new laws. Sometimes, it feels as though each time we win a battle, the battlefield becomes obsolete.

Writing this book reminded me of the incredible community our activism created, the powerful love and trust we shared, and what we lost when that was ripped away. But it also reminded me that throughout the period covered by this account, successive repressive laws, from the Criminal Justice Act of 1994 to the Police, Crime, Sentencing and Courts Act of 2022, have tried and failed to stifle political dissent. From the cost-of-living crisis to the climate emergency, from Black Lives Matter to the genocide in Palestine, people continue to take to the streets. No amount of state oppression will stop people coming together to challenge the status quo, and wherever there are injustices, people will fight – for what they love, for their families and friends, for the vulnerable and the voiceless, and for the planet that sustains us. There are lessons to be learnt from what we lived through, but it will be the next generation of dissidents who really figure out what they are.

Kate Wilson, January 2024

References

p.8   Dublin Grassroots Network. 'Press Release', 30 April 2004.

p.9, 10, 13   Black Bloc. 'Dublin Mayday: Why we pushed through police lines', Statement, 5 May 2004.

p.18   Perot, R. 'Clinton-Bush-Perot Presidential Debate'. Michigan, USA, 19 October 1992.

p.19   Notes from Nowhere collective. *We Are Everywhere: The Irresistible Rise of Global Anticapitalism*. New York City: Verso, 2003.

p.20   'Hallmarks of Peoples' Global Action', nadir.org. Available at: https://www.nadir.org/nadir/initiativ/agp/free/pga/hallm.htm [accessed 3 February 2025].

p.21–2   Corporate Watch and Reclaim the Streets. 'Squaring Up to the Square Mile: A rough guide to the City of London', booklet, April 1999.

p.29, 30   'Pancho and Lefty' by Merle Haggard and Willie Nelson (Epic), originally by Townes Van Zandt (Poppy). Lyrics by Townes Van Zandt © 1972 (Sony/ATV Music Publishing LLC).

p.32   Graham, C. 'How beautiful redhead girlfriend blew eco-spy's cover after finding passport with his real name'. *Daily Mail*, 16 January 2011. Available at: https://www.dailymail.co.uk/news/article-1347561/Undercover-policeman-I-loved-lady-I-really-did-Then-passport-real-it.html [accessed 3 April 2025].

p.35–7   Graham, C. 'I had to have sex with eco-warriors to keep my cover: Undercover officer's lovers sue over "degrading deceit"'. *Daily Mail*, 31 December 2011. Available at: https://www.dailymail.co.uk/news/article-2080733/I-sex-eco-warriors-cover-Undercover-officers-lovers-sue-degrading-deceit.html [accessed 3 April 2025].

p.44   The Honourable Mr Justice Tugendhat, In the High Court of Justice Queen's Bench Division. 'Approved Judgement', 17 January 2013.

REFERENCES

p.45–6   The Home Affairs Select Committee. 'Undercover Policing, Interim Report', Prepared March 2013.

p.47   Hattenstone, S. 'Mark Kennedy: Confessions of an undercover cop'. *Guardian*, 26 March 2011. Available at: https://www.theguardian.com/environment/2011/mar/26/mark-kennedy-undercover-cop-environmental-activist [accessed 3 April 2025].

p. 49–50   Evans, R. and Lewis, P. *Undercover: The True Story of Britain's Secret Police*. London: Guardian Books, Faber & Faber, 2012.

p.56   Evans, R. 'Woman suing police over relationship with undercover spy finds tracking device in her car – reports'. *Guardian*, 11 March 2015. Available at: https://www.theguardian.com/uk-news/undercover-with-paul-lewis-and-rob-evans/2015/mar/11/woman-suing-police-over-relationship-with-undercover-spy-finds-tracking-device-in-her-car-reports [accessed 3 April 2025].

p.61   Metropolitan Police, video of a statement from assistant commissioner Martin Hewitt, 20 November 2015.

p.62–3   Casciani, D. 'Woman wins undercover officer case against Met Police'. BBC News [online], 19 January 2016. Available at: https://www.bbc.co.uk/news/uk-35350095 [accessed 3 April 2025].

p.68–9   Claimant's Statement of Grounds, 10 April 2017.

p.84   'Every Breath You Take' by The Police (A&M Records). Lyrics by Gordon Sumner © 1983 (Universal Music Publishing Group).

p.85   R (Saha) v Secretary of State for the Home Department (Secretary of State's duty of candour). UKUT 17 (IAC), 2017. Quoted in Steele, I. Public Law Project, 'The Duty of Candour: Where Are We Now?' 2017. Available at: www.publiclawproject.org.uk/content/uploads/2018/02/The-duty-of-candour-where-are-we-now.pdf [accessed 8 April 2025].

p.192   Electronic Frontier Foundation, 'EFF Challenges Secret Court Order', October 2004.

p.203   BBC *News*, various correspondents including Gareth Furby. BBC *News* Report, 26 December 2004.

p.237   National Coordinator for Domestic Extremism (NCDE), 2008.

p.237–8   SOCA (Serious Organised Crime Agency). 'Review of Undercover Deployment in support of HMIC review of the National Domestic Extremism Unit', 2011.

p.238–9   HMIC. 'A review of national police units which provide intelligence on criminality associated with protest'. www.hmic.gov.uk, 2012. Available at: https://s3-eu-west-2.amazonaws.com/assets-hmicfrs.justiceinspectorates.gov.uk/uploads/review-of-national-police-units-which-provide-intelligence-on-criminality-associated-with-protest-20120202.pdf [accessed 8 April 2025].

p.252 Graham, C. 'How undercover officers squandered millions of pounds, with flash cars, luxury flats and up to 14 hours' overtime a day'. *Mail on Sunday*, 23 January 2011. Available at: https://www.dailymail.co.uk/news/article-1349647/How-undercover-officers-squandered-millions-pounds-flash-cars-luxury-flats-14-hours-overtime-day.html [accessed 3 April 2025].

p.269–70 Post by merrick, 'ratcliffe trial: prosecutor and police conspired'. Bristling Badger blog, 10 August 2013. Available at: https://bristling-badger.blogspot.com/2013/08/ratcliffe-trial-prosecutors-and-police.html [accessed 3 February 2025].

p.277–8 Evans, R., Hill, A., Lewis, P. and Kingsley, P. 'Mark Kennedy: secret policeman's sideline as corporate spy'. *Guardian*, 13 January 2011. Available at: https://www.theguardian.com/environment/2011/jan/12/mark-kennedy-policeman-corporate-spy [accessed 3 April 2025].

p.283–4 IMC UK Features. 'Mark Kennedy/Stone exposed as undercover cop', Indymedia UK, October 2010. Available at: https://www.indymedia.org.uk/en/2010/10/466705.html [accessed 3 April 2025].

p.307 Steafel, E. 'Sarah Everard vigil: How the police turned on women paying tribute to murdered woman'. *Telegraph*, 15 March 2021. Available at: https://www.telegraph.co.uk/news/2021/03/15/sarah-everard-vigil-clapham-common-protest-vigil-protest-sarah/ [accessed 3 April 2025].

p.326 Wilson, K. Post as Kate Wilson (@fruitbatmania) on X.com (formerly known as Twitter), 26 April 2021.

p. 332–3 Investigatory Powers Tribunal. 'Case No: IPT/11/167/H: Approved Judgment', 20 September 2021. Available at: https://www.judiciary.uk/wp-content/uploads/2022/07/Wilson-v-MPS-Judgment.pdf [accessed 8 April 2025].

p.335–6 Category H Core Participants. Undercover Policing Inquiry, 25 April 2022.

Acknowledgements

A full list of the people without whom this book could not have been written would require a history of the groups and movements that were spied on; the brave activists and investigative journalists who uncovered the first spycops; the ongoing struggle and support of thousands of people and the work of dedicated campaign groups that have kept the issue alive. Rather than trying to thank them all, I encourage you to check out these websites and get involved:

Police Spies Out of Lives – https://policespiesoutoflives.org.uk/
Campaign Opposing Police Surveillance –
https://campaignopposingpolicesurveillance.com/
Undercover Research Group – https://spycops.info/
NetPol – https://netpol.org/
The Monitoring Group – https://tmg-uk.org/
Blacklist Support Group – https://www.facebook.com/groups/blacklistSG/

We could never have won without the work of Charlotte Kilroy KC and the solicitors at Birnberg Peirce and Freshfields Bruckhaus Deringer, all of whom went far above and beyond the call of duty in their work on my case.

I also want to thank my family: Lily (who loaned me her name for a while), John, Esme, Adam and Caitlin; Pauline and Dave (aka Mum & Dad) who always supported me, gave me the values I hold dear, taught me to never give up, and never once blamed me for bringing those men into their homes; and Ben, who stuck by me while I wrote the book, listened supportively as I read each and every new bit out loud, and always said the right thing in response.

There are dozens of people who deserve recognition for the work they did on the disclosure while the case was ongoing, for the support they gave me, and for reading, commenting and contributing to this book, particularly: Eleanor, Dónal, Kate T, Harriet, Helen, Axel, TomBFowler, Oscar, Joel, Spencer, Ronny, the folks at Wild Peak, Merrick, Red, Frances, Alison, Naomi, Ruth, Rosa, Lisa, Loukas, Sebastian, and Rob Evans.

Finally, special thanks to 'Lisa', 'ARB', Sarah, Loukas, Harriet and Eleanor for allowing me to use parts of your witness statements in this book. I am sure this is not how you would have chosen to tell your own stories outside of the courtroom, and I am sorry if it feels uncomfortable or incomplete.